SLEY

PIS LANE

THE

ro Widbury

To Bowling Green

TITHE LAND

NEW ROAD

KIBES LANE

WARE MANOR

ST STREET

BRIDGE FOOT

STAR STREET

AMWELL END

ROAD TO LONDON

THE
HISTORY OF WARE

BESIDE THE LEA AT WARE

THE
HISTORY OF WARE

BY

EDITH M. HUNT

With a New Introduction by
DAVID PERMAN

Illustrations in Halftone and Line
Coloured Frontispiece from a Watercolour by May Hammond

HERTFORD
STEPHEN AUSTIN AND SONS, LTD.
1986

DEDICATION

To all those born beneath the roofs of Ware,
In olden times, to-day, or years to be ;
To those who enter in and, loving, share
The native pride in their town's ancestry.

Then, after these, to church and ancient street,
To cowl and barge, to kiln and cart and sack,
To my home-bringing bridge, from which I greet
This malting town which calls her children back.

First published in 1946
Reprinted 1949
New Edition 1986

© Stephen Austin and Sons

ISBN 0   9509259   1   8

CONTENTS

ILLUSTRATIONS

ACKNOWLEDGMENTS

In this short History of Ware I have tried to present the chief links in the chain of our town's life story, and to show where the clues may be found. The story does not claim to be exhaustive. Channels are left open for scholars capable of deeper research. For instance, Ware town manor alone is dealt with, whereas, to begin with, Blakesware (or Grimbolds), Mardocks, Cosyns, Braughyns, New Hall, and Westmill or Halfhide, were all " held of the manor of Ware ".

During the time spent on this work I have had generous help from many people, and in many ways. I wish to acknowledge with gratitude my indebtedness to :—

1. Those who in the past had already collected material on Ware and left valuable fruits of their industry, particularly—the late R. T. Andrews, A. B. Bannister, W. B. Gerish, and E. E. Squires.

2. Many of my fellow townsmen who have unhesitatingly allowed me to invade their premises, take photographs, and ask questions.

3. The Librarians and Keepers of MSS. at—The British Museum, Somerset House, Public Record Office, Guildhall, Westminster Abbey, Dr. William's, Trinity College, Cambridge, St. Albans Public Library, Hertford Museum, and Hertford County Library and Muniment Room.

4. The producers and editors of the *Victoria County History of Hertfordshire*, and the *Quarter Sessions Records*.

5. Many distinguished scholars and personal friends who have contributed unfailing help and sympathetic interest, including—Dr. G. R. Owst, Dr. E. C. Messenger, and the late W. G. Bell, also the late Mrs. B. M. Ridout (*née* Fanshawe) ; very especially to those Hertfordshire Worthies and Historians, H. C. Andrews, M.A., F.S.A., and Reginald L. Hine, F.S.A., F.R.Hist.S., who stood over me and tried to keep me straight from the beginning of this enterprise, and, over all, to my father, Ernest H. Hitch, who helped to develop an abiding love for our ancestral town.

Further, I am indebted to Miss French for the gift of photos on the River Lea, by the late Rev. J. W. Fall, and many town photos by M. P. Hitch. Also to Mrs. Bambridge and Messrs. MacMillan for permission to quote lines from Rudyard Kipling, and to Eleanor Tyler for designing the end papers.

WARE · HERTS.

INTRODUCTION

Secretary of the Ware Museum Trust

It is forty years since Edith Hunt's " History of Ware " was published and it still remains the only comprehensive history of this small, ancient Hertfordshire town. That fact alone is enough to justify its re-publication. But the book also has the distinctive flavour of a strong emotional bond between the author and her subject, which no reader can fail to detect. Whatever its deficiencies from the modern historian's point of view—and they certainly exist—Mrs Hunt's book distilled the essential spirit of Ware as its older residents still remember it. She extended their knowledge and deepened their pride in their home town at a time, when (as Reginald Hine wrote in his original introduction) Ware was " a shadow of her former self" and noted mainly for her " picturesque grubbiness ". Edith Hunt finished her history during the 1930s (publication was held up by the war), when the once-dominant malting industry was in depression and when the old yards and streets of crowded cottages were being swept away in slum clearance schemes. She wrote to record what was left and to salvage as much as she could from " the waters of oblivion ". But her book was much more than that. It was an act of personal and family piety towards a dearly loved friend. As she wrote later: " As far back as memory will carry me, my home town has been much more than a mere background to the normal happenings of a child's life, it has been a personality and a companion to me. " That comes from " Memories of a Malting Town ", which first appeared as a magazine article and was republished along with other articles and twenty of her poems in the late forties in aid of the St. Mary's Church Restoration Fund. One of the poems is entitled " A Request ":

> Oh big round Moon, you're looking down
> All through the night on my own town . . .
> Big Moon, the times I am not there,
> But kept from my own town of Ware,
> Then, Moon, keep watch with steady light
> That nothing harmful come by night;
> Wrapped in my cloak of Love, so strong,
> Bathed in your beams, naught shall be wrong.

*   *   *   *   *

xiii

Edith May Hunt was born in 1888 and was a maltster's daughter, but that was not her only inheritance from her father, Ernest Hollingsworth Hitch. He was a churchwarden of St. Mary's, a councillor and for a short time chairman of Ware U.D.C. and a member of a long-established Ware family, engaged in malting, brickmaking, building and barge construction. Through her father's family, Edith was related to Robert and William Andrews, co-founders of the Hertford Museum and leading lights in the East Herts Archaeological Society, as she was to be later. It was they and her cousin, Herbert Caleb Andrews who encouraged her in her earliest historical activities which, we are told, was copying inscriptions on the mouldering gravestones at Thundridge. Within her family she was known as " Topsy " and she had a happy childhood, as is evident from " Memories of a Malting Town ". There she described the games children played in the maltings when they were not in use in the summer, the " delicious scent " of the malt when they were in use and the winter memories of her father having a snowball fight from the parapet of their Georgian house with a neighbour across the street. Later she went to Girton College, Cambridge, and during the First World War she worked as a cook in the V.A.D. hospital for wounded soldiers established in The Priory (see page 93).

In 1911, she married Thomas Cyril Hunt, who won the M.C. during the war and became South American export manager for the Metropolitan Vickers Company. He too was a churchwarden at St. Mary's and he was the anonymous donor (mentioned on page 49) who paid for the gas lamps to be replaced by electric lighting. Edith Hunt later renewed and extended the church lighting in her late husband's memory. They lived for a while in Broxbourne, then at Haycocks in Baldock Street with her father and, best of all, at 6 Star Street. As her friend, Gordon Moodey, wrote: " she never seemed more happily at home than when she and her husband lived for a while in a cottage in Star Street that had been her father's offices, with his nameplate still affixed on a bedroom door and a view of the maltings from the window. " Later she traced the history of this building back to the holdings of Robert the Welshman from the Manor of Sandon in 1260. On her husband's retirement, they moved to a new house at 15 Widbury Gardens, but he died shortly afterwards in 1954. They had no children.

Edith Hunt lived for another eight years and was active in local history to the last. She delighted in showing visitors the unexpected medieval features behind the modern shop fronts of Ware High Street. " But she herself enjoyed the joke when in 1949, to her utter astonishment, the French Horn was found to contain a spectacular Jacobean staircase of nine flights, richly carved, unknown to any but its unappreciative occupants. "

*   *   *   *   *

One of the major deficiencies of her history is not Mrs Hunt's fault. Following earlier writers, she assumed that Ware had been founded as an outpost of Anglo-Saxon Hertford and that the Roman finds discovered by archaeologists near Ware Lock were no indication of the age of the modern town. In the last ten years, however, excavations in the town centre have shown not just that the Romans were active far to the east of Ware Lock but that Ware was also a substantial pre-Roman, Iron Age settlement and a thriving post-Roman, Saxon town until the Danish invasions of the ninth century A.D.

It is the deficiencies at the other end of the history of Ware which are less acceptable. Apart from incidental references to malting, Mrs Hunt displayed little interest in the town's industry. Brickmaking—the traditional activity of Ware malt-makers in summer—is not mentioned at all, which is doubly curious when one recalls that her own great-grandfather was Caleb Hitch, whose patented inter-locking bricks introduced a new concept to the construction industry. Perhaps she never quite forgave him for being an accessory to the drastic restoration of St. Mary's in 1847–49 (see page 48). Indeed her recording of the nineteenth and twentieth centuries scarcely extended beyond the walls of the Parish Church. There is virtually nothing about the coming of the railway in 1843, which transformed the economic and social life of the town and caused the diversion of the Turnpike along the new Viaduct Road and over the new iron bridge, designed by George Stephenson. There is little about the Ware's social revolution whereby a solidly Radical town, whose bargemen had marched into Hertford during the 1832 Reform Bill election to do battle with the Tory Lord Salisbury's estate workers, was transformed by the influx of the professional middle classes.

Indeed, for 19th century events, she relied mainly on the writings of the Australian James Smith—although it is largely due to Edith Hunt that James Smith is still remembered in this country.

These are substantial deficiencies, but they are outweighed by the strengths of Mrs Hunt's history. She rediscovered Ware in the days of its greatness—its medieval prosperity, its importance as a posting and coaching town, " the guested towne of Ware ", before it became the main supplier of malt to London's 18th-century brewers. Her meticulous recording of the inns, which at one time stretched in an unbroken row from Ware bridge to The Priory, makes fascinating reading. Above all, Edith Hunt painted a vivid picture of Ware's people, the gentry and the gossips, the lords and layabouts, the criminals, religious fanatics, maltmakers, saints and rogues.

*   *   *   *   *

Like the town she loved so much, Edith Hunt was serious without being too grand, for ever busy, and always able to inspire great affection. She is still remembered in Ware, rushing about in her tweeds and brogues, wisps of hair coming loose from her bun and from under the straw hats she wore in summer. The *Hertfordshire Mercury* said that Ware had lost " a much-loved and respected antiquarian ". Indeed, the republication of her " History of Ware " is due to the devotion she inspired in one man. David Stockwell's mother worked for Mrs Hunt and he assisted her in 1939 in her historical and archaeological researches. It is through David's persistent efforts since her death in 1962 and through the generous response of Stephen Austin and Sons, her printers, that the " History of Ware " is now re-published in aid of two causes which would have gladdened her heart—the St. Mary's Church Restoration Fund and the newly-established Ware Museum. Finally, I would like to thank all Edith Hunt's relatives and friends who have helped me to write this memoire of a remarkable lady.

THE MANOR

"I have considered the days of old, the years of ancient times."

Psalm 77, v. 5.

It seems safe to assume from the circumstantial evidence of antiquarian remains, in and around the site now known as Ware, that a settlement for human habitation has existed here from prehistoric times. Scattered flint implements and fragments of early pottery are occasionally revealed, and there is considerable witness to extensive Roman occupation both to the north and south of the River Lea, beside Ermine Street.

Traditionally it is held that the foundations of our present town were laid by Alfred's son, Edward the Elder, in A.D. 914, also that the writer of the *Anglo Saxon Chronicle*, under the date 896, is describing Widbury (Whitberwe = the white camp, or camp on the chalk hill) in his account of how the Danes " wrought a work by the Lea, twenty miles above the city of London ". (The remains of these earthworks were examined and described a few years ago by members of the Buxton family. See *Herts Mercury*, 14th November, 1911.)

But other Saxon records seem to refer to this Leaside settlement which, from its geographical position, must have been something of a key-point in the Danish campaign. The village grew beside the ford on the Roman road, and, on account of the fall in the river here, the construction of primitive locks or weirs gave some control to the waterway and, apparently, led to the early name—WARAS (see note on Place-name), the local pronunciation, " Weir " strengthens this theory of origin. In Alfred's Peace, drawn up with Guthrum the Dane in A.D. 879 or 885, is written :—

> " This is the peace that King Alfred and King Guthrum and the Witan of all the English Nation and all the people in East Anglia have all ordained and with oaths confirmed . . . as well for born as for unborn . . . 1. Concerning our Land Boundaries : Up on the Thames, then up on the Lea unto its source, then right to Bedford, then up on the Ouse to Watling St." *Stubb's Select Charters*, p. 63 (ed. 1900).

This Peace was broken in 892.

> " In 894 the pagans brought their ships up the River Thames and after that, up the River Lige and began to throw up their fortifications near the river at the distance of 20 miles from London." *Roger de Hoveden*, trans. by Riley, p. 58.

After Saxon days, the village developed into a celebrated malting centre, the local barley coming in increasing quantities to be malted and dispatched to London from this river port, until its fame spread far and wide. There are few references to the trade, as is common with an industry of natural growth which is taken for granted in its own locality, but those that are to be found (or most of them) will be quoted in their time and place during this chronicle.

The first documentary evidence of the existence of Ware as a town may be found in the pleasingly terse and familiar language of William the Conqueror's great survey, Domesday Book, A.D. 1086 :—

" Hugh de Grentmaisnil holds in Waras 24 hides. There is land for 38 ploughs. In the demesne there are 13 hides and on it are 3 ploughs. There could be 3 more. There are 38 villeins and a priest and the reeve of the vill and 3 Frenchmen and 2 Englishmen have 26 ploughs and a half-plough. There are 27 bordars and 12 cottars and 9 serfs. Under the Frenchmen and the Englishmen are 32 men between villeins and bordars. There are 2 mills worth 24 shillings and 400 eels less 25 and other men have 3 mills producing 10s. yearly. Meadow is there sufficient for 20 plough teams, woodland to feed 400 swine. There is an enclosure for beasts of the chase and 4 arpents of vineyard just planted. The total value is 45 pounds, when received it was 50 pounds. This manor Anschil of Waras held and 1 Sokeman, his man, had there 2 hides and another sokeman, earl Guert's man, held half a hide. Either could sell. These two, after King William came, were attached to this manor. They did not belong to it in King Edward's time, so the shire moot testifies."

Eight years previously there is documentary evidence of the existence of Ware Church, when Hugh handed it to his alien Benedictine Priory in 1078. (See Chapter on that foundation.)

After the Conquest, Ware, an independent Saxon village, was put under the Bailiff of Hertford and the story of the manor for roughly two hundred years may be summed up briefly as one long wrangle with the Bailiff concerning rights and tolls of road, river, and market, until independence was finally established during the reigns of King John and Henry III, chiefly through the energetic championship of Sayer de Quincey, Earl of Winchester. (Details of the road and river squabbles are given in the chapters on the River, p. 16, and the Highway, p. 26.) This ancient rivalry between the two Saxon hamlets has continued, very much alive, all down the centuries, and at times has led to both amusing and violent incidents. One classic example was a cricket match between the two towns in 1820, when a Ware man was so upset at his home team finally losing what seemed at first a victory that he came home and burned his trousers ! Another historic incident was the notorious Hertford parliamentary election of 1832, when Hatfield men were hired to come over and help to drive off the " invaders " from Ware, and right down to the close of the nineteenth century a football match was always liable to develop into a free fight. (The 1832 election has been most amusingly dramatized by P. H. Ilott of Hertford.)

Although Hugh de Grentmesnil was the ancestor of the lords of Ware Manor from 1086 to 1485, apparently the first Norman owner was Ralf Taillebois who, after a few years of tenure, exchanged Ware for lands in Bedfordshire. (*V.C.H. Herts*, i, 283.)

Hugh's son, Ivo, being in disgrace, did not inherit Ware, and it was in the king's hands by forfeiture in 1173 (Pipe R. 19 Hen. II, 20) but the lands came into the possession of Parnel, or Petronil, his daughter who married Robert, Earl of Leicester. In 1190, their second son, Robert Fitz Parnel, succeeded to the property, and in 1199 he obtained a grant for a weekly market in Ware (Cal. Rot. Chart., 1199–1216 (Rec. Com.), 56), having served as steward at the coronation of King John. This charter is dated 23rd July, 1199, at Verneuil.

Robert died in 1207, and his mother, Petronil, held the manor in dower until 1212, when the husband of her daughter Margaret, Sayer de Quincey, Earl of Winchester, became lord of the manor. Sayer's ownership was an outstanding period for Ware, and of all those who have held this manor, he deserves most to be remembered. He was in opposition to King John from the first, being Justiciar of England from 1211–14, and owing to his energetic intervention, Ware was made practically independent of the Bailiff of Hertford. There were lively incidents at the Bridge and the Ford (see also " The River ") when Sayer broke the chain placed across the water by the Bailiff, threw it in the river and promised the Bailiff he should follow the chain if he offered further

opposition. De Quincey died on a Crusade, and his widow,
Margaret, spent much of her time in Ware at the Alien
Benedictine Priory. Hertford bailiffs made various attempts
to regain their authority over Ware, and references to the
trouble begin to appear in the records. (For details see " The
River ".)

Apart from this family strife by ford and bridge, Ware
found other ways of annoying their would-be overlords at
Hertford, and the next complaint tells of extra and illegal
market days starting up in Ware, on the same days as Hertford
held market, " also," it is said (Cal. Hun. Rolls, 191, Ed. I),
" that the Lady and bailiff of Ware held fairs in the town of
Ware twice in September—ad magnum nocumenti burgi de
Hertford." Margaret de Quincey was evidently as firm a
champion of Ware as her husband had been.

In the Herts Assize Roll (318 m., 6 d.), the Jurors note that
never before the war between King John and the Barons
used any cart to cross at Ware bridge, " There used to be a
certain bar closed and near the bridge there used to be a
certain iron chain " ; also (313 m., 6 d.) : " Before the Barons
War no dyers, weavers or tanners in vill of Ware, but after
there were dyers and weavers but no tanners." These various
comments almost suggest a picture of Hertford's worthy
" burgi " shaking their heads over the good old days when
Ware was kept in its proper place.

When Margaret died, in 1235, she was succeeded by
Roger de Quincey. During his period as lord of the manor a
famous Tournament was held in 1241, in spite of the
Prohibition of such entertainments (Cal. Pat., 1238), when
Gilbert Marshal, Earl of Pembroke, met with a fatal accident
and was taken to Hertford Priory, where he died. John Scott,
the Quaker poet, devotes some forty lines of his poem
" Amwell " to a description of this Tourney. From Nichols'
History of Leicester (vol. ii, 372), we learn that another tournament was held in Ware, in 1276, when Ernald de Bois, of
Weston-in-Arden, was killed. It would be of great interest
to know which of the many excellent town meadows was
chosen for these knightly competitions.

In 1253, Roger granted the tenancy of the manor to his
brother Robert, who only lived to enjoy it for four years.
He had served King Henry III in the French wars and the
King, by a charter dated at Bordeaux in 1254, granted the

licence for an annual fair to be held " on the eve and day of the Nativity of the Virgin Mary and the three days following ". (Cal. Pat., 1247–58, p. 324 ; Chart R. 37 and 38 Hen. III, m. 7.) This annual event carried on until 1936, when it had to be dropped for lack of available ground.

After Robert de Quincey's death, the manor was held for a time by Roger's three daughters, Margaret, wife of Wm. Ferrers, fifth Earl of Derby ; Elizabeth, or Isabel, married to Alex. Comyn, Earl of Buchan ; and Helen, or Ela, wife of Alan la Zouche of Ashby-de-la-Zouche. Ultimately, the whole manor came to Margaret and she settled it on her second son, William. These members of the Ferrers family do not seem to have had personal connection with Ware, and in 1284, there is an order to the escheator not to meddle with the manor of Ware, as the King learns by inquiry that Joan, late wife of Humphrey de Bohun, tenant in escheat " held the manor of Wm. de Ferrer and nothing of the King ". (Cal. Close Rolls, 1279–88, p. 250.) This Joan was Robert de Quincey's elder daughter. Joan de Bohun resided at the Benedictine Priory, and added to the buildings. These additions were demolished by the Prior directly after her death, and it seems reasonable to suppose that it was from this time that the Rectory and Town Manors were separately administered. The manor then passed to her sister, Hawise, widow of Baldwin Wake. John, son of Hawise, succeeded as a minor in the custody of Queen Eleanor in 1285, and did homage for his lands in 1290, but died in 1300. During the minority of the heir, Thomas Wake, the manor was assigned to William Trente, 22nd March, 1310 (Cal. Pat. Rolls, 1307–13), to hold for three years, in discharge of a debt due to him for wine from the King's butler, Henry de Say. By 1338, we find Thomas Wake giving land in Ware for the establishment of the Franciscan Friary, and his widow, Blanche, gave more land in 1349, (See " Franciscan Friary ".) For a time Thomas was custodian of Hertford Castle. Margaret, his sister (widow of Edmund, Earl of Kent, youngest son of Edward I), inherited the manor, but also died in the year of the Black Death, 1349. She was succeeded by her second son, John, who died three years later, when the property came to his heiress, Joan (wife of Thomas de Holand, Earl of Kent), known as the Fair Maid of Kent. She married, secondly, Edward, the Black Prince, and became the mother of King

Richard II, "Joh'a principissa Wallie mater Regis," as is written in the records. (Cal. Inquis. 9, Rich. II.)

It is traditionally held that the Lady Joan took an active interest in the building of the present church, owing to the emblazonment of her badge in both north and south aisles (see "The Church"). During this time also, as we might expect, there is mention of Ware men in the service of the Prince of Wales—in 1364, Robert de Ware was paid 1½d. a day for helping and labouring with William Spirk, keeper of the Black Prince's stud at the manor of Risbergh, and, in 1365, Robert was paid 3d. a day (and his page) for the keeping of two horses, and 2d. a day, " from now onwards for the wages of the said Robert so long as the horses stay there and he remains their keeper." (Black Prince's Reg., F. 47, 275d. and 287.)

After the death of Joan, in 1385, the manor passed to her son (by the Earl of Kent) who died in 1397 and was succeeded by his son, also Thomas, Earl of Kent. (Chan. Inq. p.m. 20, Rich. II, No. 30.) He was created Earl of Surrey, but was imprisoned and beheaded at Cirencester in 1399, presumably for his sympathies towards the unfortunate King. His lands were forfeited by Henry IV (Cal. Pat. Rolls, 1399–1401, p. 195) and granted to his son, John. Later, the manor was restored to Edmund, Earl of Kent (brother and heir to Thomas), who died in 1408. (Chan. Inq. p.m. 10, Hen. IV, No. 51.) Ware manor was then inherited by his sister, Alianore, wife of Thomas Montagu, Earl of Salisbury, who is supposed to have presented the font to the church. (Chan. Inq. 7, Hen. VI, No. 57.) Their daughter, Alice, married Sir Richard Neville, and their son Richard, who also held the manor, became famous as Earl of Warwick, and "Kingmaker"; he was killed at Barnet in 1471. His heiress, Anne, married, firstly, Edward, Prince of Wales (killed after the battle of Tewkesbury) and, secondly, Richard, Duke of Gloucester, who became King in 1483. Hence Ware manor was claimed and kept as Crown property, and in 1485, Sir Robert Brackenbury, Constable of the Tower, was appointed Steward of the manor, with fees of £5 per annum. (Cal. Pat. Rolls, 1476–85.) Queen Anne died in 1485, and was succeeded by her nephew, Edward, Earl of Warwick, but he did not hold Ware, as King Henry VII granted the property to his mother, Margaret, Countess of Richmond, for her life. (Pat. 2, Hen. VII, pt. i, m. 21.) It is part of town tradition that the beautiful old Tudor house, sometimes called Gilpin House, and now (1946) used as Blue Boot Store, was built by Henry VII for his mother. She, too, is held to have taken an active interest in the church. At her death, in 1509, the manor was put into the hands of Sir T. Lovell, treasurer of the household (L. & P. Hen. VIII, i, 285), the following year William Compton, groom of the state, was made bailiff of the town and manor, keeper of the park, meadows, fishery, and two mills. (L. & P. Hen. VIII, i, 992, 1395.)

In 1513, Lady Margaret Pole, sister and heiress of Edward Plantagenet, Earl of Warwick, was reinstated as Countess of Salisbury and Ware manor was restored to her (Exch. Inq. (ser. 2), file 299, No. 9, 10 ; Chan. Inq. p.m. (ser. 2), xxviii, 71), but Henry VIII regarded her with some suspicion and jealousy as being a member of the old royal house of England, and she was beheaded in 1541.

Again the King held the manor, appointing, in 1542, Thomas Wrothe as bailiff and keeper of the park, after Oliver Frankleyn, who had held them by grant from the Countess of Salisbury (L. & P. Hen. VIII, vii, 1251 (15)), and John Noode was granted the fishery or " Tronkage " in the rivulet at Ware (L. & P. Hen. VIII, xiv (2), 1354, 15), which fishery was formerly worth £7 a year and afterwards let for 73/4d. (Mins. Accts. Hen. VIII, 6869.) The two corn mills were leased to Thos. Lennard for 40 years ; (L. & P. Hen. VIII, xix (2), 166, 19) these two mills still carry on business, one on the south side of Ware bridge, and the other down Mill Lane, beside the Roman road just above the ford. This establishment (now owned by Messrs. Allen and Hanbury) still has one portion standing on ancient foundations of stone and timbers which may well date from the time of Thomas Lennard, or perhaps earlier.

In 1515, the value of the Manor was assessed as follows :

Farm of the fishery with agistments of the park £8. 13. 4d.
Increase of rents 19. 6½d.
Issues of the Manor 101s.
Farm of the mill 26. 0. 12d.
Farm of a pasture called Woulekechyn (?) 6. 8d.
(Mins. Accts. 6, Hen. VIII.)

The fishery business seems to have developed as time passed, as the value has increased considerably since 1384, when the manor, then held by Blanche, widow of Thomas Wake, is described (Chan. Inq. p.m. 4, Rich. II, No. 59) in size and value :

Extent 576 acres 3 rods of arable land worth	£9. 4s.	
48 ,, meadow each worth		18d.
40 ,, in the park ,, ,,		12d.
36 ,, wood ,, ,, ,, and without ,,	20s.	
a water mill and a fulling mill ,, £10		
Perquisites of court	100s.	
Fishery from Stretende to Newmededych and		
½ a fishery from Stretende to Bemeford	6s.	
Sum	£58 2. 8d.	

On 17th May, 1548, the manor was granted by King Edward VI to his elder sister Mary (Pat. 2, Ed. VI, pt. v, m. 32) who, on her accession to the throne in 1553, handed over the property to Francis, Earl of Huntingdon, and his wife, Katherine (Pat. 1, Mary, pt. vii, m. 20), the manor, park, and three mills. Probably the third mill was that which stood below Ware Park. This transfer of property was confirmed by Queen Elizabeth in 1570, with the exception of the park, mills, and fishery. (Pat. 14, Eliz., pt. iii.) But by 1575, the Huntingdons were so deeply in debt that they sold the manor to Mr. Thomas Fanshawe, Queen's Remembrancer, who acquired all the property and revived all rights of the lord of the manor by 1587 (Feet. of F. Herts Hil. 29, Eliz.).

Information concerning the financial concerns of the Huntingdons is contained in a letter to Sir Francis Willoughby, whose daughter, Dorothy, was to marry Henry Hastings, nephew of the earl, stating that :

" the earl is about £20,000 in debt, which may greatly charge his land, and that much of this money must have come by the credit of bonds of others. That in respect of procuring such " sumes " of money there may be hidden mortgages upon the land, except the earl upon his honour do confess them. The sale of Ware and Ware Park made by the earl to Mr. Fanshaw may teach you to beware." (*Hist. MSS. Comm.*, MSS. of Lord Middleton, Wollaton Hall, Notts., p. 587.)

Thomas Fanshawe seems to have taken considerable pains to establish himself as an active lord of the manor, soon after acquiring the property there is a note in the Sessions records (Hil. 21, Eliz.) : " T. Fanshaw claims fines paid at the Sessions by the tenants of his liberty at Ware for charging too much for beer, etc." Claim allowed.

In connection with the sale of the property, besides the doubtful financial status of the Earl of Huntingdon, Mr. Fanshawe had to contend with somebody named Stephen Harvye (Star Chamber Proceedings, Elizabeth, Fanshawe *v.* Harvye ; F. 16/35 ; F. 31/2). In the account of the lawsuit Fanshawe is described as appealing to the Crown, stating :

> " The said Stephen Harvye to molest and slander your subject at St. Mary Bowe in the Warde of Cheape, London, did falsely affirm and publish that the said Countess (Huntingdon) before the said feoffment made by her to your subject had assured the said manor to Lady Mary her daughter and Mr. Walter Hastings her son and afterwards to the use of the son of Sir George Hastings, whereas the said Countess in troth had not made any such assurance, by reason of which false slanderous words your subject was greatly hindered in the sale of the said manor. . . .It was ordered that the said Harvye should swere all the aforesaid matter be true whereupon the said Stephen Harvye the 28 November last past of devilish mind and not having the fear of God before his eyes, to the intent he might gain more credit to his slanderous words to the utter discrediting of your subject's state and title in the said manor did falsely and corruptly ' swere upon his corporall oathe ' that the matter of his said plea was true whereas the same is altogether false therefore the said Stephen hath committed wilfull perjury."

Stephen denies he is guilty of perjury but prays to be dismissed with costs.

When business transactions were finally settled Mr. Fanshawe set to work to build himself a country house in Ware Park, though apparently keeping the old town manor for a time as a dower house. (This ancient house, now almost certainly identified as standing on the site of Blue Coat House, must not be confused with the old Rectory Manor, north of the Church, formerly the Alien Benedictine Priory and now rather misleadingly known simply as " the Manor House ".) The old manor, largely rebuilt for Christ's Hospital in the seventeenth century, still retains most interesting features, including carved timbers reaching from floor to roof (ending in a king-post similar to that in the Franciscan Friary), being remains of the great Hall, and also the panelled screens. The magnificent entrance doorway has been dated by an architect as not later than 1400. Brayley, writing in 1808, *The Beauties of England and Wales*, says : " The ancient Manor House, which had been the retirement of the Fanshawes and the occasional residence of their predecessors in the possession of the manor was pulled down by Th. Byde Esq. with the Chapel and long gallery. . . . Sir Rich. Fanshawe, the 10th child of Sir Henry, was born in the ancient Manor House at Ware." (The historian, Dugdale, also mentions this.) The old house seems to have become known as " Ware Place " ; it was the subject of a family lawsuit in 1640 (Parker *v.* Parker, P.R.O. Chancery Bills & Answers, Charles I, 1640, 15th May, P. 46/24). In the minutes of Christ's Hospital, it is noted that " Ware Place " was purchased from William Collett, 1685 ; the house was in great part ruinous, and was ordered to be pulled down and rebuilt with cottages for the nurses and children. (J. F. B. Sharpe.) These buildings still stand, but, in their turn, are being allowed to fall into decay. They are fully described in an article by W. H. Lee, in the *Transactions of the E. Herts Archæ. Soc.*, Vol. VIII, part 3, with reproductions of eighteenth century sketches by Horsnell.

Sir Thomas Fanshawe only lived until 1601, when his son Henry succeeded him at Ware Park. He followed his father in the office of King's Remembrancer, and was knighted in 1603, but died in 1615. During this short time as Lord of the Manor, Sir Henry became noted as a great horticulturist, and his gardens were noted far and wide. We find (Cal. S.P.D., 1611–13) in a letter written by Chamberlain to Carleton : " Earl of Arundel with Inigo Jones the Surveyor paid a visit to Ware Park and were so pleased with the grapes and peaches that the King has sent for them twice a week ever since." Sir H. Wotton, in his *Elements of Architecture*, 1624, wrote :

> " Though other countreys have more benefits of sunne than wee, and thereby more properly tryed to contemplate this delight ; yet have I seene in our owne a delicate and diligent curiositie surely without parallel amonge foreigne nations ; namely in the garden of Sir Henry Fanshaw at his seat in Ware Parke, where I wel remember hee did so precisely examine the tinctures and seasons of his flowers, that in their setting the inwardest of those which were to come up at the same time should be always a little darker than the utmost and so serve them for a kinde of gentle shadow, like a piece, not of Nature,

but of Arte : which mention (incident of this place) I have willingly made of his name for the deare friendship that was long betweene us ; though I must confesse, with much wrong to his other virtues, which deserve a more solid memoriall than amonge these varant observations.''

It was Sir Henry who brought a suit against a certain Henry Osbaston for ploughing up part of Berry Close (the Bury field), a ground that was used for the mustering of trained bands. He also had trouble with the townsfolk for using it as a recreation field without leave.

Another Thomas Fanshawe succeeded his father, and was knighted after the coronation of Charles I, in 1625. He, and all his family, remained staunch Royalists through the troubled years ahead and suffered severe losses, which finally led to the sale of Ware Manor to Sir Thomas Byde in 1668. In a pamphlet, " A perfect Diurnall of the Proceedings in Hertfordshire from the 15th August to the 29, 1642," printed for W. M., 1st September, 1642, we get a little insight into the loyal activities of the lord of the manor :

" On munday the 29th August . . . at Sir Thomas Fanshaws house were found two Peeces of Ordnance, with severall barrels of Powder, Muskets and Pikes : and is thought in the country that he is a great deal better provided, having kept two Gunsmiths these three months in his house to mend and make armes clean, but for the present they cannot learn where they are bestowed." Hartf. Aug. 29, 1642. Yr. loving friend R.E. (Copy in Hertford Museum.)

On the cover of the Parish Church Register, No. 2, is written :

" July the 12th 1655. Sr. Thomas Fanshawe and Sir John Watts are both at theire Habitations accordinge to Proclimation." James Sigston. Clerk and Register the mark of Richard and Bigg Constable Willm. Crosse.

The notice is repeated inside the cover also.

One Volume of the Ware Court Rolls, 1665–1706, is in the British Museum (Add. MSS. 27–977). The last court under Sir Thomas Fanshawe was held on 9th October, 1667, after that, the signature of Sir Thomas Byde appears on the proceedings.

These Rolls contain various entertaining little accounts of petty offenders. Item from Court held 27th September, 1678 :

" Item doe put and order Richard Adams that he doe
sufficiently repaire and amend his wharfe and footpath leading
from the towne of Ware towards Baldock Streete by the time
aforesaide on paine of paying to the Lord of the Manor forty
shillings if he shall make default therein."

" Every man that shall digg any clay or sand upon the Lord's
Ways shall forfeit for every load thereof 6d. Wee paine [fine ?]
every one that shall not make his Teme against the highway 1d.
a pole for every pole that shall not be made up between this
and the first of Aprill next."

" Wee doe order them (Surveyors, Rich. Dickinson, Francis
Frost, and John Harding) to scower and clense the highway
between the Black Swan (23 Baldock St.) and the White Hart
(77, 79 High St.) on or before the first of November next on
paine of payeinge to the Lord of the Manor."

1682. " Wee present Edward Malyn the younger for the penthouse erected before his dwelling house that it is unwanted,
built upon the Lord's way, that it is also built so lowe that
persons cannot safely goo under it without hurting themselves
which is a great Annoyance to all persons that have occasion
to pass that way and we payne him to remove his penthouse
or get a license from the Lord of the Manor for the standing of
it and set it higher before the 5th day of Nov."

" 25th Sept. 1682. We present Thom. Philpott, Edward Roberts,
Ed. Philpott, Thom. Harvey the elder, Ed. Browne and John
Philpott for not scouring an ancient watercourse running
between the pound and the Priory wall."

The manor pound was at the junction of Park Lane and
Watton Road, the watercourse then flowed down into Baldock
Street.

" We present Wm. Holland, John Harding, Ed. Malyn, John
North, John Britton for making severall dunghills before their
doores and we pray that it may be ordered that the sinkes be
scoured and the dunghills be removed."

" Wee doo demand all persons that loose hoggs and lett them
goo abroad without a driver and unrung or unyoaked, ijd
an hogg, the one halfe to the Lord of the Manor and the other
halfe to them that shall take up the said hoggs and putt them
into the Lord's pound."

Note.—A further Volume of Ware Manor Rolls, 1766–83,
is in Hertford Record Office (Hawkins Coll., vol. 37, Doc. 80),
also one membrane, 1692.

Sir Thomas Byde was M.P. for Hertford in 1672, he married

a lady named Skinner of Hitchin. Their son, Skinner Byde, died during his father's lifetime and the manor came to the grandson, Thomas. His son, Thomas Plumer Byde, suffered a recovery of the manor in 1749, and his heir, Thomas Hope Byde, did the same in 1774. This Thomas Hope Byde built the present house in the fashion of that day, destroying for us what must have been far more valuable and pleasing to look on, Mr. Fanshawe's original building.

In 1787, owing to the presence of an unjust and most unpopular Excise Officer, there was almost a riot in the town amongst the maltsters. The officer, Grand, was sufficiently weak and fearful to have the military called in, but they were quickly recalled on account of the great and general indignation caused. The incident is fully recorded in the MSS. of the Earl of Verulam, now in Hertford County Record Office. (See chapter on " Townsfolk ".)

In 1828, just before his death, Mr. Byde had made a new set of official weights and measures, inscribed with his name, and these are preserved for the town.

The manor was then sold to strangers who never came into residence, and this brought to an end the continuity of a " lord of the manor ".

When Sir Thomas Byde came to Ware, he asked permission of the Bishop of London to construct his family vault in the South Transept of Ware Church. This licence was granted, and the document lies in the church safe. Sir Thomas is known outside Ware for his bookplate, described as " excessively rare " for that date ; details are given in the *Home County Magazine*, vol. v.

Ware Manor passed from the Byde family finally in 1846, being sold to James Cudden of Norwich, he parted with it in 1853 to Daniel de Castro, and in 1869 it was conveyed to George Rastrick of Woking, whose family still holds the remnant of this property.

Other documents concerning Ware Manor are held by the Steward of the Manor, and are not available to the student of historical research.

" Old " Ware, in some degree, died away with the passing of an active Lord of the Manor, and this seems a fitting date to close the survey attempted here. A final word picture of that date is fortunately given to us by a native of Ware, J. Smith, who migrated to Melbourne, and wrote articles for a paper there, describing life in the days of his boyhood. (See also in " Inns ".) He tells us :

"Old customs lingered in the town with a tenacious vitality. May-Day would not have been May-Day without the sweeps—' my lord ' in a cocked hat and a suit of the sweeps, ' my lady ' in white muslin and spangles, with a brass ladle to collect the offerings of the public in. ' Jack-in-the-Green,' a locomotive mass of foliage with his black face shining through an aperture in the leaves, while a clown, two ' innocent blacknesses ' in the shape of climbing boys, and a drummer who also played upon the pan-pipes, completed the wandering company, the members of which sang and danced and kept alive in the nineteenth century the Floralia instituted among us by our Roman conquerors. (This custom was still observed well into the 'nineties. E.M.H.) Oak-apple day was celebrated on the 29th of May by the decoration of shops and tavern doors with large branches of oak. Easter Eggs and Fifth of November processions were popular. Whit-Monday was the most important holiday. The subscription reading-room was in the Town Hall, and the London papers did not reach it until 11 o'clock. We schoolboys should have known the hour of their arrival even if we had not heard it strike in the church tower, for our master, the rector, used to take up his hat and march down to the reading-room for the first sight of the ' Times ' with the utmost punctuality, while we would leave our books open on the desk and gather round the fire. . . . Our school was close by the grand old church [this foundation dated from at least 1612]— so close that we could chivy ' Polly Gull's greyhounds '—the inmates of a female charity school inside the churchyard— round its paths, when they and we came out at 12 o'c., to their extreme terror and our commensurate delight. But they had a valiant protector in the person of Lawrence the beadle, whom we hated, as in duty bound. One of his organs of vision was immovable and had a fixed stony stare and therefore we christened him ' Chaney Eye '. We led him a miserable life I'm afraid . . . we practised ventriloquism for the sake of calling out ' Chaney Eye ' from positions where no enemy was visible and as we were fleet of foot and he was gouty, we provoked him to pursue us and mocked at his discomfiture. Another of our victims was ' Billy ' or ' Biddy ' Biggs, the postman, who must have been verging on 70, and so wonderfully like Trotty Veck in figure and feature that I think John Leach must have been acquainted with him. As the P.O. was situated at the extreme end of the town the postmaster used to collect the letters by sound of a bell at 9 o'c. every night. Biddy Biggs was

the bearer of the bell and bag, and to call him from some dark
hiding-place, to watch him stop and listen, and then resume
his progress while he ' swore a prayer or two ' was one of our
impish pastimes.

" After the death of the old whist-playing, easy-going
rector a Puseyite was appointed in his place, who preached in
a white surplice, turned round to the Communion Table when
he recited the Belief and otherwise offended the congregation,
one third of whom rose and left the Church Sunday after
Sunday as he ascended the pulpit stairs. Then the dissidents
seceded in a body and conducted divine service in the Town
Hall, and so the town was split into two factions. It was soon
after this that the railway came and the Ware of olden days
had gone for ever."

After the closing of the Manor Courts, the Reverend Joseph
William Blakesley was appointed, in 1849, under the Public
Health Act, 1848, to conduct and complete the first Election
of the Ware Local Board of Health. The number of persons
to be elected as members of the Local Board was nine, and the
qualifications for membership was that the person should be
resident within the district for which he was elected or within
seven miles thereof and rated to the relief of the poor to some
parish, township, or place of which some part was in the district
of the Local Board of Health upon the annual value of not less
than £25.

From records it appears that the Election Day was fixed
for the 28th August, 1849, and that there were twenty-four
candidates for the nine vacancies.

The first meeting of the Board was held on the
1st September, 1849. Mr. W. Parker was the first Chairman
of the Board, and Mr. Nathaniel Cobham was appointed
Clerk.

The Local Board of Health continued to function until
the operation of the Public Health Act, 1894, when under that
Act it was changed to the Urban District Council and from
the records the first meeting of the Urban District Council was
held on the 2nd day of January, 1895. The town is still governed
by an Urban District Council of twelve members.

[These notes on Local Government were kindly provided
by Mr. L. G. Southall, Clerk to the Ware U.D.C.]

THE RIVER

" By the margin, willow-veil'd,
Slide the heavy barges trail'd
By slow horses."   Tennyson.

The River Lea, Ley, or Luy, and the old North Road (Ermine Street) have both played an important part in the history of the town of Ware ; indeed, the fact of the old road following the line of the Lea Valley, and fording the river just where it did, most probably led to the origin of a settlement and later a town. Certainly, the growth of traffic to and from the north, after Saxon times, led to the growth and development of Ware and added to its prosperity, so that it became known as a resting-place to many famous people, and is mentioned in various records on that account alone.

As the river, naturally, must have existed before the road, it is seemly to give it the prior notice.

The first written reference to the Lea can be found in the *Anglo Saxon Chronicle*, though fragments of pottery and worked flints show that this stretch of the valley was known to, and inhabited by, ancient man. The Romans, too, must have been familiar with the district, since their military section of Ermine Street came to the Ware ford, joining the old road to the north from that point. But there is no evidence that they used this piece of the river for traffic.

It was the Danish invasion, and King Alfred's ensuing campaign, that first brought the Lea into prominence as a water-way, and it is practically certain that it was from this time that Ware became established as a Saxon village. The poet, Vallans, writes that Edward the Elder built a town by the river " two miles from Hertford, and two years later " (916). Two water mills were set up, one beside the ford on the Roman road, to the west of the town. There was a fall of the river at this point (where the lock was built later) and, probably, a natural division into two channels, one of which could be turned to account as the mill stream. This mill is at present the property of Messrs. Allen and Hanbury. The second mill, east of the bridge and junction with the stream from Chadwell Spring, is now worked by Messrs. J. W. French, Ltd. Both mills are mentioned in the Domesday . Book survey.

After the Norman occupation, the Bailiff of Hertford, in the name of the king, claimed the monopoly of the highway,

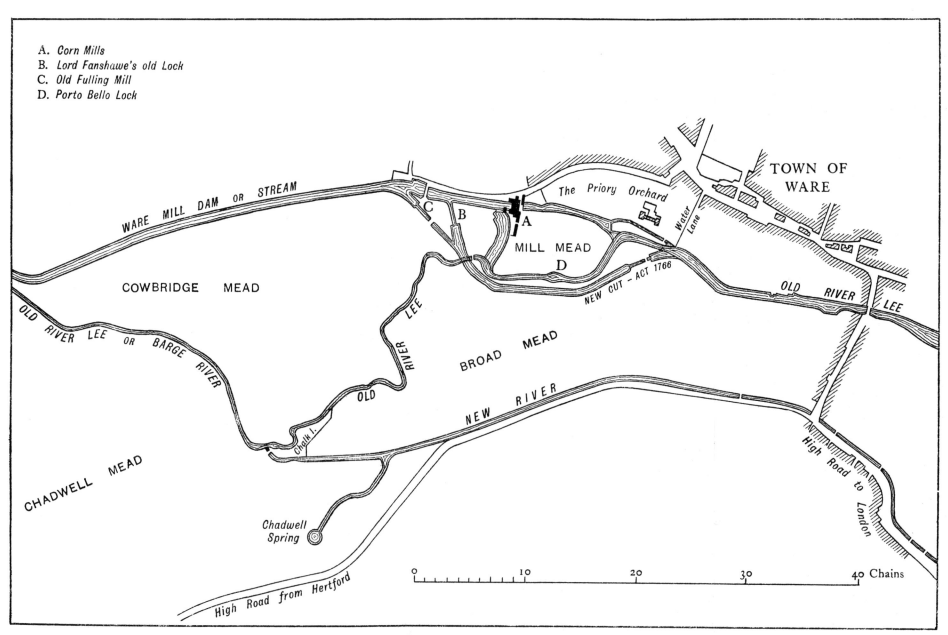

A. *Corn Mills*
B. *Lord Fanshawe's old Lock*
C. *Old Fulling Mill*
D. *Porto Bello Lock*

TOWN OF WARE

WARE MILL DAM OR STREAM

The Priory Orchard

Water Lane

C   B   A

MILL MEAD

D

COWBRIDGE MEAD

NEW CUT – ACT 1766

OLD RIVER LEE

OLD RIVER LEE OR BARGE RIVER

RIVER LEE

OLD LEE

BROAD MEAD

NEW RIVER

High Road to London

CHADWELL MEAD

Chalk I.

Chadwell Spring

High Road from Hertford

0   10   20   30   40 Chains

PLAN OF RIVER LEA SHOWING 1831 ALTERATIONS IN THE POSSESSION OF J. W. TURNER

trying to block Ware ford and chain the Bridge ; later, when the passage of the bridge had been forced, he claimed the Tolls, and by 1191, the passage of the river, ford, and bridge had developed into such a lively bone of contention between the two towns that the rivalry has never entirely died away. It was in 1191 that the men of Hertford came to Ware and broke down the bridge in their efforts to divert all traffic from Ware, trying to force travellers and traders to cross the river at Hertford. (Pipe R. 3, Rich. I, m. 12d.)

Squabbles between the Bailiffs of Hertford and the various holders of Ware manor are all that history has to relate of the Lea, until the reign of Henry VI. During the fourteenth century are several entries in the Hundred Rolls [1] all telling the same tale : " the Lady of Ware and her bailiffs have neglected the weirs of Ware so that no boats can pass as accustomed." Again, " the lady and bailiffs of Ware have altered the weirs . . . to the great annoyance of the burgesses of Hertford, and to the detriment of the town of Hertford." A truce was arranged in 1207 between Margaret, Countess of Leicester (lady of the manor), and Hertford's bailiff, and tolls from all ships laded at Ware were divided between them, reserving free carriage to the Countess for her corn, etc., and free passage for the boats from Hertford. At this time, the Countess granted to the canons of Holy Trinity, London, " free " carriage of their corn by ship from Ware to London at the same price as they paid to her father and mother—1d. on a quarter of hard corn. (Cur. Reg. R. 94, m. 17 (Hil. 10, Hen. III).)

But Ware's neglect of the river led to its own misfortune. The historians Camden and Norden relate that there was a great flood in 1408 (Salmon gives it in 1403), when the town was almost destroyed " by the great inundation of waters that from the upland pass by the town, since which time there was great provision made by wayres and sleuces for the better preservation of the town ".

Although barges were using the Lea in 1423, several petitions were launched in Henry VI's reign to try to improve the condition of the river (3rd Hen. VI, c. 5) : " For authorizing Commissions to be awarded to retain persons to reform the river Ley, running from Ware to the Thames." (9th Hen. VI, c. 9.) " For authorizing the Chancellor to

[1] See " Manor ", p. 4.

grant his Commission to retain persons to scour and amend the river Ley . . . ," and in 1440 a commission was granted to Sir Ralph Cromwel, Knt., John Fray, Robert Rolleston and others to remove all the shelves and shoals in the river. (Dugd. Fens. fol. 81.)

In both these petitions of 1423 (or 1424) and 1429, the river is referred to as : " the Ley one of the great rivers which extends from the Town of Ware to the water of Thames," and, " the river of Ley which runs from the bridge of the town of Ware to the river of Thames." As there is no word of the existence of Hertford, it points to the trade of Ware being far in excess of that of the county town.

The work done at this time does not seem to have been of any lasting quality for, by Tudor times, corn and malt leaving Ware for London was carried by road as far as Enfield before being loaded into barges and, in 1571, the Lea was again the subject of an Act of Parliament. The Introduction of this Act reads :

" Act for bringing the River of the Lee to the North Side of the Citie of London,"

" For as much as is perceived by many grave and wise men, as well of the Citie of London as of the country, that it were very commodious and profitable, both for the Citie and the country, that the River of the Lee, otherwise called ' Ware River ', might be brought within the land to the North part of the said Citie of London, the same to be cut out of the said river in the most aptest and meetest places of the said river Lee, to convey from thence the leading and the passage of the said water through such a convenient and meet cut as may be secure for the navigation of barges and other vessels, and for the carriage and conveying, as well of merchandise, corn, and victuals, as other necessaries, from the Town of Ware unto the said Citie of London, and from the said Citie to the said places and the Towne of Ware. And also for Tiltbotes, and Wherries, for the conveying of the Queen's subjects to and fro, to their great ease and commoditie." (Stat. of Realm (Rec. Com.), iv(i), 553).

What with purchase of ground and erection of locks, the work involved by this act cost the city £80,000.

The restoration of the barge traffic to Ware roused serious opposition amongst the Enfield " loaders ", who resorted to violence in their efforts to retain the trade, damaging the new locks and trying to sink barges with gunpowder. Items from the Cecil papers in the Lansdowne letters show that Ware

men were mixed up in these disturbances. The names of
barge owners are given also and certain details of their trade.
In vol. i, f. 42, no. 33 :

" Barge owners. Robert Leonard, 1
            Richard Brooke,   1
            John Mathysomm, 1 boate
            John Whiskhood,   1
            John Spencer   1 boate
            Richard Sibborne 1 boate

R. Broke, of Ware, hath two barges, the *Great Blue Lion*, the
burden whereof is 42 qrs. and worketh with 5 men, and the
Little Blue Lion of 28 qrs. with 3 men. Masters of barges are
44, the servants working in them 7 score and odd.

The burden of the barges are 1 m. 1 c. The numbers of
men occupied lc.xxiii. A gret barge costeth xiL. with all
furniture. A small barge costeth xi marks with all furniture.
The greatest barge laden draweth xvi ins., the leist barge laden
draweth xvi ins. A cart loaden holdeth at Ware viii qrs. of
malt, 5 qrs. of wheat. For 1 qr. of wheat xi*d.* for 5 bushels of
wheat viii*d.* Five bushels of wheat meal is as heavy as 8 bushels
of wheat. They take for every hundred iiii*d.* and per ton
vi*s.* viii*d.*, for a caldron of coals or a wey of salt vi*s.* viii*d.*, for
carriage of one person vi*d.* The masters do give to their
bargemen, to the stearman x*s.* or viii*s.* or ix*s.*, to every other
viii*s.*

They lade on Saturday, on Monday go down to Bow
Bridge to tarry the tide. From the Bow with the tide they will
pass in 4 hours, if they row away. They come on to London
with flood and return at an ebb to the creek mouth, and then
with a flood. The lock at the Bow opens at the first beginning
to flow. They shut it at the highest of the flood. They come
from Bow to Waltham in 6 hours and from Waltham to Ware
in another 6 hours."

No. 34 contains a petition (1583) of the inhabitants of
Ware to Lord Burghley, for a commission to hinder damage
done to the river, signed by Richard Pegram, Thomas Hoode,
Richard Brooke, Thomas Gold, and Walter Tuck.

No. 38, 32 is an answer to Enfield concerning carrying
grain by water : " the highway to Ware by land is more
possible for those that ride post and all others, than before
when it was pestered with malt horses besides very many other
commodities and great saving of unnecessary expenses."

Letter 37. " Richard Shephard, servant of Richard Brooke, confesseth that Isabell Modham did tell him that her brother Richard Cowper did tell her that James Browne did tell him that he was one of them that cutt mardich [a ditch or cutting ?] and that afterwards Richard Cowper told this examynant so muche."

Letter 35. " John Styer of Ware, waterman, dothe affirme all the speache and confession of his fellowe Richard Stringer saving the wishing of a barrell of gunpowder (gonne) under the bardge and sayeth further that he sayd he would give fourtie shillinges to know who did attempt to burn ye locke to which penifather sayed what were you the better if that you did know for [if] yourself did know who did it you could but hange him amongst you and if he were hanged you would have evill going by the River after."

William Vallans (see " Celebrities ", p. 148) writes of the interest taken by Thomas Fanshawe, Lord of the Manor (1575–1601), in this Lea Navigation scheme and also tells of a stone-arched bridge. It is not known when this bridge was replaced, but, through the occurrence of an accident, another bridge is mentioned in *The Gentleman's Magazine*, two hundred years later. The incident is described as follows : " In the evening as the St. Ives waggon was passing over Ware bridge, just as the horses were over, some of the planks gave way and let in the waggon. Fortunately the pole-pin breaking in the instant disengaged the horses, and the waggon with contents were received into an empty barge under the bridge and all recovered except the hind wheels, which flew off and sunk in the river, whence they were not got out till some time after. The bridge was new-built of timber not above 25 years ago." (*The Gentleman's Magazine*, 5th January, 1788, vol. 58, p. 79.) In different parts of the town pieces of stone can be seen which may well have come from the Elizabethan structure, in old gateways placed against the timber to protect it from collision with cart-wheels.

In 1665, at the time of the great Plague, Ware River and Ware bargees made a name for themselves in history. They continued carrying corn to London all through the period of that dread scourge, helping very largely to save the city from starvation. For this gallant service Charles II granted certain privileges to Ware to be enjoyed for all time.

From this time onwards, Ware barges have been entitled

to enter the Thames without taking the service of a Lighterman, and Ware bargees on their return home from a " voyage " may demand refreshment at an Inn at any hour.[1]

In 1667, the Dutch were in the mouth of the Thames, and " Ware River " again played a part in provisioning London. Coal which usually reached the capital from the Midlands via the East coast was unshipped at King's Lynn, and notes on the situation are found in a communication from Edward Bodham to Williamson (Arlington's secretary).—July 5th, " Arrival of 60 sail of Colliers. Thinks the coal will be carried from Lynn to London. Price is 30s. per chaldron. Water carriage to Cambridge, 4s., land carriage thence to Ware 20 or 25s. and water carriage from Ware to London 6s. or 7s. per chaldron." (Cal. S.P.D., 1667, p. 268.)

In 1669 is the first official mention of the water taken from the Lea to augment the supply from the New River. (Cal. S.P.D., 1669, 9th November, p. 573.) " Approval of the King of the subjoined decree of the Commissioners of Sewers for the R. Lee and the New River, published at the sessions of sewers, St. Andrews, Holborn, viz. that the two pipes for conveying water from the R. Lee to the New R. by Chalk Island, near Ware, be one 6 and the other 8 inches bore, and that turnpike jetties be set up by the New R. Co. to raise the water of the Lee high enough to pass through the pipes, yet not so as to endanger any vessel, or to cause inundation of the meadows ; the decree to be certified in Chancery." (Eleven signatures and note of the king's approval. Corroborated by an Order in Council, Whitehall, 1st December.)

In 1675, the Thames Watermen Bill was passed, which stated that " in times of imminent danger . . . no person shall row between Gravesend and Maidenhead except . . . (various vessels named) and the Ware River barges ". (House of Lords Cal., 15th May, 1675.)

By 1694, the river was again the subject of petitions for repair, over and over again the complaints of the maltsters and barge-owners of Ware may be found telling the tale of neglect, leading to much delay and inconvenience to navigation. They are fully recorded in a MS. book, " Extracts from Records relating to the Lee and the New River," now

[1] Although these privileges have been exercised since 1665, and are recognized by the Port of London Authority, no documentary evidence has ever been traced.

in the library of the Guildhall, London.   A few quotations
will amply illustrate the state of affairs.

"Tues. 31st July, 1694. Rine Willi. et Marie Angli. etc.
sexto.

Upon the humble petition of Richd. Dickenson and
other Navigators upon the R. Lee, alias Ware R. and Traders
in and aboute the Towne of Ware in the Co. of Hertford
complayning of Severall Locks Wears Turnpikes and Ditches
made and erected in or nere the said River to their great
Charge and prejudice contrary to the true intent and meaning
of an Act of Parliamt. made in the 13th yeare of the Reigne
of Queene Elizabeth.   And Therefore praying this Court to
request the Right Honble. the Lord Keeper of the great Seale
of England to appoint Sixteene Commissioners Pursuant to
the said Act for the Putting the said Act in Execution to the
End the Said River may be cleansed and for the future be
kept Navigable.   It is by this court referred to Sr. Robt.
Geffery Sr. John Ffleet Sr. Peter Daniel Sr. Thomas Lane
Sr. Edward Clarke Sr. Humphrey Edwin Sr. Richd. Levett
and Sr. Wm. Gore Kts. and Aldermen, or any Three of them
to Consider of the said Peticion and ye Account of the said
Locks Weares Turnpikes and Ditches now delivered in by the
said Peticion and what is fitt to be done by this Court therein
And to Report their Opinions unto this Court and John Nix
to warne and attend them."

Tuesday, 14th August, 1694.   "This Day the Committee
lately Appointed by this court to consider of a Peticion
delivered by Severall Navigators and Maulsters in and aboute
the Towne of Ware in the County of Hertford. . . . Pursuant
to an Order. . . . Wee the Committee . . . have mett and
considered the said Peticion and Find there are severall
Locks Turnpikes and Ditches by Incroachment on the Old
Cutt and are of opinion this Honble. Court may Peticion the
Rt. Honble the Lord Keeper to appoint and Authorize
Committees under the Great Seale to Inspect and remove
the Incroachmt. on the said R. Lee Pursuant to an Act of
Parl. made in the 13th yeare of the Reigne of Queen Elizabeth
All of which Nevertheless Wee Submitte to the grave Wisdome
of this Honble Court."

After this, Mr. George Seracole "who hath Surveyed the
River up to Ware and is skilled in such affairs" reports :
"It appears there is a fall or declivity of the Water from Old

Ford to Bromley Lock of at least Fifteen Foot by reason whereof the highest Penn of Water they can make at Bromley (altho' thereby they drowne the Lands and Spoile the City Mills) will not fetch the Ware Barges off from the Flatts of Old Ford without the help of a Spring Tyde. But they lay there sometimes Twelve or Sixteen Days before they can gett off To the great Damage of the City in the Excessive hightening of the Water Carriage from Ware which as we are now Informed is now Nineteen s. p. Tun and the Lands Carriage but 20s. p. Tun. but we are informed both by the said Bargemasters and by the said Mr. Seracole and in our own Judgments do believe that if the said intended Lock be sett up . . . that the largest Barge may come over the said Flatts and fall down into the Tyde."

In 1720, an Act for improving the Navigation of the Lea was " proposed ", but in 1736 the complaints were as loud as ever, on 27th July of that year : " A Petition of several Malsters Barge Owners and Navigators of the town of Ware in the Co. of Hertford . . . was . . . this day presented to this Court . . . that at a certain Bridge called Temple Mills Bridge near the lower end of Hackney Marsh . . . has caused the Eddy to cast up such great quantities of Sand and Gravell that the same is become a Bank whereby the several Barges Boats and other Vessels . . .have been Interrupted in their Passage." Petition that the Obstacle be removed. (Signed by) :

John Richford	Richd. Dickinson	Humphy Adams
John Lowen	In' Docwra	Thos. Goodwin
Edw. Mitchell Jr.	Edw. Mitchell	John Leighton
Humphrey Ives	John Carter	Robt. Thorowgood
Benj. Curtis	Edw. Fearne	James Huson
Robt. Daniell	Thos. Mitchell	Benj. Hudson
Thos. Pettit	John Brown	Jhe. North
Jn. Ives Jr.	Robt. Reason	Searth Wyatt
Josh. Mitchell	Wayte Hampson	Wm. Wilburn Sr.
William Leek	George Hagger	Wm. Harvey
Jn. Adams	Thomas Scott	James Mitchell
		Wm. Tyms

The Petition was referred to the Aldermen, attended by Mr. Waterbayliff, who agreed that the work was necessary. In 1738, they were still thinking about it—" at an Especial Court held on the Feast of Saint Mark the Evangelist (that

is to say) Tuesday the 25th day of April 1738 ". And though
an Act was passed in 1739 to regulate the amount of water
supplied by the Lea to the New River (an important proceeding
which finally ended the long standing disputes between the
Corporation of the Borough of Hertford, the inhabitants of
Ware, and the Governor and Company of the New River),
the Lea was still waiting for attention. In 1741, Tuesday,
28th July : " Mr. Town Clerk acquainted the Court thet he
had received a Letter from Mr. Toller Clerk to the Trustees
and Commissioners of Sewers for preserving and Improving
the Navigation of the R. Lee . . . purporting that a Meeting
of the said Trustees will be held at the Bull Inn at Ware in the
Co. of Hertford and the Lord Mayor, Aldermen and Recorder
of the City of London being amongst other Trustees and
Commissioners he desired the Town Clerk to acquaint them
with the time and place of Meeting that they may if they
please be at it." We do not know if these distinguished gentlemen honoured the Meeting with their presence, but if they
did, nothing seems to have come of it for, 28th September,
1742, there is yet another petition " from Owners of Barges
and Boats imployed on the R. Lee, alias Ware River, and of
several Malsters ". This plea was postponed again and again
until 1760, when malt was being carried by road from Bell's
Wharf to the City. An inquiry made in December of that year
" declared that it was absolutely necessary that the New
Cutt . . . should be immediately cleared of Obstructions . . .
that the same should be effectually performed in six months
in such manner as that it should endure for the Age of Man ".
A laudable but somewhat ambitious proposal. In 1766, the
river was still reported as very dangerous, in spite of various
attempts at improvement and then, after these interminable
delays, the work was entrusted to and successfully carried
through by Messrs. Smeaton and Yeomans.

Ware Lock was again rebuilt in 1831, when various objects
of great antiquarian value were discovered and described in a
letter from W. Chadwell Mylne, Esq., dated 22nd October,
1831, printed in *Archæologia*, vol. xxiv, p. 350. There were
found :—Skeletons, a portion of steel-yard, apparently Roman,
a brass coin of Domitian, a brass candlestick, an iron axe-
head, a finger ring, a hairpin, a Roman key, a brass coin of
Severus, two grindstones of Herts Conglomerate or concrete
stone.

During the Great War, 1914–18, " Ware River " again took a part in national affairs, special boats for the carriage of ammunition to France being built and launched in Ware docks.

The following note on the derivation of the name **LEA** is to be found in *English River Names*, by Eilert Ekwall :

> " LEA, first found written LYGEAN, how it developed into LEA is not known. Various forms go back to O.E. LYGE, M.E. LUYE. LYGE may be derived from LUG = light, it is also held to be the base of LUGU (in Gaul), O.Ir. LUG, Welsh LLIN, the name of a deity ; the name may mean either ' the bright river ' or ' river dedicated to Lugus '."

So the later controversies as to whether the river should be referred to as LEA or LEE seem to be unnecessary, neither form of spelling bearing much resemblance to the early name. As late as 1711, the spelling LEYE is used.

THE HIGHWAY

" And up and down the people go."
In " The Lady of Shalott ", Tennyson.

It is clear that from very early times a track wound along the west side of the Lea Valley in the narrow belt between the marshland and the forest, from what is now London to what is now Ware, then forded the Lea and turned north. Presumably it was found convenient, judging by contours, to make the crossing between the Rib and the Ash Valley on low-lying ground, where the hills approach more closely.

Down the length of the valley, relics of prehistoric man have been found, and it seems likely that the Romans used the existing track until the need arose to cut the straight military road from London to Ware, known later along its whole length as " Ermine Street ". No satisfactory derivation of this name has been found ; among various offered is the idea that the Romans, somewhere on the road, had a temple for the worship of Hermes.

Ermine Street was one of the four great through roads to enjoy the King's Peace from the eighth or ninth century. These roads (including the Icknield Way, Fosse Way, and Watling Street) were the " Quatuor Chimini " of the Norman laws. (*Origins of Eng. History*, C. I. Elton, 2nd ed., 1890.)

Ware, as we have seen, owing its growth and prosperity to its position on river and road, naturally gets many a mention by travellers to and from the north and, as the name " Ermine Street " faded out of general speech, the route became popularly known as " The old North Road ".

Up and down this ancient Trackway, Roman Street, Saxon and Norman highway, and first Turnpike in England, have passed many figures known in English history as well as the varied travellers of humbler rank, including merchants, students for Cambridge, vagrants, friars, pilgrims on this " waie to Walsingham ", and many another, all of them coming through Ware and some of them leaving a few words concerning their journey.

Probably the earliest episode of importance to occur on this road was King Harold's desperate march south when, straight from victory at Stamford, he and his Saxon followers came down the road to their tragic defeat at Hastings. By then Ware must have been a well-established village (as described in Domesday Book twenty years later) and probably men of Ware attached themselves to the last of the Saxon kings at his passing through.

It is written in the Hundred Rolls (3 Ed. I) that: " the bridge of the town is part of the king's highway and beyond the bridge which was established in the presence of king Henry (III) and 24 knights in the time of Roger de Quincy, earl of Winchester." These records also mention houses built on the king's highway and, again : " the bailiff and men of Ware have turned aside the way that used to pass by Hertford to Ware to the detriment of the town of Hertford." But well before this date, during the reign of King John, Sayer de Quincey had established the freedom of the highway for Ware and, though the complaints from Hertford continued for a time, their bailiff was powerless to re-establish any lasting authority.

In May, 1455, another distinguished visitor arrived from the north by this high road—Richard, Duke of York, bringing his demonstration of armed troops, stayed in Ware whilst a messenger was sent to London with letters to the King, Henry VI, asking that a conference might be arranged. This message was kept from the King by his advisers who, with the King, left for St. Albans. The Duke of York, receiving no reply, and taking this as a challenge, followed through Hertford to St. Albans and so began the fateful Wars of the Roses ; this calamity was hanging in the balance whilst the Duke was in Ware.

In the sixteenth century, and almost certainly from much earlier days, a beacon was maintained by the Lea from monies drawn from the White Hart and Saracen's Head inns, but whether this stood by the bridge or ford is not known. (Aug. Off. Misc. Bks., xiv, f. 127.) Apparently these monies were not always forthcoming, for there is a complaint from the county feoffees (Aug. Off. Proc. 31/29) : " to Sir Richard Sacvyle, (Chan of Court of Aug.) as to tenements in Ware called the White Hart and ' Sarsonshed ' for lands, the issues to go towards the reparation and maintenance of a bridge called Ware bridge and towards maintaining a beacon near the said town etc. The king takes 40 marks yearly in toll for the maintenance of the bridge but never repairs it." (See also " Guilds ", p. 63.)

Information concerning the kind of trade passing along the road is given in a lease of 1485 to a certain John Scarlett :

" the following customs on all things going through the bills
of Ware, Hattefeld-Bishop, Thele, and elsewhere in divers
places in the Co. of Hertford ; that is to say twopence for
every cart carrying woolen cloth, hides, wine, and other
merchandise and things for sale passing over the bridges of
Ware and Hertford or elsewhere : for every pack-horse laden
with things for sale, of which the pack is bound with cord
or other fastenings under the horse's stomach one penny, but
if there be no fastening, then one halfpenny, except the horse
be carrying corn for itself, then one farthing ; for every man
going over the bridge and elsewhere and carrying on his
back merchandise and other things for sale the value of which
exceeds four sterling, one shilling." (From notes collected
by E. E. Squires.)

During the reign of Henry VIII, there was much coming
and going from the north on our old road, and consequently
much traffic of importance and interest passing through
Ware. The following references to our town are written in the
Letters and Papers of Henry VIII.

8th March, 1534. John Rokewood writes from court :
" Scotch ambassadors have not yet arrived but are at Ware,
a Bishop and an abbot with others to the number of 70 horse."
8th October, 1536. Henry's great minister, Thomas Cromwell,
travelling north on account of the rebellion in Yorks
writes : " This night I am lodged at Ware with 100 horsemen
and have appointed Thurston and Goodwyn and his brother
Thomas as guides to 40 handguns which lie this night at
Waltham. Intend soon after midnight to repair to Huntingdon
and gather such company as I can." A week later,
15th October, John Freman writes to Cromwell, " Propose
to lie this Sunday night at Ware and after speed to Lincoln."

On 18th April, 1537, is noted my Lord Darcy's counsel to
Aske at his coming to the King at Christmas " to leave a
horse and man at Lincoln, Stamford, Huntingdon, Royston,
and Ware to give warning in case Aske should be taken."

In 1538, Sir William Kingston writes to Cromwell :
" This day Roose herald of Scotland came to the king and
delivered letters from his master desiring passport for certain
ladies and also gentlemen which the king desires he shall
have. They are now at Ware and you are to appoint some to
keep them company there and get knowledge how they have
been entertained in Scotland." The people concerned were

Madame de Montreuil and suite, who had accompanied Madeleine, James V's first queen, into Scotland, and were returning to France. On 14th September, 1542, the Duke of Norfolk writes to the council, from Scrobie, "the French Ambassador's kinsman (Jean de Formes) brought the Scottish Ambassador to Ware hitherwards."

A note as to personal travelling expenses is given in the accounts of the Duke of Rutland (Rutland MSS., Hist. MSS. Comm., p. 367) : "The xiij of December, anno quarto Edwardi Sexti, by th' andes of John Baate for ij post horses from Ware to London with the gyde iij*s*. viij*d*."

A lively little incident which took place in the High Street, in 1601, evidently at one of the posting-houses, is related by one, "Captain" John Skynner, who had married "a poor kinswoman" of Cecil's, and seems to have been employed by Sir Robert for various purposes. He writes to his employer from Ware, 6th June, 1601 : "You commanded my speed. Here at Ware, hasting after 3 hours stay for my commission to be served, and murder cried out upon those who desire speed for the horses, I went down and speaking what concerned the appeasing of a multitude disorderly collected, they fell upon me, and have wounded me in three or four places. Since, most rudely have made further and savage mis-behaviours. I humbly beseech you, if your hand have a favour, and since your place, as you to your high honour use it and not so much as you might, hath a justice, either let me not live thus foiled, wherein I must now take my fortune or comfort in all my dispositions which are yours with a good passage of my downgoing, and a just consideration of this unlawful and violent attempt against me. Here I lie at Ware till I receive comfort from that honour of yours which doeth injustice to no man." From this wordy and somewhat ambiguous complaint it seems that one poor traveller would retain only sore recollections of his visit to Ware ; what steps, if any, Cecil took to soothe his wounds history does not relate.

During the reign of James I, there are many mentions of his passing up and down the old North Road and through Ware, the first occasion being on his accession to the throne, in 1603. What excitement for Ware as the new monarch, accompanied by his Scottish retinue, came by to London. In 1612, also, the town must have been immensely interested in the funeral procession of Mary, Queen of Scots, when

King James ordered the removal of the body of his mother from Peterborough to Westminster. The cortège passed through Ware on 7th October, in the charge of Neile, Bishop of Lichfield. Going north in 1617, King James set out from Theobalds with his queen, Anne of Denmark, who travelled with him to Ware and then returned. She died in 1619, and that year Sir Lewis Watson wrote in a letter to his cousin, Sir Edward Montague, K.B. : " The king is pretty well recovered, and came last night to Ware, so to Tiballes during pleasure. The gout is gotten into one of his knees which makes him to be carried all the way in a chair." 21st April (MSS. of Lord Montague of Beaulieu, p. 96, Hist. MSS. Comm.).

Although from early times the condition of the river, as a waterway, was continually brought to public notice, it was not until the seventeenth century that serious attention was drawn to the deplorable state of the roads. This notice seems to have been due in part to King James himself making complaint for, in the Acts of Privy Council under date 16th October, 1623, is recorded : " Whereas we have formerly written letters and given directions for the amendment of highways etc. . . . these are to will you to see the passage betweene Ware and Royston to be presently amended before his Majesty have cause to come that way again by all the means that may be." Lord President, Lord Privy Seal, Lord Brooke, Mr. Treasurer, Mr. Secretarie Calvert, Master of the Rolls.

Just before the Civil War the justices sitting at Buntingford and Ware were called on by the king to suppress all wheeled traffic during the winter between Royston, Buntingford, and Ware, to give the highway a rest. This was done and all malting traffic was carried, or supposed to be, on packhorses, though occasionally the rule was relaxed and permission extended to use carts with two wheels drawn by only five horses. Even so, the bad condition of this road was well enough known to pass into a figure of speech and, in another letter to Lord Montague, we read : " 1641, Dec. The Lord Digby stood up in the Lord's House, and made a most invective speech against the Commons' House . . . and bespattered them as much as one would do his cloak in riding from Ware to London." (MSS. of Lord Montague of Beaulieu, p. 137.)

About this time, 8th May, 1639, another riotous little

affair took place in the High Street, and is related as follows :
" Lord Ker, the Earl of Roxburgh's son, riding post the other
day into the north, having letters from the Queen, came to
Ware, and the Postmaster went out to take up three horses for
his use, but out of malice would have taken a great cart-
horse which carried corn to the market, only the owner, a
poor countryman, would not part with it, saying his horse
was not to ride post. The Postmaster and he being in strife
together in the market, three Deputy-Lieutenants, Justices
of the Peace, namely Sir Richard Lucy, Sir John Butler, and
Sir John Watts, convening there about country business, saw
this contention out of the window of the inn, and they relieved
the countryman, bidding the Postmaster seek out other horses
more fit for the service, whereupon the Postmaster in a great
chafe goes back to Lord Ker and tells him the Deputy-
Lieutenants had taken one of those horses he had taken up by
his warrant. Lord Ker frets at this and learns of the Postmaster
where the Deputy-Lieutenants' horses stand and commands
three of these horses to be saddled to ride post with. The
Deputy-Lieutenants have notice of this and will not let their
horses be saddled, whereupon a great contention ensued
between the Lord and these Deputy-Lieutenants, so hot
grew Lord Ker, who had a case of pistols by his side, that he
and his two men challenge the three justices into the field
to end the difference. Sir John Butler and Sir John Watts
had good stomachs to go out with them, but Sir Richard
Lucy, a more temperate man, would rather use his authority
than his courage that way, as being much the more justifiable
course, and so sent out to provide post-horses for them which
were brought to the gate. Sir Richard then tells Lord Ker
there are post-horses for him and if he will not take them
himself, will make his Lordship fast and take from him the
Queen's letters and send them to His Majesty and do his
errand, which would be little to his Lordship's advantage.
Whereupon Lord Ker cools a little, and, grumbling at being
thus thwarted, takes the horses provided for him and away
he posts. These justices wrote a letter forthwith to Lord
Salisbury, then Lord Lieutenant, relating the whole passage,
which they sent post after the Lord, to be at Court as soon
as he should be." (From notes collected by E. E. Squires.)

Evidently during the disturbed years that followed, the
malting trade in Ware increased considerably and the

regulations concerning the size of waggon wheels and teams were ignored, but it was not until after the Restoration that serious steps were taken to remedy the existing condition of decay. J. H. Hinde, writing of the old North Road in *Archæologia Æliana* (part ix, 1858, pp. 237–255), says, " In 1663, it was represented to Parliament by the Justices of the counties of Hertford, Cambridge, and Huntingdon, that ' the ancient highway and postroad leading from London to York and so into Scotland . . . by reason of the great and many loads which are weekly drawn in waggons to Ware (whence there was water-carriage to London) and the great trade in barley and malt . . . is become so ruinous and almost impassable that the ordinary course appointed by all former laws and statutes of this realm is not sufficient for the effectual repairing of the same '.   On this petition Parliament fell back on certain medieval precedents, among them the erection of three gates and tolls (one to be at Wadesmill) for the next eleven years. The revenue to be devoted to repairs.   The other gates were at Caxton, Cambs, and Stilton, Hunts.   Only one was successful.   At Stilton, the idea raised such local opposition that the gate was never erected, that at Caxton was put up but easily evaded, so the third at Wadesmill was the first effective toll-gate in England."   Further records of these complaints as to the decay of the road and the setting up of the Tolls may be found nearer home, in the documents of the Herts County Sessions, in 1646–7, where it is noted that : " The great decay of all the ways arises through the unreasonable loads of malt brought into and through Ware to Hodsdon from remote parts, and the bringing of great loads of malt from both the Hadhams, Alburie, Starford, all the Pelhams and Clavering, through Ware Extra, and the excessive loads from Norwich, Bury, and Cambridge weekly, the teams often consisting of 7 or 8 horses.   There is a great increase of malsters in Ware.   The surveyors neglect to warn all owners of teams in the parish, and others that have draft horses, to perform their day's work, and also neglect to present defaulters in this respect.   Moreover, landholders in Ware hire teams from other parishes to plough their lands, which lands are amenable to contribution towards the repair of the said ways.   If the malsters would carry lighter loads with only 4 horses as they used to, and each person would duly perform his works, the ways could be sufficiently amended.   The surveyor and inhabitants of Ware Extra are content to help the surveyors of Ware Infra on such days as may be spared, but not to neglect their own highways." In spite of this assurance of " content " from the surveyor of Ware Extra (Wareside) he seems to have more than enough trouble in getting any work done in his own area, judging by a delicious little account also in the Sessions records :

May, 1672. An account of what was laid out by Thomas Bird, surveyor of the Upland, for the mending of the highways :—

Given to the shovell men to drinke to encourage them	£0. 1. 6d.
Given them more in the highway to encourage them to work hard	£0. 0. 6d.
Given to eleven carts [carters ?] to drinke to incourage them	£0. 1. 6d.
Paid 3 men digging 30 load of gravel at Widbury Hill	£0. 8. 0d.
Paid 6 men in the highways 3 days at 10d. per day	£0. 15. 0d.
Paid Goodman Bray for 1 teame 1 day, and 2 teames 2 days at 7s. per teame	£1. 15. 0d.
Paid to a shovell man for 2 days to shovell in the cart rakes	£0. 2. 0d.

Shortly before the inauguration of the Toll, Samuel Pepys, in his famous Diary, makes several references to Ware and the road to Cambridge : " *Feb. 24, 1660*, the way exceeding bad from Ware to Puckeridge. *Aug. 2, 1661*, I set out and rode to Ware, this night, in the way having much discourse with a fell-monger, a Quaker, who told me what a wicked man he had been all his lifetime till within this two years. Here I lay and got up early the next morning. *Sept. 17, 1661*, [with his wife] we got to Ware, and there supped, and to bed very merry and pleasant. The next morning up early and begun our march ; the way about Puckridge very bad, and my wife, in the very last dirty place of all, got a fall, but no hurt, though some dirt. At last she begun, poor wretch, to be tired, and I to be angry at it, but I was to blame ; for she is a very good companion as long as she is well. *Oct. 15, 1662*, Will (his servant) and I . . . came to Ware about three o'clock in the afternoon, the ways being everywhere but bad."

After the Toll had been working for some twenty years, a Petition from Innkeepers and other inhabitants of Ware was presented at the Sessions court, 1693, showing that a turnpike was set up at Wadesmill, to the procuring whereof the petitioners contributed " what in them lay ", hoping to have some advantage thereby in the way of trade : but that now when any waggon, cart, or carriage comes " loaden " through the said turnpike to Ware and pays for such passage as the act directs, in case the same waggon, cart, or carriage returns empty the next morning through the same turnpike, the persons who collect the toll compel the same payments for such returning passage when empty as before when " loaden ". By this means the petitioners' constant customers, by whom, in a great measure they and their families subsist, do not stay all night at Ware as usual, but return beyond the said turnpike as soon as they have unloaded, to prevent repayment, to the great prejudice of the petitioners and of the trade of the town of Ware in general. The petitioners pray that, in consideration of their great rents, and also as they have always readily and cheerfully, for many years past, for their majesties service, entertained and quartered great numbers of soldiers, often to their great loss and damage, that an order be made for their relief in the matters complained of. At the foot of the document is a note : " Whereas there is a clause in the act, that when any waggon or cart goes through the turnpike loaded, and doth come back the same day, such waggon is not to pay, now the court is of opinion that if such waggon return empty within 12 hrs. such returning shall count as the same day and shall not be liable to pay."

In spite of funds provided for the road from tolls, there could not have been any solid improvement for Ralph Thoresby, F. R. S., wrote in his diary, in 1680 : " Ware, 20 miles from London, a most pleasant road in summer, and as bad in winter, because of the depth of the cart ruts." And again, 17th May, 1695 : " Rode by Puckeridge to Ware, where we baited, and had some showers, which raised the washes upon the road to that height that passengers from London that were upon the road swam, and a poor higgler was drowned, which prevented our travelling for many hours, yet towards evening adventured with some country people." (1830 ed., p. 275.)

Defoe, writing of his Tour through Great Britain in 1724, gives a better account of the road between Ware and Royston, he says : " though this road is continually work'd upon, by the vast numbers of Carriages, bringing Malt and Barley to Ware, for whose sake indeed, it was obtained ; yet, with small repairs it is maintain'd and the Toll is reduced from a penny to a halfpenny."

One more muddy incident seems worth the telling before leaving the old North Road to develop, through various stages, to the condition of tarred billiard table with which we are familiar to-day. Among the MSS. and letters of Sir Harry Verney, Bart., Claydon House, Bucks, is a note, dated 5th May, 1669. " Tom Elliott won his match at Newmarket ; but that that likes me better is that Sir Th. Fanshaw being on the road from Ware to London in the company of my Lord Fanshaw, Sir John Morton and others, uppon a sudden crack of Sir John's to ride to London with any horse there to London, being about 16 or 17 miles, for 1000L, Sir Tho. undertook him for 100L and beat him and his horse all to dirt, for he was so bedasht that neither horse nor man would be known, for which the King and Duke did not laugh a little at him." (Hist. MSS. Comm., 7th Report.)

And because no old road can tell a complete tale without reference to a highwayman, history obligingly gives at least two.

There is an early note of highway robbery in a complaint from William de Walden, Clerk to Edward II, stating that he and his servants were assaulted and robbed at Cheshunt and Ware on his way to the king at York. (Cal. Pat. 7th December, 1312.)

Among the Acts of Privy Council is found, dated 8th April, 1582, this note : " One Richard Bacon in the prisonne at Newgate lately apprehended and committed for a robberye by him and others uppon a servante of the Lord Clinton not farre from Ware forasmuche as his pacte touching the force on the highe waye is not tryable but in the countye where the same hathe bene committed their Lordships thincke mete that he be removed from London into that countye." And in *Lives of the Highwaymen* by Captain Johnson, 1734, is written : " A Highwayman known as ' the Colonel ' and friend left London for Scotland, walked to Ware and at an inn took advantage of the bustle during the arrival of a coach to help themselves to a countryman's horse and rode off to Cambridge. After many adventures abroad the ' Colonel ' made money in Virginia, obtained the king's pardon and returned."

One glimpse at the Vagrants who have passed upon this ancient highway is given in the Herts Co. Records when, in 1711, Thos. Hoy, constable of Royston, is presented at the Quarter Sessions for " receiving vagrants on horseback and letting 'em travell to Ware on foote."

Note.—John Wesley records in his *Journal* (Standard Ed., vol. vii, p. 214) that he passed through Ware on Tuesday, 10th October, 1786.

Finally it must not be forgotten that the old North Road, for one stretch, is Ware High Street itself, and its early condition here does not seem to have been in any way superior to that of the outskirts ; a complaint is brought to the Quarter Sessions in 1628 that : " the highway in the common street of Ware leading into and through the said town is in decay and that the inhabitants within the town from time immemorial have repaired and still ought to repair and cleanse the said highway severally and respectively next to their several houses."

Also, it should be remembered that until about 1820, the Upper and the Lower Bourne both flowed as open streams for the whole of their lengths. The Upper Bourne (from High Oak and Musley meadows) ran down the back of various properties in Baldock Street, through the farmyard attached to the old Rectory Manor (now the Church Schools), in front of the Church and the old Forge, across the High Street, and down Water Lane (now the Priory drive) to the Lea. This stream was the main source of the flooding that occurred periodically.

The Lower Bourne, which flows from the Poles Lane meadows, through Canons Farm, down Canons drive and under Watton Road to the water-course skirting the Recreation ground, under Mill Lane and the Priory grounds to the Lea, used originally to turn down Watton Road into Baldock Street, and join the other brook in Water Lane.

A detailed plan, made in 1818, when these streams were diverted and mostly put underground, is preserved among the Ware documents at Trinity College, Cambridge. (Box 44, vi, 1.) A copy is held by Ware U.D.C.

At times, deliberate flooding for cleansing purposes was caused by turning water from the Mill down Mill Lane into the High Street. The town still retains the right to use Mill stream water in this way should the Council consider it advisable.

But this old road, though undoubtedly first in importance, is not the only " through-fair " to Ware, and in Norden's map of 1598, all five roads converging on their junction in the town are represented as of equal size.

The Ware Extra, or Upland, road to Wareside and on to Widford, Stortford and the East was witness to a notable historical scene (apart from the rich incident of the difficulties of a Surveyor and his voluntary bands), when the funeral procession of Humphrey, Duke of Gloucester, rested for the night in Ware on its way from Bury to St. Albans, on 29th February, 1447. In 1598, there is a presentment in the Herts Co. Records stating that : " the highway between Ware and Widford, near ' Old Hawle ', is very ruinous and that the inhabitants of Ware ought to repair the same." This familiar complaint applies to all the roads in turn for the same story comes up in connection with the road to Hertford, the continuation of the Lea Valley track westward. This road does not appear to have particular mention until after the construction of the New River, but after that the appeals for repair come thick and fast :—

In 1646, " the New River lying between Ware and Hertford and between Ware and Amwell is in great decay through want of repair to the banks, to the damage of the highways leading from Ware to Hertford, through the overflow of water : and that Sir Wm. Middleton, late of Edmonton, co. Mdsx., Kt., has been accustomed ' for time immemorial ' to repair the same and should still do so whenever necessary." Apparently there was no response to this appeal, for it is repeated very shortly after : " the highway leading from Ware to Hertford is very ruinous and in great decay through lack of repair to the New Rivulet in the parish of Great Amwell and that Sir Wm. Middleton, Kt., ought to repair so much of the said highway as lies next to the said New Rivulet . . . as he had been accustomed to whenever necessary." The next century tells the same tale in the records : " 1718, 20th April. The New River, running from Chalden Head to London near the highway from Limekiln Hill, between Ware and Hertford in the parish of Amwell, is dangerous to the liege subjects of the King travelling there and that the Proprietors of the New River ought to fence in the same." Later in the same year, the Proprietors of the New River were summoned for not fencing the river where it joins the highway at the foot of Limekiln

Hill. In 1722, they are again presented at the Herts Quarter Sessions for " not setting posts and rails on that side of the river next the King's Highway from Amwell to the limekiln between Ware and Hertford, which also wants ' worfing ' [wharfing] and is very dangerous, some men being lately drowned and waggons, carts, and horses often falling into the said river." It would appear that the journey from Ware to Hertford was something of an adventure at that time. A further reference to this road occurs in a " Letter to the Inhabitants of Hertford ", 1771 : " In 1768 a road in Herts which had for time immemorial been suffered to remain impassable by all carriages (narrow-wheeled carts and waggons excepted), became the subject of universal complaint but nothing was done. At length . . . a person who frequently suffered inconvenience from the road, availing himself of the powers granted, as Surveyor of Amwell, by the late General Highway Act (1766) and assisted in the execution thereof by some gentlemen in the Commission of the Peace . . . applied the whole statute duty of the parish, with the addition of parochial rates and liberal subscriptions of his own, to improving that part of the road . . . which, by these means and the generous aid of a gentleman in Ware, was completed to the satisfaction of the public." It is supposed that the anonymous benefactor was John Scott, the Quaker poet, who built Amwell House, though it is difficult to understand why, even at that time, he should have chosen his site right upon the road, never a wide one, and so precluded any possibility of widening the route without destroying the house in the process.

The remaining road, running north-west to Watton, and eventually leading into the great North road, has a strong interest of its own as being constructed by Sayer de Quincey, Earl of Winchester and Lord of the Manor of Ware, in the reign of King John, and endures as a lasting testimony of the independence he secured to Ware, a triumphant step in the overthrow of the dominance of Hertford. Until this road was made traffic from the north-west had to pass through Hertford for Ware but, after, Hertford was left on one side and Ware's prosperity increased rapidly.

An outstanding incident of this road, and certainly the most important when judged by its lasting effect upon the welfare of the country, took place on a June night in 1215,

when the great " Magna Charta " Barons were invited to
enter London and came from Bedford, as Matthew Paris
records for us, " through Ware by night." (Hist. Min., ii, 156,
Rolls, 44.) Presumably this route was chosen owing to Sayer
de Quincey, lord of the manor, being one of their number.

What a picture, what a string of questions, those few words
of the old chronicler conjure up for us.—Did they partake of
refreshment in Sayer's manor that night ? Had he fresh horses
waiting ? Was there much peeping and whispering after
Curfew amongst the townsfolk, or was it a dark and secret
passing ? Was it guessed that the end of that " march by
night through Ware " was to be the humbling of the villainous
and hated John ? And after, when all England knew, was our
town a little proud to have had a personal share in this mile-
stone of history ? It is pleasing to think that the sturdy
independence which has always been a marked characteristic
of Ware may have its roots in the energetic example of our
own champion of liberty, de Quincey, of whom another old
historian wrote : " he was not the kind of man to be frighted
by the Pope and his excommunications." (Brady.) Matthew
Paris also remarks that King John hated Sayer " worse than
viper's blood ".

Other references to this road may be found in the Herts
county records ; about 1620, there is a presentment that
" the way called ' War Wismil Hil ' in Ware parish, ought to
be repaired by the said parish ; it is so much decayed and
out of repair that it is impossible to pass through there with
horse and cart, without great danger." By 1772, it had become
a turnpike road and an order by the Trustees for this road
states that " any number of horses, not exceeding ten, may
be used for drawing up waggons and carriages with 9 in.
wheels ; and not exceeding six for waggons of less breadth for
the purpose only of drawing up three hills in that part of the
road between Watton and Ware, from and to such parts of
them as are hereafter mentioned . . . from Ware to Watton,
from the pound at the bottom of the first hill to a ' Gravill
Pit ' at the top of the same hill ; from Ware to Westmill to a
black-smith's shop at Turnhill (Tonwell) and from Sacomb
turnpike gate to the corner of Woodhall Park." The pound
referred to was at the corner of Watton road and Park Lane,
and, being the property of the manor, was known as " the
Lord's Pound ".

Although these notes on the highways have tempted us to wander beyond the confines of the town itself, perhaps they may be excused when we turn round again and find that they also lead us into Ware. Nevertheless, when we consider that the large majority of these notes and records call attention to the almost impassable conditions of olden days, it does seem a problem and a mystery how those travellers of all kinds and ranks ever did succeed in reaching their destination.

THE CHURCH

" Surely the Lord is in this place."
Gen. xxviii, v. 16.

On approaching Ware by any one of the several roads of entry, the first thing to draw and hold the attention is the beautifully proportioned tower and spire of the church, dedicated to St. Mary the Virgin.

Dominating the cluster of homely little houses by which it is surrounded, this lovely building gives Ware the appearance of a cathedral town in miniature. In spite of restorations and cleanings and rebuilt windows, the outline may be regarded as identical with that first proud view the fourteenth and fifteenth century builders must have rejoiced in.

Of the earlier church, presumably on this same site, there is no description whatever. We only know from sparse records that Ware had a church by 1078, perhaps similar in design to those of Great Amwell and Bengeo. This early reference occurs in the charter given by William I to Hugo de Grentesmesnil, granting permission to found a cell of the Benedictine Abbey of St. Evreul, Normandy, in Ware and handing over the church to the alien priory.

During the existence of this Priory in Ware (1078–1415) there are accounts of difficulty in providing a parish priest and details concerning tithes (see " Alien Benedictine Priory "), but no word as to the nature of the building, or information concerning enlargement or rebuilding.

The dimensions of the present church were given in *The Builder*, December, 1847, as follows :—

Length of Nave, inside, to Chancel Arch,	81 ft.
Width,	22 ft.
Width of aisles,	12 ft. 9 in.
Whole width of church inside, including main columns, 3 ft. in diameter,	53 ft. 6 in.
Length of nave aisles to transept,	57 ft. 9 in.
Transept from N. to S. (23 ft. Wide)	72 ft.
Chancel length,	40 ft. 6 in.
,, width,	23 ft. 3 in.
Tower height,	78 ft.
Spire, about,	30 ft.

The *Victoria Co. History* (p. 392) gives in addition the measurement of the vestry and organ chamber, 23 feet by

23 feet, the west tower and south porch 15 feet square, and the south chapel, 25 feet by 15 ft. 6 in., all internal dimensions.

In the same volume the church is described in architectural detail and it is stated that,

" The church consisting of chancel, nave and transepts, was probably erected in the 13th century ; the west tower and perhaps the nave aisles were built about the middle of the 14th century ; the south chapel dates from the close of the 14th century ; the clearstory was added about 1410, and the nave arcades appear to have been rebuilt at the same time, and probably also the south porch and the old vestry, now part of the organ chamber ; the rest of the organ chamber occupies a chapel built late in the 15th century between the old vestry and the north transept. During the 19th century the present vestry was partitioned off and the whole of the external stonework renewed and a great deal of stonework internally.

" The five-light traceried east window of the chancel is modern. In the north wall is a 15th century doorway opening into the vestry, with continuous mouldings to arch and jambs, with carved heads inserted at the springing of the arch. The oak door is original, but has been painted ; the door had originally three stock locks of oak, one of which is still in position and another is in the vestry cupboard. To the west of the doorway is a coarsely moulded arch of late 15th-century work opening into the organ chamber. In the south wall is a modern three-light window. Adjoining it is a large round-headed arch [similar to that in Chelmsford church] subdivided beneath into two lancet arches resting on a central shaft of Purbeck marble ; the arches are well moulded and the spandrels of the inner arches are filled with tracery. The central shaft is composed of four grouped shafts separated by hollows ; the work is of the late 14th century. Part of a 13th century window still remains to the east of the arch. The chancel arch is of two moulded orders, the outer one continuous, the inner one carried on grouped shafts with moulded capitals and bases ; it appears to have been rebuilt in the early part of the 15th century. The 15th-century clearstory has three windows on each side, of two cinquefoiled lights, much of which is modern stonework. On the south side of the chancel is a 15th-century piscina with moulded jambs and arch under a square head. The chancel roof is modern.

" In the east wall of the south chapel is a five-light traceried window, and in the south wall are two three-light windows, all of which are of modern stonework. In the south wall is a late 14th-century cinquefoil-headed piscina, which has been restored. Adjoining it is a sedile with cinquefoiled head ; the moulded label forms an ogee arch over piscina and sedile.

" The nave has north and south arcades of five bays ; those opening into the transepts are wider and loftier than the others. Both the eastern angles of the nave are splayed to receive the doorways to the stairs—of which there are two—to the rood-loft and roof above. Both turrets are carried well above the roof and are finished with embattled parapets. The north turret has still the lower and roof doorways, but that to the rood-loft is blocked ; the south turret doorways are blocked. The arches of the arcades are of two moulded orders, the outer being continuous, the inner carried on shafted jambs with moulded capitals and bases. On each side of the nave are four clearstory windows, each of three lights under a segmental arch, but most of the stonework is modern, only the inner jambs and arches being original. The roof belongs to the 15th century but has been restored ; the trusses have traceried spandrels, supported on stone corbels carved with half figures of saints or apostles. There are some heraldic shields as bosses at the intersection of the timbers.

" In the north wall of the north transept is a large five-light traceried window, nearly all of which is of modern stonework ; the inner jambs are original and have an early 14th-century wave moulding with stops. Beneath the window are two recesses ; the first is about 3 ft. 6 in. in width, 2 ft. 7 in. to the springing of the arch, and 3 ft. from the floor. The arch is segmental and cinquefoiled with leaf sub-cuspings. Over the arch is an ogee crocketed label with head stops and foliated finial. The jambs are shafted with carved capitals and moulded bases. Part is much decayed. It may possibly have once formed a reredos over an altar in the east wall. The other recess is 6 ft. 3 in. wide with moulded jambs and segmental arch ; this was probably a recess for a tomb. Both recesses are of 15th-century work. An 18th-century arch in the east wall opens into the organ chamber, and opposite is an arch of two chamfered orders opening into the north aisle. The clearstory is modern.

" The five-light window in the south wall of the south transept is of modern stonework, all but the inner jambs and rear arch, which have a 15th-century double ogee moulding. A late 14th-century arch with two chamfered orders opens into the south chapel, and on the west side is a plain arch opening into the south aisle. In the south wall is a small piscina with a moulded cinquefoiled arch of the 14th century ; there is no bowl, and the mouldings are much decayed. The clearstory is modern.

" The three side windows and the west one of each aisle are all of modern stonework, as are also the north doorway and the windows and archway to the south porch ; the south doorway is of 14th-century work, repaired. The roofs of aisles and south porch retain many of their original 15th-century timbers.

" The west tower is of five stages with buttressed angles, with embattled parapet and small lead-covered spire. The tower arch is of three hollow-chamfered orders, with splayed jambs having moulded capitals and bases ; it is of the 14th century. The west doorway is of modern stonework, and above it is a window with two cinquefoiled lights. The third stage has narrow loop-lights on three of its faces ; the fourth stage has a window of two trefoiled lights on the north and east faces and clocks on the other two. On each side of the belfry is a window of two cinquefoiled lights with cusped opening in the head."

To this precise account it is possible to add a few further notes and descriptions.

The Font. This lovely piece of stonework is octagonal, and in each of the sunken panels is carven a figure under a moulded arch with a crocketed label. The figures represent St. Margaret, St. Christopher, St. George, St. Katherine, St. James, St. John the Baptist, and two panels contain representations of the Annunciation. Although expert opinion places this font at about 1380, local tradition ascribes the gift of it to Thomas Montagu, Earl of Salisbury, husband of Alianore (a grand-daughter of Joan of Kent), who inherited Ware manor in 1408. Cussans pointed out that the figure of St. George is wearing armour similar in detail to that of the Black Prince on his tomb at Canterbury Cathedral. At each angle are half figures of angels, four with musical instruments and four with emblems of the Passion ; behind each angle is a crocketed pinnacle. There is a delightful floral ornament running round the rim of the moulded base, upon which the panels rest. Beneath the figure at the foot of each panel is a square quatrefoil.

The oak pulpit is of early seventeenth century workmanship. The late seventeenth century carving incorporated in the reredos of the Lady Chapel and panelling the south wall was taken from the old manor pew and may have been presented by the Byde family. One panel from the pew has inset the initials ' S B 9 5 ', which may be read—Skinner Byde, 1695.

The royal arms now attached to the pulpit was found in

the vestry and probably dates from the time of the Restoration, 1660.

Among the papers of the late W. B. Gerish (the property of the St. Albans and Herts. Archi. and Archæ. Soc.) is a letter dated 1903, mentioning supposed frescoes visible in dry weather on the nave walls of Ware church and describing them.

N. of Chancel arch, Diaper pattern and figure.
S. ,, ,, ,, a Saint.
   Between the arches of Nave arcade, East to West, Conventional flowers, a Lily, a Lady's head with butterfly headdress, a Gothic H. (first letter of an inscription) a Crown, two Wings (?).

The roof decorations are described in the following notes by the Rev. H. P. Pollard :—

   " *The Nave Roof.* Until 1849 much original painting was retained. References are made to it in Clutterbuck's ' Hertfordshire ', the ' Antiquarian Itinerary ' (1815, vol. 1). Add. MSS. 9062/4, B.M., ' The Ecclesiologist,' 1849, ' The Builder,' Sept. 1849, etc. The Nave roof is a king-post one, of chestnut, with arch wall pieces under each tie-beam supported by corbels, the spandrel formed by the wall piece is filled with open tracery. The 18 bosses have coloured and gilt conventional designs, lions' heads, human heads, and 3 shields, viz., 1, argent, a cross gules ; 2, argent, a fess between two chevrons gules, possibly a shield of a member of the de Clare family ; 3, modern France, or perhaps the Fanshawe ' Fleur de Lys '.

   " The aisles have open timber roofs, in each are four finely carved foliage bosses ; the six bosses in the south transept are ornamented with conventional designs and heads ; the six in the north consist of a lion's head, five conventional designs and a shield argent, a cross gules.

   " The nine bosses of the chancel consist of the arms of the see of Rochester, twice ; Trinity College, Cambridge, twice ; a figure holding a shield gules ; foliage with head in centre, two ; lion's head ; angel holding a crown.

   " The ceiling of the Lady Chapel is divided into 24 panels with tracery at the angles ; 33 of the bosses have gilt foliage, one a grotesque human head (similar to one in the nave roof at Kelshall), and one is missing. Until the 1849 restoration each panel had a grey ground, and was occupied by a seated figure representing the Apostles and minor prophets ; the former had each a Latin sentence from the Creed in black letter ; the latter, verses also in black letter. In the ' Ecclesiologist ' it is stated that these figures were on record with a view to their future restoration."

There are still pleasing remnants of original colouring on the Lady Chapel roof.

The screen between the South Chapel and Transept incorporates a certain amount of the original rood screen. The Jacobean carving included in the new panelling on the east and south walls of the chapel was taken from the old manor pew.

The Altar rails, from Benington, were presented by Mr. R. H. Pickering.

The Corbels
Nave, South side, from the west end.
 1. St. Jude. 2. St. John. 3. St. Peter. 4. doubtful. 5. St. Bartholomew. 6. St. James the Great.
Nave, North side, from the west end.
 1. Doubtful. 2. St. Simon. 3. query. 4. St. James the Less. 5. St. Matthias. 6. St. John the Baptist.

These figures are said to date from about 1865, it is not known if they are copies of originals.

South Transept, west, 1. Abraham. 2 and 3. query.
     east, 1. A winged ecclesiastic in cloak. 2 and 3. query.
North Transept, west, 1. St. Philip (?). 2. query. 3. St. Matthew.
     east, 1. A winged ecclesiastic in cope.
       2. A figure with compasses in right and plan in left hand.
       3. Query.
 South Aisle (these corbels and those in North Aisle and Chancel are ancient, 1380). 1. A grotesque head. 2, 3, 4. Arms of Richard II, a hart lodged, chained, and gorged. 5. A head.
 North Aisle. 1. Head. 2 and 4. A nondescript animal. 3. Richard II's badge. 5. Head.
 Chancel. A fine series of 8 angels, holding musical instruments.

There is some account in existence of repairs necessary after unusually stormy weather in 1703, and the late H. R. Wilton Hall, in Herts Archæ. Notes and Queries, August 1918, gives the following notes :—

 " Repairs to Ware Church in 1703. The autumn of the year 1703 was, apparently, from the accounts which have come down to us, memorable for the violent storms which swept over the country and the devastation which they wrought. Amongst the many churches which suffered severely Ware Church was one. On or about Nov. 27, 1703, the Parish Church of Ware and Chapel of St. Mary thereto belonging received much damage by a storm. The ' biggest ' window of the church ' being very large ', was almost blown down and six or seven other windows damaged in their frames and ' shattered in glass '. Some of the pews in the church were much damaged by the stones from the wrecked windows falling on them, and the church, chapel, and steeple received ' other considerable damage '. The church-wardens, apparently, lost no time in taking steps to get the damage repaired and seem to have thought that this would be a good opportunity for carrying out some other improvements in the church and its fittings. They erected a new pew at the lower end of the church near the church door, where some old benches formerly stood for a Churchwardens pew, ' to perform Divine Service and hear sermons,' and thought that the church-wardens sitting there were better able to perform part of their duties than they had been before. At the same time the old church doors which were very ancient, out of repair and much patched, were by the churchwardens' direction pulled down, ' and new substantial ones put up,' of tight, good and sound work. Up to that time the church porch had been open, the windows unglazed, and the outer doorway unprotected. To preserve the new doors to the church they set up a door at the entrance to the porch and shuttered the windows, ' which are useful and absolutely necessary to preserve the same from several abuses.'

" Trouble arose when the time came for payment to be made for these repairs. On March 20, 1703–4, the Vestry ordered the workmen employed on the repairs to finish their work and bring in their bills. Another Vestry meeting followed, April 3, 1704, and some examination of the bills was made. Colonel Plummer proposed a rate of 6d. in the pound, but Mr. Churchwarden Lamas said that this would not be sufficient. In spite of his protest Sir Thomas Byde and Colonel Plummer signed a rate of 6d. in the pound before the rate was figured ' or any sums therein inserted '. Apparently on the following day another Vestry meeting was held and a rate of 9d. in the pound was made. A great dispute followed in which the legality of both the sixpenny and ninepenny rate was called in question and the matter came before the Court of the Arch-deacon of Middlesex. From the bills, allegations and answers which this course of procedure involved, we gather that Colonel Plummer headed the opposition to the ninepenny rate. He says that the storm did some damage to the windows, and many quarries of glass were broken, but he knows nothing of any damage done to the pews, and he contends that if any damage was done to the pews they should be repaired by the owners or proprietors of the same. He does not believe that the whole church was damaged ; some few stones fell from the battle-ments, and some lead was unrolled ; and, further, that he never heard of any chapel belonging to the church of Ware called St. Mary's. The Vicar of the parish, he contends, has nothing to do with ordering pews, and that the new pew is not so convenient for the churchwardens as their old seat was, for it hides the font so that several persons in the church cannot see baptisms performed. There were several empty pews in the church which the churchwardens could have appropriated to their use and they had spent about six pounds upon the erection of this new pew. The old doors, he declares, were better and much stronger than the new ones, being of sound oak or of some other substantial wood battened across each way ' in the nature of check work ', whilst the new doors were of slight thin work and made of deal, and he declares that if the old doors were broken or shattered it was done in carelessly taking or casting them down. He objects to the new doors and shutters set up in the porch, and believes ' there never were any before, at least for time immemorial '.

" Alexander Sigston, parish clerk and schoolmaster, said that the old church doors were so very ancient and out of repair that new doors were necessary, and that the new porch doors and shutters to the windows were absolutely necessary, for boys had been used to play therein, defacing and spoiling the pavement and walls and leaving filth therein. He had been obliged to clean the porch on Sunday mornings in consequence. This was borne out by Thomas Millet, of Ware, blacksmith, and Mephiboseth Robins, also of Ware, barber."

This Clerk, Alexander Sigston, was buried in the porch, 1707.

To return to the Church as a structure, the century or so following the repairs of 1703-4 seems to have been a period of general neglect and consequent decay and it is not surprising to learn that by 1847 the condition of the building was very serious. It was then that the parishioners, under the leadership of the Vicar, the Rev. J. W. Blakesley, and the Churchwardens, Messrs. Hitch, Hudson, and Waller, awoke to the danger of the situation and set about restoration on a large scale and put the ancient building into a sound condition once more. The account in the *Hertford Mercury* for 1st January, 1847, gives a very good idea of what was necessary.

" In the north transept is an ugly lumbering gallery, blocking a large and elegant ' imbricated ' window ; it was built for the blue-coat boys of Christ's Hospital, ' by a Governor,' in 1687.

" The west end of the church is disfigured by a similar ugly adjunct, containing the organ. The pulpit, pews, and stoves, all want revision.

" The outside of the church is in a truly deplorable, and partly a dangerous condition. It is constructed of flint work, with dressings of clunch, and the whole has been covered in modern times with rough cast, which has separated from the walls, and is now ready to fall on the heads of passers by. The stone mullions and tracery of the windows have mostly disappeared, and have been replaced by wood and cement, and all the strings and mouldings were cut off for the convenience of rough casting. The copings are loose, and the roofs decayed. . . . All that is to be done is absolutely necessary for the preservation of the fabric."

I think it may be stated with confidence that such a disgraceful state of neglect would never be allowed to occur again.

Mercifully the delicious little imps running round the south and east windows of the Lady Chapel managed to escape the general destruction at the time of the rough-casting.

Since 1847 various other repairs and improvements have been carried out. The royal Coat of Arms on the pulpit was found in the vestry, and put there as being a more prominent position. It probably dates from the time of the Restoration when the Royal Arms were placed in every church.

The excellent oaken pews were installed soon after the Rev. E. E. W. Kirkby became vicar. The gas was replaced by electric light through the gift of an anonymous donor in 1936.

A print of the Church in its plaster covering hangs in the vestry. Other well-known nineteenth century drawings of the church include those of Buckler (Hertford County Library) and Oldfield (in possession of the Dimsdale family).

The south transept window repaired in 1704, and replaced before 1836 (see J. C. Buckler's drawing), is shown in a sketch dated 1803, which is the work of J. Baskerfeild. (Add. MSS. 9062, B.M.)

When we consider the proportions and age of this building, notes and records seem remarkably scarce. There must at

E

one time have been a ruthless sweeping away of documents, probably during the early years of the careless and conscienceless eighteenth century, perhaps by the same hands that purloined most of the monumental brasses. In fact it was not until the middle of the nineteenth century that Ware Church began to receive the attention and care due to it.

One most interesting detail is written in the records of the Herts Quarter Sessions :— " *1652*, 20th April. The Inhabitants of Ware met at the Stone in the Parish Church " and chose the following officers : Isaack Halden, Arthur Patnell, and William Cartwright, for Churchwardens ; William Collett, Richard Uthwayte the elder, John Grigges, and Robert Spencer of Upland for overseers ; Yeallop, innkeeper, Edward Heath, and Thomas Skyngle for surveyors of the highways. This suggests that, at any rate at that time, the Church was recognized as the centre of the life of the town. If only we knew what kind of stone it was, and whereabouts in the Church it stood, we could perhaps show a traditional link with very early history indeed.

The records of the Archdeaconry of Middlesex also give a descriptive note of the Church in the seventeenth century :—

" 1663, Ware. It is ordered that the canopy of wainscot and the benches, with the rubbish at the upper end of the Chancel now above the communion-table, be taken down and carried away, and the communion-table be placed north and south at the upper end of the chancel."

1667. Another order for the removing the communion-table to the east end of the chancel, and taking down the canopy. (Showing that the order four years before had not been obeyed. Urwick's *Nonconformity in Herts*.)

A contemporary note was written about 1840, by James Smith (see also " Inns ") who migrated to Melbourne and wrote accounts of his native town. He tells us that the Church was hung with tattered banners and rusty helmets, but otherwise says nothing of its condition.

So, with written records giving but a meagre story, we are forced back on to our own constructive ability to build a consecutive and not altogether unreliable life history of this glorious place from its first mention in 1078.

The architectural evidence shows us thirteenth century Transepts and remnants of a Chancel window, this indicates a considerable enlarging, if not total rebuilding, since that

Early Norman date, which may have been carried out whilst the de Quinceys held the Manor. We may recall that Margaret, widow of Sayer, spent much of her time at the Benedictine establishment near by. The Nave aisles, the South Chapel and the west Tower belong to the fourteenth century when Joan, the Fair Maid of Kent, was Lady of the Manor and her Arms are on the corbels of the aisles. Tradition has always connected these additions with her patronage. Again, in the fifteenth century, additions and alterations were made, and have been connected with the generosity of Margaret, Countess of Richmond. But as her son, Henry VII, did not grant her the Manor until 1485 it seems to make the date a little later than the witness of the building would say. The good seventeenth century Pulpit may have been a gift from the Fanshawe family.

From the time of the Reformation, 1538, Ware Church, in common with the rest of the country, began to lose its internal beauties ; ornaments, furnishings and, probably, stained glass were ruthlessly swept away ; three centuries later, at the 1847–9 restoration, still more treasures were removed, most of the brasses had already vanished and tombs had been removed, and the hatchments and considerable remains of wall paintings went the way of the rest. It seems almost a miracle that we have even the Registers and a little Plate left to us.

But still, emptied and ravished as it has been from time to time, the lovely proportions of the building are as appealing as ever and, although we may not see what our ancestors saw — the colours, the jewels, the furnishings, the stately tombs and banners — St. Mary's lacks nothing as a centre for inspiration and great love. Particularly, perhaps, on a Christmas morning, the bells dying down, the volume of the organ swelling through the arches and down the aisles to the waiting choir in the porch, until, as the procession gradually approaches the chancel, voices and organ blend at the transept crossing of the nave and the sound reaches to Heaven itself. Following them, surely, not only the joyful and triumphant faithful of our own day, but all those others who loved, and helped to build and maintain through the centuries, this temple for the worship of God ; foremost among them those two fair ladies—Joan, Princess of Wales, accompanied by a little lad who is destined to become the tragic King Richard II, and Margaret, the saintly and gracious mother of King Henry VII. To them, more particularly, we direct our grateful thoughts for the heritage of this glorious and ancient building.

In St. Mary's, Ware

In quiet I contemplate this lovely House
And turn to you, Ladies of long ago,
Who watched in love the growth of wall and tower,
Saw stately pillar rise and arches spring ;
Then brought, in royal hands, your jewelled gifts
And lovely furnishings—Fair Joan of Kent,
Princess of Wales as wife to England's heir,
Margaret of Richmond, mothers, both, to kings—
I hold no manor, wield no royal power,
Nor riches have to bear as offering ;
Look on this work (though centuries roll between)
And gently guide the pen which is my tool.

Church Brasses and Monuments

Until about the year 1800, there were at least ten Brasses in the Church. Mention is made of some of the inscriptions in Weaver's *Funeral Monuments*, and Chauncy's *Hertfordshire*, but the most careful account is the following from Salmon's *Hertfordshire*, 1728 :

" 1. An old stone below the rails in the place where the Arms and Name used to be, hath this—Credo quod Redemptor meus vivit, etc.

" 2. Another, more in the body of the church, brasses lost, only the coronet remains, supposed to be what carried this inscription, preserved by Mr. Weaver :—Hic jacet Rogerus Domory Baro tempore Edwardi secundi et Elizabetha tertio filia Gilberti Clare comitis Gloucestriæ et Johannæ uxoris ejus filiæ Edvardi primi vocat Johan de Acris. . . .

" 3. Another, Hic jacet Johannes Holper secundus Capellanus Helenæ Bramble, Qui ob. Octob. 7, 1477. Cujus animæ propitietur Deus. Jehu Mia. (Rev. H. P. Pollard suggests that this may be a printer's error for Mci.)

" 4. Another for Henry Ayr gent. upholster who died 1645. [This stone lies in the chancel and was uncovered in 1892 when the mosaic was laid. The inscription was then noted and reads :—' Here lyeth the body of Henry Ayre, Gentleman and Maulster, who lived in Marriage Estate 23 years, and departed this life the 18th day of November Anno Domini 1645, being aged 48 years, and left issue 7 children, 5 sonnes and 2 Daughters, Henry, Edmond, Richard, Francis, John, Letitia and

Isabell, which Isabell departed this life the 31 of January 16–9 aged 20 weekes.

"And thus like graine in which he dealt he is made,
Full ripe cut down and in gods garner is laid."

Evidently Salmon was in error with his "upholster", E.M.H.]

"5. In the North side of the Church an altar tomb of black Marble, Arms and Inscription defaced, at the End hath been a shield, lozenge wise. This I take to have born the Epitaph in Weaver—Hic jacet Thomas Bouchier Miles filius Henrici Comitis Essex ac Isabella uxor ejus nuper comitissa Devon filia et hæres Johannis Barry Militis qui ob . . . 1491 et Isabella ob mar. 1, 1488, quorum A etc.

"6. Another, Jean Lucas gist ici Dieu de s'alme eit merci.

"Weaver speaking of this (6) says, 'This is an ancient monument so is the family.'

"7. Clutterbuck, 1819, says, 'In a wooden frame fastened against south wall are the effigies of a lady in brass and beneath her this inscription (to Elene Bramble) in black letter which have been removed hither from some part of the church. . . .'

"8. The brass of William Pyrrey was also in this frame.

"9. Clutterbuck also informs us that there was this inscription on a brass tablet on one of the pillars of the north aisle :— Hic jacet corpus Nathaniel Godfrey jun. qui obiit 23 May 1715 ætat. 26.

"10. Small figure of a lady, *circa* 1400, mentioned in Haines' 'Manual'.

"Two other brasses are mentioned by Weaver, viz.

A. "Here lieth Thomas Heaton & Jone his wife which Thos. died xix Aug. Mccccix & Joyce. . . .

B." . . . Will Litlebury & Eliz. his wife, he died xxii of July cccc. "

But it is not at all clear whether these were in St. Mary's Church or in that of the Franciscan Friary.

Soon after the year 1800, the brasses began to disappear ; Cooke's *Topographical* informs us that " most of the ancient Brasses were pillaged by a knavish Sexton ".

In 1848, the Church was restored and the majority of the remainder vanished. In Add. MSS. 9062/4 in the British Museum (Sir T. Baskerfeild's copy of the *History of Herts*) are preserved many of the inscriptions on the gravestones and drawings of the matrices of brasses Nos. 2 and 5, the cross, No. 11, now in the South aisle, and two, 12 and 13, that have entirely disappeared. No. 2, which seems to have been originally at the west end of the chancel, is now in the south-east corner of the south transept. No. 5 is shown as a large black marble tomb with six oblong panels on the side, and a lozenge containing a quatrefoil on one end ; on the slab are the figures of a man and his wife, with a child between them, all arrayed in shrouds, and having labels issuing from their mouths directed towards a Trinity matrix : at each end of the slab are two shields. This tomb probably stood under the arch in the north wall of the north transept. No. 12 shows a man and his wife, above their heads is a large cross fleurie on two steps and inscription. No. 13 is a man and wife, and judging from the lady's head-dress, dates from about 1473. The matrices of Nos. 1, 4, and 6 have entirely disappeared ; that of No. 3 (or a similar figure) was lying broken on the east side of the porch some years back but by now has also vanished. Brass No. 9 has also gone.

Thus of ten brasses in existence up to 1800, and thirteen matrices in existence up to 1848, only three of the former and two of the latter remain.

With regard to the brasses, No. 7 was removed from its original position to the wooden frame in the vestry, then placed on the floor near the pulpit, and is now fixed to the east wall of the north transept. The inscription reads :

"Orate pro āiā Elene quondā filie Johīs Coke et Margerie Consortis sue. Et pro āiābus Willī Bramble filij sui que quidem Elena obijt vicesimo sexto die mensis Octobris anno dnī Millimo CCCCliiij. Quor' āiābus p̄piciet deus amē. . . . " (Four characters follow which appear to be a very early example of the use of Arabic numerals.)

Brass No. 8 was first removed to the wooden frame, then placed on the floor in the nave, and is now on the east wall of the south transept. The brass represents William Pyrrey and his two wives with their ten children, the inscription reads :

"Orate p anā Willi Pyrrey et Agnet ac Alicie uxor' ei' quiq̄dem Willms obiit—die—Ao dm mcccclxx—qr āiābz— p̄picietur deus. Amen."

(These inscriptions were copied by W. F. Andrews, 1903.)

No. 10 was near the pulpit, then was put in the arch of the north wall of the north transept. It is now on the floor immediately in front of the arch.

With regard to the matrices, No. 2 is a Purbeck marble slab about 8 ft. 10 in. long and 3 ft. 4 in. wide, the indent shows a man with short hair, wearing a close fitting garment with stiff collar, he also has a broad waist-belt ; the lady has her arms raised from the elbows, the hands were probably joined in an attitude of prayer, she wears a narrow waist-belt, on each shoulder is a small semi-circular projection : each figure is under a finely crocketed, cinquefoil headed canopy ; at each side of the slab is a border terminating in a crocketed finial ; the sketch in the British Museum (Add. MSS. 9062/4) shows two shields above and two below the figures ; it appears, therefore, that the slab has been cut at each end to fit its present position on the floor of the south transept.

No. 11 is a Purbeck marble coffin-shaped slab, about 5 ft. 5 in. long ; the indent shows a fine floriated cross with a long narrow stem terminating in three steps, the head of the ecclesiastic commemorated was probably represented in the centre of the cross ; a similar instance may be seen at Lewknor, Oxfordshire. It is a pity that this slab lies in the north aisle where it gets a great deal of wear.

(This description of brasses is taken largely from notes collected by the Rev. H. P. Pollard.)

There is in the garden of Canons Hotel a small alabaster figure of a man in Elizabethan costume, kneeling, which must at one time have been taken from the Church and from one of the larger monuments lost to us.

A very good idea of the Hatchments and Coats of Arms that used to hang in the Church is given by the sketches in the Oldfield collection, c. 1800, in the possession of the Dimsdale family.

These drawings have been described in heraldic detail by H. C. Andrews, F.S.A., and the following account is taken from his notes, of which I hold a copy.

The plates show :

1. The exterior of the Church from the north-east.

2. Tabard hanging on the south wall of the Church. Arms of Fanshawe.

3. Tabard showing Byrde or Bird arms. Thomas Bird acquired Mardocks Manor before 1666, he was buried at Ware in 1699.

4. Arms of Battell (?), a Ware maltster in the seventeenth century, at one time owner of Ware Friary.

5. Arms of Battell (?).

6 and 7. Arms unidentified.

8. Arms of Alison (?).

9. Arms of Hadsley.

10. Arms of Briscoe. Clutterbuck records a slab to the memory of Philip Briscoe, 1698, on the floor of the north aisle.

11. Arms of Batell, as No. 5, impaling Withie (?).

12. Arms of Fanshawe.

Four achievements showing arms of (i) Sir T. Byde ; (ii) Byde impaling Skinner ; (iii) Byde quartering Skinner impaling Villiers (Skinner Byde married secondly the Hon. Mary Villiers) ; (iv) Byde quartering Skinner, quartering Plummer (Thomas, son of Skinner Byde, married secondly Catherine, daughter of John Plummer of Blakesware).

Four Achievements showing arms of (i) Byde quartering Skinner, impaling arms resembling those of Buckeridge. (Clutterbuck records an epitaph to Elizabeth Buckeridge who died in 1757) ; (ii) Bromley of Westmill, Ware ; (iii) Ball, and Lewis (?) ; (iv) Lewis (?) as above, impaling Andrews (?).

Three achievements showing arms of (i) Byde impaling Skinner, as above ; (ii) Byde alone ; (iii) Byde impaling Grimdall. (Susanna Grimdall was the second wife of Sir T. Byde.)

Three achievements, (i) Tredenham, impaling Lewis (?) as above.
        (ii) Tufton, impaling Lewis (?) as above.
        (iii) Farewell, impaling Lewis (?) as above.

These shields indicate the three husbands of one lady. Seymour Tredenham was the third son of Sir Joseph Tredenham, a leaseholder of Ware Rectory by assignment of Alex. Mead, from the Master and Fellows of Trinity College, Cambridge, who died in 1797. His wife was a daughter of Thomas Lewis of Westminster.

Three achievements showing (i) Arms of Battell as above, impaling White (?) ; (ii) and (iii) Batell (?) as above.

The Church Plate at present consists of :—A paten, 1806, a small cup, 1806, a Sheffield plate paten, 1755, two modern chalices and patens, a spoon, and a cup, 1618, bequeathed by William Armstrong.

" I bequeath the great silver and gilt cuppe worth £5 13. 4. with my name engraved and set thereon to the parish church of Ware to remain for ever for a communion cuppe for the parishioners of the parish of Ware." (P.C.C. 116, Meade.)

The Inventory of Furniture and Ornaments in Ware Church as set down by the Commissioners of Edward VI give some idea of the articles of value once contained here. This Inventory was made :

" the xth day of Novembre (1553) &c And John Inglis of Ware &c belonginge to the P'ishe church of Ware &c

Impis A chalis all gylt wayinge	xxxj ounce
Itm An other chalis of gylt wayinge	xxv ounce
P' ecclia It An other chalis gylt wayinge	xx ounce qrt
It An other chalis parcell gylt broken wayinge	xv ounce di'
It A crosse of marie and John parcell gylt waying	lx ounce
It an other crosse parcell gylt wayinge	xxxij ounce
It iiijor pipes of syluer for the crosse staffe the knoppes gylt wayinge	lxv ounce iij qrt
It An image of or Lady gylt wayinge	xxiij ounce di'
It ij payer of syluer cruetes wayinge	xx ownce
It A pax of syluer pcell gylt waying	ix ounce iij qrt
It An other pax of syluer pcell gylt wayinge	v ounce di'
It a basen of syluer pcell gylt wayinge	xix ounce
It a payer of sencers of syluer pcell gylt wt. a plate of yerne in yt wayes all togyther	xxxviij once
It ij other payers of sencers wt. yerne and all wayes	lij once
It ij shippes of syluer for ffrankensens wt. ther spones to them wayes	xxij once
It A payer of Candelstyckes of syluer pcell gylt wayes	xlv once
It A pyx of Syluer gylt wayinge	xliiij ounce
It v Rynges of syluer gylt wt. stones in them ways	j ounce iij qrt
It A crysmatory of syluer pcell gylt wt. a lytle box of syluer all gylt wt. oyle in them wayes all togyther	xxiiij ounce
It ii lytle crosses wt. stones and serten peases of copper in them wayes all togythers	viij ounces

It ij other crosses of syluer plate set
    upon wood wayes all togythers
    with stones and all   j ounce di'
It A peace of syluer pcell gylt lyke
    a pattent of a challys garnesht wt.
    stones wayes in the hoole   iiij ounce di'
It A lytle box of syluer lyke a nedle
    case wt. lytle peases of syluer in
    yt wayes all together   iij qrts of an ou
It a peace of syluer pcell gylt like a
    cradell wayinge   ij ounces di'
It a gyrdell wt. xxv lytle barres of
    syluer wt. a shelde of syluer
    hangynge at yt wayes all togythers j oz di
It ij clapses of syluer pcell gylt for
    a booke wayinge   j onc j qrt

And there is divers countrphet stones and other Robbissh
contyned upon pcell of the said plate.

Ornaments

It ij copes of clothe of tyssue
It ij copes of crymsen vellet   another of tawney vellet
It one cope of whyte Damaske
It one blewe veelet cope
It thre owlde towell of Diaper
It vij awbes
It x amyses
p' ecclia   It a payre of organes
It fyve great belles
It one lytle belle to calle for ye priste Clarke or sexten when they
                      arre absent
              JOHN YNGLYSHE

Besides these items Hugh Chapman, alderman of
Cambridge, left the following instruction in his Will, 11th
March, 1520 :

"Item, I will that ther be bought and made ij garments of
fyne redd satten purselled with blake velvet withe flowers of
silke and golde browdered in the best manner for ij images of
Our Ladie in Ware Chaunsell in the countie of Harffortte ;
the one image at the highawtre on the north and a nother at the
Chauntre on the northe parte."

The gild or brotherhood of Jesus owned three velvet coats
embroidered with gold for the image of Jesus in the church
(Aug. Off. Misc. Bks., xiv, fol. 127.)

THE CHURCH REGISTERS

Ware is fortunate in the possession of Registers complete from 1558. These were transcribed in part and many interesting notes made upon them by the late Mr. A. Bannister, who presented his work to the Vicar and Churchwardens of Ware. It is much to be regretted that Mr. Bannister did not live to finish his work. Besides the many items of general interest picked out the volume contains : Extracts from Baptisms, 1558–1812, extracts from Marriages, 1558–1754, and a complete copy of Burials, 1558–1843.

In the Burial registers we find :

> 1658. Humiliation Scratcher, a nurse child. (The number of deaths among nurse children is very high.)
> 1688. Richard Browne, Butcher, kild by a hooke in his Eye.
> 1688. Anthony Davie, a Blackmore child.
> 1695. Sam. Hogg drowned by Pressmasters.

During the Great Plague, 1665–6, 202 burials marked with the ominous " P " appear in the register. Between 1683 and 1696 twenty-two French children were buried. They were Huguenot refugees, for a time housed in Ware. There is also steady mortality among the " blew " boys from the Bluecoat nursery school which, during the seventeenth century, was contained in the remains of the old Ware manor house. A new volume for " Burying onlie in Woollen " was started in August, 1678, and contains thirty-eight entries especially noted.

In 1802 John Marsh was killed from a fall off the Box of the North Mail Coach.

Items of general information interspersed among the entries give us :

> 1661–2. Jan. 30. The great Flood.
> Feb. 17. The great windee Tuesday
> 1680. Dec. 10. The Blazing Starr seene about 3 weeks togeather. (Halley's Comet (?).)
> 1692. Sept. 8. An Earthquak.
> 1697. May 4. A great Storme of Haile 9 inches about.
> 1698. July 31. The Great Wind at Sacomb Park.

Among Christian names that have dropped out of general use are : Annamiriah, Bettymariah, Caressa, Henerrata, Melisene, Temperance.

Occasionally a man's trade is given, all those common to

a country town are to be found, and, in frequent recurrence owing to Ware's staple trade, " Bardgman, Sackcarrier, Maltmeter, Maltgrinder," also a " Hare-weaver ", a Hopman, Shoomaker, Shearman, and Virginallmaker.

The Registers also give accounts of Collections made for the benefit of sufferers in other parishes, particularly for losses sustained by serious fires. Moneys for this object were paid out between 1658–63, to Enfield, Walkhorne, Cheshunt, Bygrave, and further afield, to Gainsbury in Lincs, Southbay in Suffolk and ffleet bridge. Assistance was sent to relatives of people enslaved in Turkey, " captives by ye Turke at Constantinople " and to folk in distress in Ireland.

Altogether the Registers may be considered as a mine of information and interest, of the greatest value to the parish.

The Chantry of Helen Bramble was founded in 1470. Her brass is now in the north transept of the church.

She was the daughter of John and Margery Cook and married first William Bramble and secondly Richard Warburton of London. By her will (P.C.C., 1 Stokton) proved 9th September, 1454, she desired to be buried in the parish church of Ware next the tomb of Margaret her mother. She left 12*d.* to the clerk and 12*d.* to the sub-clerk or sacrist, 5 marks to the fabric of the church, and after several other bequests the rest of her property to works of charity and the repair of altars. The chantry was founded by Brian Roucliff, baron of the Exchequer, and John Marchall. Mass was to be celebrated at the altar in the chapel of St. Mary for the present and future kings of England, for Brian and John and Master William Graunger, and for the souls of Helen, her two husbands, of William Bramble her son, and of her parents. The chantry was endowed with lands to the value of £10 (Cal. Pat., 1467–77, p. 420). Thomas Beal left 3*s.* 4*d.* to the repair of the chantry by his will in 1506 (P.C.C., 10 Adeane), and lands were left to its use by Richard Shirley, 1510. (P.C.C., 29 Bennett.) When the chantry was dissolved in the reign of Edward VI it had rents accruing to it from the inns called the Cardinal's Hat in Amwell, and the Bull's Head, a tenement in Myddel Row (East St.) with a garden in Kybis Lane, a tenement called Wodehouse in Gardiner Lane and a croft called Sowrecroft, amounting to £9 14*s.* 8*d.* and goods and ornaments valued at 7*s.* 4*d.* (Chant. Cert. 27, no. 6 ; Aug. Off. Misc. Bks. lxvii, fol. 726). The chantry priest's chamber was granted in 1549 to Sir John Perient and Thomas Reve. (Pat. 3 Edw. VI, pt. vii, m. 8.) At this time the serving of the church fell entirely on the chantry priest and the curate hired by the vicar, although the parish contained at least 1200 inhabitants. (Chant. Cert. 27, no. 6.) This led to the inhabitants appointing a " morrow mass priest ", whose wages were collected among them, some giving 2*d.*, some 4*d.*, and some 8*d.*, according to their devotion ; if a sufficient sum was not collected the deficit was made up from the common fund.

The returns of Edward VI's Commissioners on the Chantry Certificates of Herts have been transcribed by the Rev. J. E. Brown, and those concerning Ware read as follows :—

" In Ware 1000 Hostlinge or Houseling People," that is those who were partakers of the Host or Housel.

Helen Bramble's Chantrie (Cal. Pat. Rolls, vol. 271), Edw. IV, 28th January, 1474.

License for Brian Roucliff and others to found a perpetual chantry of one chaplain and preacher of the word of God to celebrate divine service at the Altar in the chapel of St. Mary in the parish Church of Ware, Co. Hertford, in honour of the said Virgin and St. Thomas the Martyr for the good estate of the king and his consort Elizabeth Queen of England, his first-born son Edward Prince of Wales, and his heirs and successors, Kings of England . . . and for their souls . . . and the souls of Helen Bramble alias Warbulton, William Bramble and Richard Warlburton her late husbands—to be called the Chantry of Helen Bramble and for them to grant in mortmain to the said chaplain lands tenements rents services and possessions not held in chief to the yearly value of £10.

" Elen Brombles Chauntre within the Parisshe of Ware and founded by the said Elen to have a continuance for ever. Valued in—A quite Rents for a tenemente apperteninge to the heres of—Hellam now in the tenure or John Swayne   ijs.

The Ferme of a tenemente of Inne called the Cardinall Hate with a Barne a Yarde and a Garden. And also xiiij acres of meddowe lyinge in Amwell Parisshe, j acre of errable lande in a common filde within the same Parisshe, the pasture or cowe-lese in Nedenhoo marche together with the pasture of a lytill grove letten by Indenture for terme of xxj yeres to John Esquyre by Indenture bering date viij Novembr Ao. xxxvj Hen. VIII and payeth   lxvjs. viijd.

The ferme of one Tenemente or Inne called the Bull's Heade in the tenure of Richard Bromley and payeth yerelie
iiij. li. xiijs. iiij.d.

The Ferme of one Tenemente in the Myddell Rowe with a garden in Kybis Lane in the tenure of Willm christoferson together with an oven adioyninge to the said howse which oven is holden by copie ut dicitur and payeth   xiijs. iiijd.

The ferme of a close containing by estimacon iij. acres and iij rodes lyinge in the Comon fildes geven by Richard Shirley Gent now in the tenure of Thomas Cokkes and payeth yerelie
vijs.

The Baylie affirmeth it to be parcell of ye demaynes of Ware and holden by copie.

The Ferme of a croft called Sower Crofte containing by estemacon ij acres in the tenure of Robt Crosse and yeldeth by the yere iijs. iiij.d.

The Rente or Ferme of a garden lyinge in Gardyner lane in the handes of Willm Kyrbie at will, and payeth by the yere
ijs. iiij.d.

The Ferme of a chaumbre called the Prestes Chaumbr now in the handes of Willm Dosen late Incumbent and payeth
vi.s. viij.d.

Perquiritur per JoP and THo. Reve.

(Total) ix.li. xiiij.s. viij.d. whereof.

Reprises in

Rente Resolute to the mannor or lordship of Ware viz for the Bull Heade iij.s. iiij.d. The Cardinall Hate j.d. The barne yarde and garden in the tenure of John Squyer ij.s. for an oven kome the ij.d. and for the tenemente in Mydell Rowe xiiij.d.
In all yerelie vj.s ix.d.

Rente resolute to the said lordshippe for the landes geven by . . . Shirley by the yere xx.d. Rente payed to the lordship of Amwell by the yere for the londes in Amwell Parisshe vij.d.
(Total) ix.s.

And so remayneth ix.li. v.s. viij.d. whereof Distributed at iij obites to the pore yerely vij.s. viij.d. Goodes and Ornamentes belongynge to the same Chauntre valued at
vij.s. iiij.d.

Md. that the Towne of Ware is a thorowfare wherein ther is non other prest but the Curate hyered by the Vicar havynge in Chardge and Cure at the lest a M people that done receyve the Blessed Comunyon.

Item, Willm Dosen man of lvij yeres and of honest fame is Incombent havinge no other lyvinge but the revenneus of this Chauntre.

A rente goynge out of a tente : with thappertenences within the said Parisshe geven by Willm Kinge for an obite and payeth by the yere by thandes of Thoms Kynge x.s.

whereof to the pore vj.s.

Value of Chantries by Valor Ecclesiasticus.

Cantaria de Ware ex fundac : Elene Brondley
Per ann. clare vij.li. xj.s. iiij.d.
xmande xxvij.s. j.d.

Guilds

An account of the Brotherhoods of Jesus and Corpus Christi, from the Certificate of Sir Ralph Sadler and Sir Henry Parker, Kts., two of the king's commissioners, 31 March, 4 Edward VI, 1551. (Misc. Bks. Aug. Off., 114, f. 127, *et seq.*)

Sir Philip Butler and others by a deed, 19 March, 35 Henry VIII, were seised of 2 messuages called the White Hart and " Sarrsons " Head and land in Ware and Amwell for the use of the inhabitants of the town of Ware.

William Valentine and others were enfeoffed of the same about 40 years ago and enfeoffed Sir Philip and others. The profits of said lands for 11 years have been employed in sundry kinds of ways for the common charges of the town, i.e. in setting forth soldiers, relieving the inhabitants in taxes and tallages, maintaining a beacon beside Ware and the Bridge there. (The king takes 40 marks yearly in toll for the maintenance of the bridge but never repairs it.) There were never grants of corporation of any guild or brotherhood given by any kings of England. There was in the town of Ware a brotherhood called Jesus brotherhood with " no other contynuance of being than of the charytie as well of straungers as of the inhabytauntes whose devocons of longe tyme not Augmented but Abatynge aboute xii yeres syns quasshed their sayde brotherhed."

They never knew that the above messuages were given for the finding of any priest or for the use of the gild or brotherhood.

There has been a " morrowe masse " priest in the town for the last 2 years who was appointed by the inhabitants " because they then not only conceyved the same to be necessary but also to be a profite to the whoole town of Ware for giftes to here masse " and his wages were collected among the inhabitants some giving 2d. some 4d. some 8d. some more and some less " as ther devocon was ". The wages of the last priest were 53/4 and if there was not enough to pay the wages it was taken from the common stock.

Depositions of witnesses re the same Guild, 22 Dec., 2 Edward VI.

William Spence(r ?) of Ware, the last alderman of the gild says that every year at the feast of Jesus the alderman with 4 masters and the brethren of the fraternity " did kepe feaste " at which the masters for the year past did give their account to the alderman and brethren and a new alderman and masters were chosen. [Query, was it for this occasion that the four-gallon brass pot presented in accordance with the will of Thomas Clarke, 1505, was brought into commission ?]

There was no incorporation to his knowledge.

Goods and chattels of the brotherhood included a great brasse pot, a little cup of silver " for to drynk in wyne ", and " one dosen sylver spones " which were sold about 8 or 9 years ago by one of the Masters, and also " 3 cotes of velvet whereof some Imbrodered with golde for the unseemly fornyture of the Image of Jhus " in the parish church.

Extracts from WILLS containing bequests to the Church and the Guilds.

P.C.C. 35 Marche. 1416. John Ferrour. To be buried in the parish church of Ware before the high cross there (alta cruce). To the repair and amendment of the nave of the said church 13/4. For buying a great new bell 2 marks. To the Friars minors of Ware 13/4. Land in Foulme, Camb. to be sold and the money devoted to chaplains to celebrate in the church at Ware.

1 Stokton. 1454. Ellen Bramble. To be buried in parish church of the Blessed Mary at Ware next the tomb of Margaret my mother. To the clerk of this church 12*d*. To the sub clerk or sacrist 12*d*. To the making and repair of the church or ornaments of the church of Amwell 5 marks. [No mention of chantry. Brass in North Transept.]

3 Stokton, 1455. William Martyn of Holborne, London. To the parish church of Ware a chalice price 26/8. A priest to pray for his soul in the church for one year.

24 Milles. 1490. William Pery. Buried in the church of Ware. Money left to light of the Holy Cross. To the fraternity of Corpus Christi 3/4. To lights of Blessed Virgin Mary, St. John, St. Anthony, St. Christopher, St. Clement. To sons John and William his place called Gardeners. [Brass in South Transept.]

1 Dogett. 1491. Sir Thomas Bourchier. To be buried in the parish church. Desires that the bones of Dame Isabell late his wife may be taken up and laid by his bones. Many ornaments left to the church of Ware.

5 Dogett. 1492. William Brond. To lights of Blessed Virgin Mary and the Holy Cross. To the fraternity of Corpus Christi of Ware 2 messuages in Milstrete. [Origin of Almshouses.]

6 Vox. 1493. John Claver. 20 Oct. To be buried in parish church of Ware. To the fraternity of Corpus Christi 5/-. To the light burning before the image of Blessed Mary in the same church. To the lights of St. John Baptist. To Holy Cross. To the repair of the church 20*d*.

4 Horne. 1496. William Welles. To be buried in the parish church of Ware. To the lights burning before the images of the Blessed Mary and the Holy Cross.

22 Horne. 1498. Thomas Brawinge. To be buried in the church

of Ware before the chapel of Our Lady. To the brotherhood of Jhu—

4 Adeane. 1505. Thomas Clarke. To be buried in the church of Blessed Mary of Ware, by my wife in the middle of the church. To the fraternity of Corpus Christi a brass pot of 4 Gallons and a brass pan, 3 spoons of silver. To every brotherhood in the church 12d.

10 Adeane. 1506. Thomas Beal. To be buried in the church of Ware by the sepulchre of Edym (?) my wife. To the fraternity of Jesus in the same church 20s. To the lights of the Rood and Our Lady. To the repair of the chantry of Aelyn Bramble 3/4. To Alice his wife a tenement in Dead Lane, that is to say the gate, gatehouse and barn.

17 Bennett. 1509. Alice Dele. To brotherhood of Jesus in Ware 6/8.

29 Bennett. 1510. Richard Shirley. To be buried in the church of Ware in Our Lady Chapell. To the Rood light, the Lady light, the brotherhood of Jesus. To the use of the chantry of Helen Bramble certain lands for the chantry priest to say masses or obit once a year. Tenement and lands called Raven in Ware. (An Inn ?)

13 Ayloffe. 1518. Walter Gynne. To brotherhood in the parish church (OF Jesus) 3/4. To light of Our Lady and Rood.—

25 Porch. 1527. Thomas Dorcyter. To brotherhood of Jesus Gild 6/. To painting the image of the Assumption of Our Lady in the church 6/8.

CHARITIES

The various Charities were combined into one scheme in 1909, they embraced :

1. Almshouses of Lawrence Armatridinge.—These consist of five tenements in Crib Street, inhabited by ten poor women. L. Armatridinge gave twenty twopenny loaves of bread to twenty widows out of the rent of these five tenements. (See Burial Reg., 1645.)

2. The Bell Close (Recreation Ground).—An indenture of feoffment dated 20th March, 1612, recites that a donor unknown gave the Bell Close, containing about 4 acres, for the benefit of the poor. This produces £27 10s. yearly.

3. James Birch's Almshouses.—These two houses are near the north gate of the churchyard and are for the dwelling of two poor widows. The inmates receive parish relief.

4. Charity of Ellen Bridge, founded by deed in 1628.— This consists of a garden formerly known as Pope's or Doulton's

F

Pightle in Watton Road and producing £10 yearly. (This is the ground just above the lodge to Canons, now built over.)

5. John Burr's Charity, founded by will dated 1814, whereby testator gave £400 3 per cent Bank annuities, now a like sum of consols, producing £10 yearly, the interest to be distributed to poor widows in sums not exceeding 2s. 6d. each.

6. Corpus Christi Barn.—The indenture of feoffment of 1612 also recites that a donor unknown gave to the poor a piece of ground whereon formerly stood a barn called Corpus Christi Barn.

7. Hellum or Elm Green Almshouses.—A deed of feoffment dated in 1788, recites that two almshouses were given by a donor unknown. These are inhabited by four widows who receive parochial relief.

8. Paul Hogge's Charity.—The origin of this charity is unknown, but a rent charge of 6s. 8d. is paid out of a close called Hogg's Close in Great Amwell. (Springfield.)

9. Mill Lane Almshouses.—The indenture of 1612 further recites that a donor unknown gave two almshouses in Mill Lane. The property now consists of eight almshouses in Mill Lane with garden ground let for £2 15s. yearly.

10. Sir William Robert's Charity.—By a feoffment dated 8th April, 1788, it appears that Sir W. Roberts gave three almshouses in Mill Lane and pasture land known as Widow's Mead and Mill Mead containing 8a. 3r. 3p. and producing £22 yearly. The rents are divided among the inmates.

11. The " Saracen's Head ".—The indenture of 1612 also recites that a donor unknown gave a messuage or inn called the " Saracen's Head " together with a piece of land called the netherhoe to the poor. The land was sold in 1891, and the proceeds invested in £247 6s. 8d. consols. The stock has since been increased to £276 2s. 10d. by the investment of balance of premium on lease of the present building. (This inn is now marked for demolition, 1938.)

12. Charity of Humphrey, founded by will 26th June, 1630, consists of a cottage in Kibes Lane producing £9 2s. yearly.

13. The White Hart Estate.—The indenture of 1612 also recited that a donor unknown gave a messuage or inn called the " White Hart " with appurtenances. This property, nos. 77 and 79 High Street, produces £88 yearly, and a slaughter-house producing £20 yearly.

14. Charity of Frederick Harrison, founded by will proved in London, 8th June, 1907.—The property consists of two almshouses built on part of Bell Close, called the Harrison Almshouses, and £94 13s. 5d. New South Wales 3½ per cent stock (1924), £400 Great Northern Railway 3 per cent pref.

stock, producing altogether yearly £22 6s. 2d. and called the Harrison Fund. The scheme directs that the Harrison alms-people shall be two married couples and each couple shall receive a stipend of not less than 7s. 6d. or more than 10s. weekly.

In 1619, George Mead, M.D., by his will gave £5 yearly issuing out of the George Inn, Ware, to the poor. This inn is now Barclay's Bank, Ltd.

In 1622, John Elmer by his will gave the Black Swan for the benefit of the poor of Ware and Stevenage. This property (23 Baldock Street) was sold in 1906 and the proceeds divided.

In 1722, Dame Margaret Tufton by her will gave £260, the interest to be applied in coats to six poor men and gowns to six poor women once every two years and in teaching four boys and four girls to read and write and say the catechism.

In 1749, Anne Ball by her will gave £40 to be applied to the same purposes as Dame Margaret Tufton's bequest. These legacies were later invested in consols. A portion is placed to a separate account and the dividends paid to the Ware school managers. In 1739, Mary Evans by her will gave £100, the income to be distributed in sums of 5s. to poor widows.

In 1825, William Murvell by his will gave £300, the dividends arising therefrom to be applied to the upkeep of testator's monument and the residue, together with the interest on £100, in the relief of five poor women of sixty years and upwards. The same testator gave £666 13s. 4d. consols, the interest therefrom to be applied in the relief of six poor men of sixty years and upwards. In 1907, £2 2s. was spent on the monument, it was cleaned again in 1938.

The Parish Clerk's Charity.—Four acres of land in Wainges Field, Ware, have been appropriated from time immemorial to the use of the parish clerk, being the gift of a donor unknown.

ADVOWSON

The living of St. Mary's, Ware (with Thundridge), was given into the hands of the Alien Benedictine Priory of Ware by Hugo de Grentesmesnil in 1078, and so continued until Henry V passed it over to his Carthusian Priory at Sheen, 1415. In 1538, the church and living were granted, by Henry VIII, to Trinity College, Cambridge, in whose hands it remains.

The following priests have held office in Ware :

Nicholas Speleman	1231
John de Pylardynton	1336
Richard de Pylardynton	1337

John de Colne . . .	—
Ralph —— . . .	—
Robert de Garton . .	1371
John Wengrave . . .	1372
Peter de Winstead . .	1372
Philip Hertford . . .	—
Nicholas Drayton . .	1383
Henry Vyneter . . .	1385
Robert Langeton . .	1387
Simon Say . . .	—
Thomas Graunger, B.D. .	1451
John Elton, B.D. . .	1467
John Lawesby, M.A. . .	1468
John Bennet, S.T.B. . .	1476
John Foster, M.A. . .	1480
Robert Lawe . . .	—
Stephen Leder . . .	1520
Richard Wylcockson . .	1534
John Harte . . .	1542
Robert Kynsey, M.A. . .	1552
William Dowsing . .	1558
John Bendall . . .	1559
Robert Kay . . .	1567
Charles Chauncy, S.T.B. .	1627
John Mountfort, S.T.P. .	1633
Isaac Craven, ejected . .	1634
— Young . . .	—
Richard Waugh, M.A. .	1661
Robert Bulman . . .	1670
Samuel Scattergood, M.A. .	1681
Joseph Weld, M.A. . .	1681
Roger Wye . . .	1682
William Burrough, M.A. .	1689
David Humphreys, S.T.P. .	1730
William Webster, D.D. .	1740
Thomas Franklyn, M.A. .	1759
John White . . .	1777
William Hughes, M.A. .	1781
Henry Allen Lagden, M.A. .	1790
Henry Coddington, M.A. .	1832
Joseph W. Blakesley, B.D. .	1845
E. E. W. Kirkby, M.A. .	1873
Richard Appleton, M.A. .	1904
Martin Reed . . .	1907
Noel Marsh . . .	1924
A. Lloyd Phillips . .	1928

A few personal anecdotes remain concerning some of these priests and other " clerks ".

It has been stated that in Henry IV's reign a Ware priest was hung, drawn, and quartered for declaring that Richard II was still alive.

William of Worcester records in his *Itinerary* that about 1476, Thomas, Clerk of Ware (Graunger ?), left Ware on the Octave of St. John Baptist and rode to St. Michael's Mount within ten days and returned to Ware in another ten days. (Over 32 miles a day for twenty consecutive days, a remarkable achievement for that time, which suggests dry summer conditions.)

This is the route given :

> Waare - Watford - Bekynfield - Henely - Redyng - Kyngsclere - Andever - Salisbery - Sheftesbery - Shyrdorn - Yevylle - Crokehorn - Cherd - Honyton - Excetyr - Crocornwille - Okynton - Lanceston - Bodman-Machehole-Rooderyth-Marchew.
> Margew distat per unum quartum miliaris de Monte Michaelis.

The first intimation of Protestant views being expressed in Ware comes to us from Foxe's *Acts and Monuments*, concerning Thomas Clerk and his wife, and Henry Miller of Tucke (?) by Ware—accused of " Buying and reading the Bible, dissuading from bowing to images and refusing to believe in sacrament of Altar. . . . "

> " Thos. Clerk did detect as his instructor Chris Tinker of Wickham who came to his house at Ware and told him that the sacrament of the Altar was a holy thing but *not* flesh and blood of Christ. Regarding the pieces of bread Clerk said that if every one of these were a God then there were many gods. The priest told him that till the holy words were spoken over it, it was of no power, and then it was very God flesh and blood ; adding that it was not mete for a layman to speak of such things. These words of the priest being recited by Clerk to Tinker he replied ' Let every man say what they will but you shall find it as I show good and if you will come to my house I will show you further proof of it '."

In another statement, not very clear :

> " Henry Miller of Ware did show to Roger Dods (who accused) a story of a woman in the Apocalypse riding on a red beast. He was twice abjured in 1521 when Stephen Leder was priest at Ware."

Robert Kynsey, 1552–8, is mentioned by Dr. Messenger in

an article, " Bishop Bonner and Anglican Orders," in *The Dublin Review*, January, 1936. He writes :

" Robert Kynsey had been ordained Edwardine deacon on 24th August, 1552, by Bishop Ridley at Cambridge, and Edwardine priest by the same bishop at London on 21st December, 1552 . . . the selfsame Robert Kynseye, Vicar of Ware, Herts, was ordained to the four minor Orders, sub-diaconite, diaconite, and priesthood, according to the Catholic rite, in London itself, by the Commission of Bishop Bonner, on 20 and 21 December, 1553."

While Kynsey was vicar, Thomas Fust was burnt at the stake, 1554.

William Dowsing (1558) is mentioned in the Chantry Certificate of Edward VI's reign, so must have had connection with Ware before that date. (Chantry Certif. No. 27, P.R.O.)

" Willm. Dosen a man of lvij yeres and of honest fame is Incombent havinge no other lyvinge but the revenneus of this Chauntre."

Among the collected notes of the late W.B. Gerish is this item :

" 1559. The iiij day of November was a prest maryed with a prest's widow of Ware in Herts. at Saint Botulfe with-out Byshopegatt."

The unfortunate experiences of poor Charles Chauncy which caused him to give up the living of Ware and migrate to America have passed into general history and are related in full under his name among the " Few Celebrities ".

Isaac Craven, 1634, was also subjected to persecutions and ejected. In the Calendar of State Papers, 1653–6, is given an account of yet another unsatisfactory incumbent, who does not appear in the list of regular vicars, one Richard Farrer :

" May 1, 1656. Petition of divers inhabitants of Ware, co. Herts. to the Protector. Richard Farrer, who obtained the presentation to our living, was rejected by nine of the Commissioners for Public Preachers, yet he preached till articles were exhibited against him to the Commissioners of the county for the ejection of scandalous ministers and schoolmasters, whereon the living was sequestered from him ; yet he continues to preach as publicly as before, in the town called the Fryars (?), the inhabitants of which cannot procure an able minister so long as Mr. Farrer continues at or near Ware. Beg an order for his removal.

Twelve signatures. With reference thereon to Wm. Packer, Major-General of Herts, Col. Alban Cox, Isaac Puller and Wm. Turner, to examine the parties and report.

Annexing :—

1. Articles before the Commissioners for ejecting insufficient and scandalous ministers in co. Herts against Richard Farrer accusing him of lying, indecency, extortion, fraud, and violence. Signed Thos. Meade and Humph. Packer.

2. Certificate of John Nye, registrar to the Commissioners for Public Preachers, that nine of them rejected Farrer as disqualified.

3. Report thereon by Packer, Cox, Turner and Puller, that the petition and articles are true, and that the peace of the town would be disturbed by Farrer's remaining there.

Order in Council thereon for the following letter.

President Lawrence to Major-General Packer and the Commissioners for securing the peace of co. Herts. On the above report Council recommends you to deal with Mr. Farrer agreeably to your orders and instructions, as you find most conducible to the peace of the town."

Ware seems to have been unusually unfortunate in its vicars during this seventeenth century, for John Young, 1656–61,

" On Thursday, 4th Sept., 1656, ' Att the councell att Whitehall ordered by his Highness the Lord Protector and the Councell that it be recommended to the Trustees for Maintenance of Ministers to settle an augmentation of £50 per annum upon Mr. John Yong, minister of Ware, in the county of Hertford. Henry Scobell, clerk of ye councell.' " Urwick's *Noncomformity in Herts.* (Lambeth MSS. Aug., 977.)

was also found wanting and ejected. Following his disgrace is another entry in the Cal. State Papers, 1661 :

" Nov. 4. Whitehall. Warrant for corroboration of (Rich.) Waugh, M.A. to the Vicarage of Ware, to which he was formerly presented by Trinity College, Cambridge, but which is in the King's gift by lapse."

Thomas Franklyn, M.A., 1759–77, officiated at the marriage of David Garrick.

Henry Lagden, M.A., 1790–1832, brought a suit against Jacob Robinson and James Green for the tithes of a mill. None had been demanded for many years. The judge, Sir Wm. Scott, found for the vicar.

In 1845, a great change for the better came to Ware living

in the person of Joseph W. Blakesley, B.D., afterwards Dean of Lincoln. Blakesley was the prime mover in the great restoration of the church in 1849, and was most active in drawing the attention of the authorities to the lamentable condition of the dwelling-places in the poor parts of the town. Besides being a distinguished scholar, he may be said to have instigated the first movement towards making Ware a wholesome town. He should be remembered with respect and gratitude. At that time, in common with all reformers, he met with much unpopularity and abuse, but his strong character and enlightened outlook made easier the path of all who have followed him.

From the records of Ware held by Trin. Coll., Cam., Box 44 (1. (2)).

The Feast of St. Barnabas, 1231

Roger (Niger) bishop of London (by commission of Pope G(regory) IX to him and Geoffrey (deLacy) dean of St. Paul's London, upon complaint of the parishioners of Ware, dated St. Peter's Rome iij non Feb. 1 Pope G., Indenture of decree for a Composition between William prior of Ware (an Alien, and proctor of the house of St. Evroult), in England, and Sir Nicholas Speleman at his presentation vicar of the church of St. Mary Ware, quashing a pension of 10 marks payable by the vicar to the prior (of which prior has made quit claim), and awarding to the vicar and his successor for security in case any further claim to such pension be made, the tithes of all mills of all the town of Ware and of Thundrich, the tithes of the park and groves now or late of Robert Earl of Leicester, the tithes of corn of 56 acres of arable land of the manor of Ware all adjoining, namely in a straight line from Waryno Cross to Baldoke Lane abutting on the priory, from Warymo Cros in a straight line westward beyond Godeyers londes to the river, down river to Ware mill, thence to Waterlanend, up Water lane by the high road to Baldoklanend, the heads abutting upon Warymo [1] way northward and the river called Mylwater and Milstrete southward, the tithes of corn of 40 acres, of arable land and 8 acres of meadow in Estfild from Cripestre on the west to Whytberwe Cros on the east, the heads abutting on Popes lane northward and to the south on the town of Ware at Gerneslane all the way to Whitberwe Cros ; the tithe of Salmanne croft in Popesfeld (Stephen Balke the elder) and the tithe of hay of the lord's meadows Berymede, Chaldwellmede, Millemede and " Parc Medwe ", shall all remain to the vicar and his successors, awarding him in name of his vicarage all small tithes and oblations to the church of St. Mary, Ware, and the chapel of Thundrick pertaining, tithe of corn and hay excepted, whereof the tithes above mentioned are reserved to the vicar upon the condition aforesaid, and the tithe of hay of the fees of Robert de Parco, Silvester de Aqua, and Walter the clerk unconditionally, also awarding him the tithes of trees, logs and woodfals in all groves, delles and hedges of the parish of Ware and of Thundrich, the tithes of flax, hemp, yards, fruit, wool, lambs, pigs, geese, swans, calves, cheese, butter, milk, agistments of cattle in the said parish and Thundrich, harts, conies, fish and fowls, mills, gains of trading and lodging, the principal mortuaries, all things pertaining to the altars of the said church and chapel, and a messuage called the priest's messuage with the increase of the yard which was the prior's, and he shall be ordinary charges. Power reserved to the diocesan forever to enforce this award. Witnesses—John atte Water, John Blake the elder ; Memorandum (interpolated at the end) that the tithes of corn and hay of the fee of Richard de Ware shall remain to the vicar for ever. Robert de Parco, Silvester de Aqua, Osbert de Fanham, Robert Whitberwe, William Halfhide.

Seal—two others gone.

[1] WARYMO—probably a confused spelling of WARINGHOE, now contracted to WENGEO.

THE ALIEN BENEDICTINE PRIORY

When Hugh de Grantmesnil became Lord of the Manor of Ware, shortly after the Norman conquest, he wished to give some of his property to the Benedictine Abbey of St. Evroul in Normandy (which he had helped to restore) and found a cell of that Abbey in Ware. William the Conqueror's Charter permitting and confirming this gift (with other lands also) is given by Dugdale, the Ware reference reading : " He gave three villains of Ware. . . . He gave also the Church of Ware and all tenths which belonged to it and two caracutes of land." (Charter of Will. I from Orderius Vitalis, Dugdale, Mon. ii, 966. Ed. 1682.)

This Priory was the only alien establishment in Herts, and apparently the most important of the English possessions of St. Evroul, as the Prior of Ware was Proctor for England, and the majority of the scant references to this house are in connection with the other small foundations, most of them situated in the Midlands.

Other references deal chiefly with the vexed question of finance. These Alien Priories sent much money out of England, the funds being sequestrated by the King whenever one of the frequent wars with France was in progress.

The position of Prior of Ware must have been a very uncomfortable one during the thirteenth and fourteenth centuries when the French wars scarcely ceased. Added to this, he suffered much from intrusion by his patrons, the Lords, or Ladies, of the Manor.

As early as 1219, Margaret de Quincey inherited the Manor and seems to have made her headquarters at the Priory. According to the Assize Roll of 1256 (m. 39) she built a great hall, a large chamber, and a chapel for her own convenience and held her manorial courts there. Her son Roger (or William in Assize Roll) succeeded her in 1235, and made the same use of the Priory, as did his brother, Robert, to whom the Manor was transferred.

This semi-public arrangement was evidently an inconvenience to the monks, for the same note tells us that the Prior built a small hall for his own use during the time of Robert's daughter, Joan, and her husband, Humphrey de Bohun. At Humphrey's death, Joan added yet another chamber for her own use.

By now, the Priory must have been a most interesting group of buildings and it is the greatest pity that we have no single fragment of this date remaining to us. We only know from the property subsequently transferred to Trinity College, Cambridge, by Henry VIII that they must have stood just north of the Church on land now occupied by schools, and the house and garden known as the " Manor House ", though referred to in the College records as " The Rectory ". A little later, as will be seen, there are frequent references to the Priory Farm, which must also have been of considerable size and value, and this may have been to the north of the town, on the Cambridge road, where a group of old farm buildings and maltings have always borne the name of " Canons ". A windmill stood here until about 1820, and is shown on a sketch by Bourne, owned by Rev. H. Evans. The millstones are still in the farmyard.

Joan de Bohun died in November, 1283 (Chan. Inq. p.m. 12, Ed. 1, No. 27), and when the escheator arrived at Ware to take possession in the King's name, he found the windows and doors closed against him. With help from the Earl of Gloucester's men he forced an entrance but meanwhile the Prior had had Joan's new hall pulled down. In consequence, a suit was brought against him by the heiress, Hawise Wake, Joan's sister, but we do not find that any other holder of Ware Manor resided at the Priory.

Hawise stated (Assize Roll, 1283) that her ancestors had given and granted lands and tenements to the Priory at Ware, that there was a residence and storehouse within the enclosure of the Priory, to which the said ancestors had access whenever they required.

In the general ecclesiastical taxation of the clergy in the Diocese of London made about 1291, the entry relating to the Prior of Ware states :

> Church of Ware, 60 marks
> Tenths, £4.
> Medr. (one-twentieth) 40s.

The Prior was responsible for providing a parish priest and seems to have had difficulty in finding suitable men, probably owing to the annual payment of ten marks demanded from them, and also the reservation to the Prior of the tithes of the mills of the whole parish of Ware and Thundridge, also the tithes of the park and woods of Robert, Earl of Leicester, and the tithes also of corn and hay " of the said parish to the prejudice and more destruction of the said vicarage ".

In 1228, the parishioners of Ware appealed to Pope Gregory IX, stating that the Prior had refused to let the cure of their Parish Church be served by a sufficient vicar. (Lond. Epis. Reg. Gilbert, fol. 169–170.) The Pope issued a mandatory letter to the Bishop and Dean of London to hear and determine the matter, and the Prior and men of Ware, having first sworn that they would stand by the award without appeal, the dispute was settled as follows : " The Vicar and others appointed Vicars in the same Church, shall take possession of all the small tenths and oblations whatsoever with all things belonging to the said Church of Ware and Chapel of Thundridge (except tenths of sheaves of corn and of hay, exclusive of the tenths of hay due to the Vicar and his successors from the farm of Robert of the Park, Sylvester of the Water, and Walter Clerk)." The Vicar was also to have tenths of wood of trees, of underwood, wild trees, groves, and dells, and all hedges of the parish town of Ware and Thundridge, tenths of timber and bark, growing crops, fruit, wool, lambs, pigs, geese, swans, calves, cheese, butter, milk, agistment, animals, stags, rabbits, fish, and of all fowl, mills, business, profit, and principal inns, and all other things belonging to the altars of the Church of Ware and Chapel of Thundridge. The Vicar is also to have " a messuage, that is called the Priest's Messuage, together with the increase therefrom arising which was the Prior's, and he shall sustain the ordinary burdens of the aforesaid Church ".

This endowment, with the consent of all parties, was confirmed by Roger Niger in 1231, with the clause : " and in like manner of the tenths of sheaves, growing crops and hay of the farm of Richard de Ware Senior shall remain to the aforesaid Vicar in perpetuity." (In passing, it is interesting to note the name of Richard de Ware senior, who may have been father to the Benedictine Richard de Ware who became famous as Abbot of Westminster in 1258.)

At an Assize held at Hertford in 1278, the Prior of Ware, for one caracute of land in the same town, was ordered to make two bridges, one in Hempwellesmede, 10 ft. long and 6 ft. wide ; the other in Ffoueracremade, 10 ft. long and 6 ft. wide. As these bridges were certainly too short to have spanned the River Lea they probably crossed the stream known as the Bourne, which flowed through the Benedictine property.

The sequestration of Priory funds to the King started in King John's reign ; in 1295, the Priory was again in the hands of the King (Pope Nich. Tax. Rec. Com. 2496), and protection was granted to the Prior. A King's man was put into the house to see that there was no communication with France, to answer at the Exchequer for the issues of the property and receive from the Exchequer what was necessary to maintain the house. (Ordinances for the alien religious in 1295. Cal. Fine R., 1272–1307.)

In 1324, a third seizure of alien priories took place (Mins. Accts. bdle., 1125, No. 11), two men were appointed to account to the Crown, from 8th October to 10th December, for the monastic manor and the church of Ware. The translation of the inquisition runs : " Inquisition taken at Ware in the presence of John de Enfield, Knight, and Ralph Hereward, clerk, custodians of the lands and alien houses which are of the power of the Lord King of France in the counties of Essex and Hertford, day of S. Luke evangelist in the 18th year of the reign of King Edward son of King Edward, by the oath of John at Water, William le Barber, Alexi de Spaldyng, Richard Richard, clerk, phi . . . of the priory, Godyni le Salter, Thomas Austyn, John Fitz Aldiche, Matthew the Taverner, Hugo, clerk, with Syward and John Millers of the bridge, jurors, who say that the Prior of Ware is Rector of the church of Ware in his own right with one caracute of arable land which is worth per annum £40 without reprisals, that Richard Smelt of Ware is farmer at £60 of the said priory paying for the same each year £30 at the Feast of Easter, and £30 at Saint Mary Magdalene, beginning payment on All Saints Day in the 17th year of the reign of King Edward son of King Edward up to the end of seven years next following and fully complete. . . . In the said manor there is no dovecote nor any other goods. Item, there are 30 qrs. 2 lbs. of corn worth £8 16d., per quarter 5s. 4d. which remain without reprisals. Item 15 qrs. of beans, worth 60s., per quarter 4 shillings, which remain without reprisals. Item, 5 qrs. of pease worth 16s. 8d. per quarter 3s. 4d. which remain without reprisals. Item, of oats nothing without reprisals. Item, of hay and forage 6s. 8d. without reprisals. Item, there are 2 cart horses worth 20 shillings, 4 kine for the plough, worth 26s. and

8*d*., per head 6*s*. 8*d*. Item, 2 oxen worth 20*s*., which belong to the said Richard Smelt."

The Priory of Ware appears to have been suppressed in January, 1328, when the Prior was granted protection for one year. In 1333, there was a grant that his contribution of 100 shillings towards the expenses of the marriage of Eleanor, the King's sister, to the Count of Gueldres shall not prejudice their house as a precedent.

In Edward III's reign, the long war with France again stopped relations between the Priory and the Abbey of St. Evroul (Cal. Close, 1333–7) and the property was farmed, with the exception of the advowsons to the prior, for £230 per annum.

The Prior had difficulty in collecting the money due to the King, in March, 1342, and again in June, 1343, he was threatened with the loss of the custody if he did not pay £160 immediately to one of the King's creditors. (Cal. Close, 1343–6.)

In the previous year, 21st May, 1342, protection and safe-conduct was granted until Michaelmas for the Prior of Ware going beyond the seas to a general chapter of his order, with ten men of his household, six horses, and gold for his expenses to the value of 40 marks. (Cal. Pat., 1343–5.) But his money difficulties continued, and on 18th April, 1344, a patent roll entry states that, whereas the King is informed that many of the farms, etc., are in arrears, he has appointed his sergeant-at-arms, John de Monceux, and others to collect all such arrears and cause them to be kept in safe custody for his use. On 18th January, 1345, the King directed that an annuity of £100 and arrears should be paid, beginning at Michaelmas next, out of the farm which the alien Prior of Ware pays for the Priory, for such time as the Priory remain in the King's hands on account of the war with France.

On 27th January, 1348, the King directed that John de Ravenesholm was to be paid an annuity of £140 out of the farm of the Priory of Ware. A patent roll entry of 12th April, 1348, states that, whereas the King by letters patent lately granted to the Prior of Ware, an alien, the custody of the temporalities of the Priory in England during the war with France, at the request of Queen Isabel, and for 100 marks which the Prior will pay into the King's chamber, he has granted to him all advowsons of churches and benefices pertaining to such temporalities to hold for the same time. In 1350, the money to be collected was again in arrears when, 20th April, William de Monte Sorelli and others were appointed to collect what was due from the Prior.

In a long entry (Cal. Close, 1360–4), it appears that for the five years before the peace of Bretigny, 1360, all possessions of the alien houses were given by the King into the custody of the Prior of Monte Acuto in Somerset, and that, as there is now peace between " us and the Magnificent Prince the King of France, our most dear brother ", the King directs the Prior of Monte Acuto to restore all the possessions of the various establishments. There are some 130 entries, Ware coming the thirty-third as : " Priory of Ware which is a cell of the Abbie of St. Ebrulpho in Normandy."

War began again in 1367, and in a Close roll entry of 1371, it appears that the Prior, John Gerand, held the priory for £200 annually, paid to the Exchequer ; in this document there is also reference to the Vicar's pension of 10 marks.

In November, 1377, Richard II made William Herbert, the prior, custodian of the house for £245 a year, and granted John de Ipre, Knight, 50 marks yearly from the farm of the Priory ; on 5th July, 1379, is a grant to the King's uncle, Thomas de Wodestok, Earl of Buckingham, that he may receive £1000 a year to maintain his rank as earl, from farms of alien priories, the Priory of Ware to contribute £206 13s. 4d. and, in June, 1380, provision that should he die in the next expedition against France his executors shall receive this sum for one year to discharge his debts.

When the King's mother, Joan, Princess of Wales, lady of Ware Manor, died in 1385, Herbert's rights were disregarded and the custody given to John Golofre, one of the gentlemen of the King's chamber. (Anct. Pet., No. 7262, P.R.O.)

On 4th June, 1395, another of the King's uncles, Thomas, Duke of Gloucester, was also granted £1000 from alien priories, Ware to contribute £206 13s. 4d.

In March, 1398, the King assigned the house during the war to his nephew Thomas Holland, Duke of Surrey, without rent (Cal. Pat., 1396–9), and it was probably the duke who made it over to Mountgrace, Yorkshire, for a short time. When Henry IV took the throne in 1399, he granted £245 yearly from Ware Priory to Philip Repyndon, the Abbot and the Convent of St. Mary, Leicester, and later, February, 1400, gave the Abbott of St. Evroul leave to grant in mortmain the proctorial house of Ware, with all possessions, to the abbey of St. Mary, Leicester. This arrangement did not last long, for within a few months Ware was again receiving, or trying to collect, arrears from the other foundations of St. Evroul in England.

In the September Parliament of 1402, the King and Peers resolved at the petition of the Commons that all alien priories should be resumed into the King's hands, and in the Minutes of the Privy Council for 4th January, 1403, it is noted : " Priory of Ware which remains in the hands of the King."

In 1405, Queen Joan received the custody of the priory valued at £240 per annum. (Cal. Pat., 1405-8.)

In the summer of 1406, Parliament insisted that a correct return should be made of all alien priories (with other properties) that their real value might be ascertained and proper rent paid. At the great Council of Westminster, 21st February, 1408, it was decreed that the property of alien priories or cells belonging to foreign monasteries should in future be appropriated to supply funds for the expenses of the Royal Household. In 1409, " Richard Champeney, Prior of the Priory of Ware, alien," and R. Blaby, farmers of the Priory, paid to the King £66 13s. 4d. per annum.

On 5th February, 1410, the King granted a licence to the Prior, Nicholas Champens, that he might bring a certain monk from St. Ebrulf, with a servant, for the term of their lives for " divine singing " ; they were to behave themselves well and honestly, and to attempt nothing against the King or his Kingdom. (Cal. Pat., 1408-13.)

Soon after the accession of King Henry V, 20th November, 1413, he granted £100 annually from the farm of Ware Priory to Mountgrace (presumably in place of £100 formerly granted from the Exchequer) and on 24th November, leased the farm to the Prior Nicholas Champeney, a fellow monk of his, called Richard Baussain, the Earl of Arundel, and others for 400 marks per annum. (Parl. R. IV, 3136.) But in 1414, the alien priories were finally suppressed and taken into the hands of the King, who granted Ware and all its possessions on 1st April, 1415, to his new foundation, the Carthusian Priory at Sheen. This house presented to the living at Ware until the time of Henry VIII.

After the dissolution of the monasteries, the Ware property

was presented to Trinity College, Cambridge, in 1546, with the gift of the Church living.

Priors of Ware

Richard, occurs 1174, was then proctor of St. Evroul in England (Cal. Doc. France) and probably Prior of Ware.

Hubert, occurs *c.* 1203–6 (*ibid.*).

A—, occurs 1219 (R. of Hugh di Welles : Cant. and York Soc., i, 49).

William, occurs 1231 (Lond. Epis., Reg. Gilbert, fol. 169–170), and 1234 (R. of Hugh de Welles, Cant. and York Soc., ii, 323).

Nicholas, occurs 1235–9 (Anct. D., P.R.O., H. 2447).

John, occurs 1259–60 (Harl. Chart. 84 D 56).

William, occurs 1278–9 (Reg. of Archbp. Peckham (Cant. and York Soc.), 140).

Fulk, occurs 1281–2 (Reg. Epist. John Peckham (Rolls Ser.), i, 209–10 ; ii, 432).

Ralph, occurs June, 1297 (Cal. Pat., 1292–1301, p. 270).

Hugh, occurs 1327–8 (De Banco R., 1 Edw. III, m. 42 ; 2 Edw. III, m. 237).

William Herbert, occurs November, 1377–May, 1381 (Cal. Pat., 1381–5), and 1385.

A petition from the prior (Anct. Pet., No. 7262, P.R.O.) speaks of the Princess of Wales as dead and is therefore later than August, 1385.

Nicholas Champene, occurs February, 1410 (Cal. Pat., 1408–13, p. 157), 24th November, 1413 (Parl. R. IV, 3136), and at the dissolution of the Priory. (20th July, 1414, he is called Prior of Noion of Newmarket, alias Prior of Ware. (Cal. Pat. 1413–16, p. 89.))

The seal of Prior John is in the British Museum, attached to an agreement of 1260 (Harl. Chart. 84 D 56). It is of dark green wax, the shape is a pointed oval, 1¾ by 1 in. The Prior is shown vested for mass standing on a carved corbel, with a book in his hands. Legend : S'I O H A N N I S : PRIORIS DE WARE.

The seal of Ralph (B.M., seals lxiv, 72), also a pointed oval, 1¾ in. by 1 in. when perfect, shows two figures standing in a double niche under a canopy, the one a King, the other a bishop or abbot, the one on the left with key, the other with pastoral staff. In the field on each side are three roses. In the

base, under a pointed arch, the prior kneels in prayer.
Legend : ...M R A D U L P H ... ORIS DE. ...
Clutterbuck illustrates this, also (2) a seal of Prior John
(fourteenth century ?), pointed oval, in double niche with
elaborate canopy ; two figures standing, one on the left with
key in left hand, book in right ; the other with pastoral staff
in right hand, book in left ; in base, under a round-headed
arch, the Prior kneeling in prayer to the left.

The references to this alien priory all seem to draw
attention to the troubles of its time, money difficulties, wrangles
with patrons, and change of overlord according to the fortunes
of war ; it is left to one item of information given in some
Thundridge records, by the late C. Giles Puller, Esq., to
strike the human note at all, and he tells us that in summer the
monks from Ware Priory sometimes came to Thundridge for
a change. Instantly our view and idea alters and we can well
imagine the Prior, with a few chosen companions, setting out
on a summer morning with fishing-rods on their shoulders
and worries left behind, to wander those two pleasant miles
to Thundridge. Did they take the old North road, or did they
prefer the quiet beauty of the field-path, starting alongside their
own Bourne, bringing them to the hill above Thundridge
Church with the exquisite view of the Rib Valley spread
before them ? Surely we are justified also in supplying a little
more imagination to fill in another picture or two. When,
in 1274, the Prior of Durham and Robert de Insula, the
Bishop-elect, spent a night in Ware on their way to, and from,
London, it is very likely that the Prior of Ware would pay them
the compliment of going out to meet them, and although from
their detailed accounts we know they stayed at an inn, perhaps
they joined the Ware brethren at Evensong. Which leads us to
another supposition.—When the great re-building of Ware
Church took place towards the end of the fourteenth century,
did the Benedictine brothers take part in the work ; was it a
cheery member of that small community who was responsible
for carving those vivid caricatures of his fellow workers between
the arches of the nave ? If so, he could scarcely have finished
the work that delights us to-day before the dispersing of his
house, knowing no more of that pleasant life and, perhaps,
wondering as much concerning its future as we are bound to
of its past.

Note.—The references in this chapter are taken from the

Victoria County History (Ecclesiastical) ; much of the matter was provided by the Rev. H. P. Pollard in his article on " The Alien Benedictine Priory at Ware ", printed in *The Transactions of the East Herts Archæological Soc.*, vol. iii, part ii, 1906, and used with his kind permission.

The Abbot and Convent of the Benedictine Abbey of St. Evroul, Normandy, wrote an earnest appeal to the Carthusians of Sheen in 1416, to restore the property that Henry V had handed them. They spent eleven years in vain endeavour to regain their lost English property and, in 1427, carried their case to Rome but failed.

There is a fifteenth century chartulary of Sheen Priory among the B.M. MSS. : " Registrum privilegiorum et terarum Monasterie de Shene." This gives abstracts of Charters and other particulars relative to the possessions of the alien Priories of Ware, etc.

The Old Rectory Manor

The remnant of this old house stands to the north of the church on the site of the Alien Benedictine Priory. Until at least 1670, it was a very attractive group of buildings, with a covered entrance and gatehouse, constructed round the farm. A small, rough sketch of this, showing dovecot and granary, etc., is given on a plan of the Glebe lands among the Ware documents preserved at Trinity College, Cambridge. (Box 44, vi.)

All business connected with the Tithe lands seems to have been transacted at this spot, for which reason, presumably, the present title of " Manor House " has been chosen, though until 1848, it was referred to as the " Old Rectory ".

The Rectory Manor Court Rolls exist from the reign of Edward VI to George II. These are also kept at Cambridge (Box 44), and give all details of tenants who were admitted to the holding of Tithe land " by the Rods by the hands of the Steward ".

There is a further sketch of Glebe lands among the Cambridge records, dated 1778, but it is too indefinite to be of particular value.

When the Priory farm buildings (last tenanted by Mr. Flack) were demolished, and schools built on the site, in 1849, there was enough of the Norman stone-work remaining to face two cottages on Musley Hill. They stand out, curiously striking, amid the early Victorian brickwork.

THE FRANCISCAN FRIARY

To the south of the Church, and just before High Street turns into Baldock Street, is the red-brick archway leading into the grounds of the Franciscan friary, more commonly, but erroneously, known as Ware Priory.

This small establishment of the Friars minors probably owed its existence to the fact of Ware lying on a main road.

The Friars obtained their place of settlement in Ware through the generosity of Thomas, second Lord Wake of Liddell, then Lord of the Manor of Ware. It is recorded (Cal. Pat. R., 1338–40, p. 14) that the King (Edward III) granted a licence in mortmain, 18th February, 1338, " to the Friars Minors of Ware for their habitation to hold to them and their successors in free pure and perpetual almoign for ever one messuage and seven acres of land with appurtenances in Ware for newly erecting an oratory house and other buildings then necessary." This grant was confirmed, in September, 1350, by the Pope :

> " To the Minister General, and Friars Minor. Confirmation of the acceptance by the Minister Provincial, and Friars Minor of the Province of England, of a site in the town of Ware, in the diocese of London, given to them by John (?) Wake, knight, Lord of Lidell, which they accepted by virtue of a general faculty to the Order to accept six sites—three in Italy, three North of the Alps." (Cal. of Papal Letters, iii, p. 394.)

After the death of Thomas Wake, a further licence in mortmain was given by the King to his widow, Blanche, in July, 1372 (Pat. 46 Ed. III, pt. ii, m. 32), enabling her to grant to the Friars " four acres of land in Ware contiguous to the Manse of the Warden and Brethren of the Order of Friars Minors in Ware ", and from the inquisition " ad quod damnum ", taken the 18th of May previous, it appears that Blanche Wake bought this land for the purpose of the grant, and that it was held of her Manor of Ware by the service of a half-penny yearly.

Although information concerning the Friary is scanty, the references we have help to give some idea of the course of its little history until the Dissolution, 200 years later.

The next mention occurs shortly after the deposition of King Richard II. Thomas, Earl of Kent, was Lord of the Manor of Ware at that time, and remaining loyal to Richard II, his lands were forfeited and himself beheaded. This is reflected in the following note :

" Grant to the Friars Minor of Ware of the underwood of 1 acre within the foreign wood late of Thomas, late Earl of Kent, by the town of Ware, and 2 cartloads of hay in the meadows, late of the said earl there—so long as they are in the king's hands by his forfeiture—with all the fishery of the water running along the length of their house during the same time." (Cal. of Pat. Rolls, 1399–1401, p. 394.)

There are notes of several legacies bequeathed to the small house among the records of Wills in the Archdeaconry of St. Albans, and published in the volumes of the *Herts Genealogist and Antiquary* :

Vol. I, p. 47 A Legacy to " Fratribus minoribus de Ware " from the Will of Johannes Brykendon, 4th May, 1416.

p. 316 A Legacy to the Friars at Ware, from Willelmus Hichman, sr., 22nd October, 1423. To friars at Ware, from Almaricus Weste, 1432.

p. 318 To Friars minors at Ware, from Willelmus Remyngton, 17th August, 1433.

Vol. II, p. 91 Legacy to Friars at Ware, from Joan Walsch, 14th March, 1435. Legacy to Friars at Ware, from Thomas Lundon, 1st June, 1433.

p. 238 Legacy to Friars at Ware from Thomas Hale, Thursday in the feast of St. Gregory the Pope, 1438.

Vol. III, p. 274 To the Convent of the friars minors of Ware, from John Wagstaffe, 29th August, 1448.

We learn of an earlier bequest, 1355, when Elizabeth de Burgh, Lady Clare (who founded Clare College, Cambridge), left our Friary 40 shillings. (Nichols, *Royal Wills*, 23, 33.)

And, from the Court of Hustings, that on 18th October, 1348, Roger de Forsham left residue of certain money to Convent of the Friars Minors. In 1361, also, Richard Cully left a bequest to the Order of Friars.

An obit, of a later date, 1526, is preserved in the British Museum. This interesting document gives full instructions from Thomas Hyde, concerning masses and prayers to be said during his life and after his death. It has been transcribed by Dr. G. R. Owst, and is given in full below.

" Thys indenture made the iiith day of October, yn the xvii yere of the reyne of King Henry the viiith be twene freer Paule, warden of the gray freeres yn Ware, and the convente of the same place off the on parte—and Thomas Hyde of the other partye, for dyverse causys, consyderacyons, and covenauntes here after folowyng, by the fore namyd warden and covente and there successores truly to be performyd and fulfylled ; —that ys to say the fore namyd warden and covent by thur one assente and consente, with the assente and agremente of Rychard Brynkeley, thur mynyster, by thes presentes, covenaunthe and graunthe to and with the fore namyd Thomas Hyde, that the sayde warden and hys successores with thur holle covente byndyth them selfe perpetually that who so ever schall syng the seconde masse by fore the common autore (altar) onyse yn the wek, that ys to say the thyrsday, shall specyally pray for the good estate and prosperus welfare of the forsayd Thomas Hyde and Jone hys wyfe, durying ther lyvys, and for thur sowlys after they be departyd thys world, and for the sowlys of John Hyde, and Maryon hys wyfe, father and mother to the forsayde Thomas, and for the sowle of Elyzabeth and Helyn sumtyme wyvys to the forsayd Thomas, and for alle the fryndes and benefactores of the forsayd Thomas :

" Also farthermore, the same warden and covente with thur on assente and consente, by thes presentes, covenaunthe and graunthe with the same Thomas Hyde, that the sayde warden and hys successores with the hoole covente shall kepe perpetually onnys yn the yere after the date here of, with yn the conventuall cherche of freeres yn Ware, a soleme and a dewoth (devout) obyte for the sayde Thomas Hyde and the sowlys before rehersyd, at suche day and tyme as here after ys expreesyd, that ys to say, the Sonday immedyately folowying Estur Day callyd ' Dominica in Albis ', a soleme Dyryge, and, the nexte day folowyinge, mass of requiem by noote (with music). And ferthermore the sayde warden and hys successors shall yerely ii thymys yn the yere perpetually rede or cawse to be redde this presente indenture yn the chaptur howse afore all the covente, that ys to say, ' in quindena Omnium Sanctorum, et in quindena Pasche ', to the yntente that the sayd Obbyte with other the premyssys truly may be observyd and kepte acordyng to the agremente and covenaunte afore expressyd, with owte pretendyng of ony ygnorancy yn the same.

" In wytnesse wherof to the on parte of these yndentures with the sayde Thomas Hyde remaynyng, the sayd warden and covente have sette too ther covente sealle, and to the other parte of these yndentures with the same warden and covente remaynyng, the sayde Thomas Hvde have sette to hys sealle, and for a confyrmacyon and more surety of the premyssys, the fore namyd Rychard Brynkeley, mynyster of Yngla(n)d, have sette hys sealle, gevyn the day and yere above wryttyn."

(Add. Charter 36070.)

Attached to this document are three seals, those of Ware Friary, Thomas Hyde, and Richard Brynkeley : that of the Friary has been drawn and described by Dr. Owst as follows : " The kneeling figure of Lord Wake, the founder, with his arms emblazoned upon his shield, is unmistakable. But the central figure which he adores has been erroneously described as representing Christ Crucified. (*V.C.H.*) The outstretched wing is itself sufficient with the general posture of the body to identify it with the Seraph of St. Francis' famous vision on Mount Alverna, during which he was said to have received the Stigmata. . . . It is the present writer's belief that a careful examination of the original seal will convince his readers further that the figure kneeling opposite to that of the Founder is not the Lady Blanche, but St. Francis himself. Even the rays of light which stream from the Seraph's stigmata to those of the Saint can be traced here, as in other representations of the scene."

The legend on the seal reads, S/ Gardiani (Fratrum) minorum de WARE.

The Friary also received fees from lay burials within its grounds. John Weever (*Ancient Monuments*, p. 312) mentions in 1631, that " at the North end of this town was a Frierie, whose ruines not altogether beaten downe are to be seen at this day. . . . Here lieth Thomas Heton and Jone his wife, which Thomas died xixth Aug., 1409, and Joyce. . . . William Littlebury, and Elizabeth his wife ; he died xxii of July, 14 . . " Other instructions for burials are found in the wills of (1) John Chichester, Ware, Herts, 1524. To be buried within the Friary of the order of St. Francis in Ware. (21 Bodfelde) and (2) William Rowse or Rous, Ware, to the Grey Friars of Ware, 1527, to be buried in the chancel of Our Lady in the Church of Ware. This latter seems an unusual request to have made to the Friars who would not have had much, if any, relations with the parish church. (22 Porch.)

But the chief means of livelihood was begging, and we have an interesting record of the limits set for the Ware brethren, which arose from a disagreement with the house at Cambridge, in 1395, as follows :

" At the recent petition of the Custos, guardian, and brethren of the house of Friars Minor at Cambridge, containing that from of old they have, on account of the University there, been wont to receive a very great multitude of brethren of the order, of divers regions and provinces, and to minister to them food and other necessaries out of the procurations of alms from the bounds of their house ; and that near the said bounds, in or near Ware, in the diocese of London, a certain small house of the Order, has been founded, whose brethren extend the bounds of their procurations so far towards Cambridge and other parts that the said multitude incurs very great loss—Inhibition to the said brethren of Ware to extend their bounds for the purpose of making procurations of alms or preachings, more than 5 miles towards any part, which before their foundation belonged to the bounds of the house at Cambridge, except to the town of Poketich (Puckeridge) in the said diocese." Concurrent Mandate to the Archbishop of York, and the Bishops of London and Ancona.

(Cal. Pap. Lett., iv, p. 517.)

References to the little house are scarce. In 1430, Roger Donwe, Deue, or Daw, " Doctor of Oxford," thirty-fifth Minister Provincial of the Order in England, came here to end his days. (Kingsford, *Greyfriars of London*, p. 194.) We have record of one distinguished visitor when, after the battle of St. Albans, during 1455, the King, Henry VI, and his Queen, with the infant Prince proceeded to Hertford Castle, and " mine lord York to the Friars at Ware " (Paston letters, p. 335, ed. Gairdner Letter, No. 243), from Royston.

There is a note from T. Cromwell to Henry VIII, 23rd July, 1533, stating that : " The Friars Observants that were with the Princess Dowager, and were subtilly conveyed thence, were first discovered at Ware by Cromwell's spies, and thence dogged to London." (Cal. S.P.D., vol. vi, 1533, no. 887.)

Of the Wardens we only know three, Paul, whose name occurs in The Obit of Thomas Hyde, 3rd October, 1525, and who appears to have held certain Protestant opinions, according to the following note :

Paul, Warden of Ware Friary, *c.* 1525, mentioned by Fox for getting into trouble with Bishop Stokesley, of London. He was accused of saying :

" It is a pity that there be so many images suffered in so many places, where indiscreet and unlearned people be, for they make their prayers and oblations so entirely and heartily before the image that they believe it to be the very saint in heaven.

"Item, that if he knew his father and mother were in heaven, he would count them as good as St. Peter and Paul, but for the pain they suffered for Christ's sake.

"Item, that there is no need to go on pilgrimage.

"Item, that if a man were at the point of drowning or in other danger, he should call only upon God and no saint, for saints in heaven cannot help us, neither know they more what men do in this world, than a man in the north country knoweth what is done in the south country."

Paul was forced to abjure. The historian Cox, 1720, gives a rather inaccurate account of this incident.

Of John Bawde nothing is known beyond his burial in the London House, c. 1530. (Kingsford, *Greyfriars of London*.)

With Thomas Chapman, S.T.B., we draw near to the end of the history of this little Friary as a Franciscan settlement. On 5th May, 1534, the Ware Friars in their chapter-house, under the signature of Thomas Chapman, S.T.B., made "Declaration of Obedience to Henry VIII and Queen Anne, and of the lawfulness of their marriage, with repudiation of the Bishop of Rome's authority, and acknowledgment of the King as Supreme Head of the Church." (L. and P. Hen. VIII, vol. vii, no. 665.)

Chapman was friendly with Lord Hussey, who was convicted and sentenced to death by Henry VIII for failing to help in suppressing the Pilgrimage of Grace in 1537. He wrote to the King to settle his debts and duties in view of the impending forfeiture. In this letter, preserved among the Hussey Papers, he mentions how : "I spake with the Warden of Gray Freers at Ware" for his help in the business. The Warden replies, "with commendations to him and to my lady." He has made the arrangement required, and adds a note.

"Where I promised you a fair bible you shall have it. I thought some of your servants should have been with me ere now. After Easter I will deliver it to Percival your servant." (Lett. and Pap., Hen. VIII, vol. vii, no. 665.)

At the time of the Dissolution, among the Friars Observants remaining in the kingdom were :

Frater Robertus Neseweke est apud Ware
   ,,   Henricus Sotyll   est idem
   ,,   Walterus ffreman   ,,   ,,
   ,,   Johes elstenys   ,,   ,.
   ,,   Johes hore   ,,   ,,

The actual date of the surrender of Ware Friary was 9th May, 1535.

On the 25th September, 1538, John Hilsey, Bishop of Rochester, writes to Thomas Cromwell from Bury, Suffolk, saying he will bring back with him the surrender of various monastic houses, " and Ware also." (L. and P. Hen. VIII, vol. xiii, pt. ii, no. 437.) But, about two months later, Richard Ingworth, Bishop of Dover, came " to receive to the King's use the Black Friars of Dunstable, the Grey in Ware ". (Gairdner, *Lollardy and the Reformation*, vol. ii.)

When, in the summer of the year following, the King's Commissioners toured the religious houses, they made detailed expense accounts of their journeyings, and the Bill of their visit to Ware is preserved in the Public Records Office, Augmentation Office. It has been transcribed by the Rev. W. H. Walcott in his article on the Dissolution of the Monasteries, printed in *Archæologia*, vol. xliii, and runs :

At Waltham, xx daye of June xxxR. Hen. VIII
At Ware that nyght.

For Sopper		iiijs.
for wyne and suger		ijs.
the mynystrels		iiijd.
fyre in chambres		viiid.

Saturday in the morning.

For brekefaste	ijs.	iiijd.
horsseshoinge		xvid.
mendinge saddels, gyrthis, male gyrthes, bridels and other neces- saries to the same belongings		vs.
horsemete	iiijs.	iiijd.
a Kerchiffe wasshinge		jd.
a bridell ther bought with a pewterell afterward		xx(?)
paper		ijd.

When the Friary passed into secular hands, the first owner was Robert Byrche and was valued at 29*s.* 8*d.* a year, the

" osierhope " was farmed for 20*d*. (Mins. Accts. Hen. VIII, no. 1617 ; 32 and 33 Hen. VIII, no. 71, m. 2.) In 1544, the site and " osier hope " were granted to Thomas Byrch, a yeoman of the Crown and to his heirs and assigns. (L. and P. Hen. VIII, xix (1), 610 (68).)

It has been suggested that the modern house by Ware Lock, called " Hope House ", may derive its name from the osier " hope " or plantations, which probably occupied this site.

Thomas Byrche, grandson, sold the site and osierlands to Job Bradshaw in 1628 (Com. Pleas D. Ens. Hil. 4 Chas I, m. 5d.) From Bradshaw, the property passed to Richard Hator ; in 1685, it became the property of Robert Hadsley of Great Munden and remained in this family until 1868. The Friary was then sold to Clement Morgan, and again to Mr. T. Gwyn Jeffreys, conchologist, who lived there until 1881, when the property was sold to the late Mr. Robert Walters, the last private inhabitant. Mrs. R. B. Croft then acquired the property and presented it to the town.

The only interesting reference during the years the old house was in secular ownership was made by Lady Anne Fanshawe in her *Memoirs*. The Fanshawes were tenants at the Friary for the year of 1658, and Lady Anne makes no secret of her rejoicing on hearing the news of the death of Oliver Cromwell, which occurred during their stay in Ware.

The building itself is admirably described in the *Victoria County History* (vol. iii, p. 392). As this publication is at present out of print it may be of interest to give the description as found there :

" The house, which is a residence of two floors with attics, lying a little to the south of the church, is constructed out of nearly the whole of the southern range of the cloisters of the Franciscan friary, not quite half of the western range, and the great hall which runs westward at right angles to the western range. A small two-storied wing projects on the south side of the south range. The rubble walls of the house are plastered and have stone dressings ; the roofs are tiled. Nothing earlier than late 15th century work survives. The modern additions are of brick and timber plastered.

" In the S.W. angle of the cloisters, which were about 8 ft. wide, a modern porch has been erected, which forms, with the two ends of the cloisters, the present entrance hall of the house. The south wall of the southern range, on the ground floor of which is the drawing-room, is not original. On the first floor of this range are bedrooms formed out of the ancient frater. The small wing projecting southward contains a smoking room on the ground floor and bedrooms above. The modern staircase is at the western end of the southern range, and beyond it are the kitchens and offices. On the ground floor of the western range is the dining-room with bedrooms above. The undercroft of the great hall is now occupied by six rooms and a corridor. The hall over it, measuring 48 ft. by 22 ft., was in four bays with an open timber roof. (See *The Builder*, 21st July, 1849, when this magnificent hall was ruined.) Above the rooms now occupying this space are attics formed by the insertion of a floor at the level of the old tie-beams. The north side of the southern range has six of the original cloister windows of three cinque-foiled lights, but these have been much altered, and some of them are blocked. In the northern (western ?) range only two of the cloister windows remain ; one of them, which lights the dining-room, has been almost entirely renewed. The end window in this and the southern range, having had their tracery removed, are now arches between the modern porch and the entrance hall. One other window in this part of the house is old, but it is now blocked. It is on the west side of the kitchen, between it and the modern pantry, where its external label shows. In the hall wing are six original windows of detail like those of the cloisters ; all have been plastered and restored. One is on each floor on the south side of the wing, three are on the upper floor of the north side ; one on this side is so considerably above the ground level that it has the appearance of an old stairway window. The rest of the windows of the house are modern, those on the north side of the hall wing being imitations of the original windows. Of the thin ashlar buttresses which divided this wing into four bays, four remain, three on the south and one on the north side. The inside of the house has been so greatly altered that little original work is visible. There is, however, a 15th century doorway in the south-west corner of the cloisters, a little niche survives in the north-east corner of the (great) hall, an old doorway, now blocked, is in the cross wall of the undercroft, and most of the roof timbers about the house appear to be old." One fine king-post remains.

There is only one further item to note ; during the summer

of 1934 it was recognized that a fourteenth century refectory table still survived, in the scullery. It was cleaned and restored by permission of the Ware Urban District Council, and is now cherished and valued for the treasure that it is. This remarkable piece of furniture is older than any part of the surviving Franciscan buildings and must have been here since the beginning of the little house. The top is ash, a splendid piece of timber, showing the heart of the tree and the original saw marks can be seen ; the trestle ends are of oak, showing the original adze marks, and the cross-bar is of poplar wood ; a wonderful testimony to the honest workmanship that went to its making, a living link with those old brothers of St. Francis who laid the foundations of the pleasant gardens we all enjoy to-day.

To WARE FRIARY, V.A.D. HOSPITAL DURING THE GREAT WAR
1914–19

Old red-roofed Friary, set among fair trees,
A haven, now, of rest to all of these
Who heard the call and counted not the cost,
Restore in full the health they risked and lost.
Give perfect cure for wounds or weary mind,
Helping dispel dark thoughts war leaves behind,
That they remember after—gardens by a stream
Where they might rest awhile, and think, and dream ;
Finding, bequeathed by them of old, that air
Of sweet tranquillity which comes of prayer.

A COOK, 1917.

(*Note.*—Much of the matter in this chapter was printed in Dr. G. R. Owst's article on " The Franciscans in Herts ", in the *Transactions* of the St. Albans and Hertfordshire Architectural and Archæological Society for 1925, and is reproduced here with his kind permission.)

Translation of a DEED, dated 1479, A letter of CONFRATERNITY sent from WARE FRIARY. Found in an old chest in a cottage at Cherry's Green, Westmill, Buntingford. The property of the late Mrs. Thomas Greg of Coles Park :

" Brother John, Warden and servant of the Convent of the Grey Friars at Ware to John Aleby vowed to Christ and God, and to Alice Aleby greeting, and may you by the merits of your present life gain the heavenly kingdom. Whereas the most holy in Christ father and lord SIXTUS the FOURTH by divine providence Pope has by his apostolic dignity graciously granted not only to the brethren and sisters of our order but also to the allied brethren and sisters of the same who have suffragal letters that each of them may choose a suitable Confessor who shall have power to absolve them and each of them from all and every crimes excesses and sins in cases reserved to the Holy See once only in this year of the issue of the papal letters, reckoning namely from the Fourth day of the month of April, and once in the hour of death ; and in every other case being truly of a like nature power to absolve them from other sins as often as there shall be need ; and to enjoin wholesome penance.

" And whereas he has benignly granted that the same or another confessor shall be able to bestow full remission of all their sins in the hour of death.

" THEREFORE considering the love and the devotion which you have for our order by reason of your reverence of Christ and of our Seraphic father Francis I receive you by the tenour of these presents into our fraternity, by all and every the Suffrages of the Brethren of the English provinces so that you may enjoy in the present life and at death for the welfare of your soul the said apostolic privileges and all the benefits of spiritual goods according to the form and effect of the same. Adding nevertheless for a special favour that when, after your death, exhibition of these present letters shall be made in our local chapter the same commendation shall be made for you as is commonly wont to be made there for our brethren. FAREWELL in Christ Jesus and pray for me.

" GIVEN AT WARE the 29th day of the month of October in the year of our Lord 1479."

Note.—This document is now in Hertford County Records Office. A copy is at Ware Friary.

INNS

" Wassail, wassail, to our town,
    The cup is white and the ale is brown.
    For the cup is made of the ashen tree
    And the ale is made of the good barley.
    Wassail, wassail, to our town ! "

                                        Old Song.

Anybody attempting to give a full list of the Inns, Taverns, and Alehouses that lined the streets of old Ware may well be compared to Noah reciting the roll-call of the Ark, with a few heraldic beasts and miscellaneous objects added to the muster, so numerous and varied were the signs.

The majority of the small houses have died away, the names surviving only through mention in the Church registers, in wills, and charity bequests, and the few remaining larger ones are modernized and largely spoiled. But we have some useful and very interesting records and descriptions of the great Inns, known far and wide during (and even before) the coaching days, left to us by travellers and writers, and we can form a very fair idea of their appearance when at the height of their prosperity.

The fullest of the contemporary accounts were written by a Ware man, James Smith, who left his native town for Australia and wrote picturesque memories of Ware as it was before the coming of the railway, for the *Melbourne Argus*, in 1880. These notes were reprinted in the *Hertfordshire Mercury*.

Among the variety of names, there is nothing particularly rare or unusual ; the symbols of the four evangelists are present in the Lion, Angel, Bull, and Eagle ; the " Flower de luce " represents the arms of the Fanshawe family, and the " White Hart " the arms of Joan, widow of the Earl of Kent, and, later, of the Black Prince, who held Ware manor, whilst the " Eagle and Child " are the arms of the house of Stanley. Two pleasing old names, the " Shovel " in Crib Street, and the " Bird in Hand " at Bridge Foot, were known within living memory.

The Inns, situated as Ware is on a great highway, have played a large part in the life of the town from very early days and mention of them appears in many records of the town or of the many distinguished travellers who have passed this way. As far back as 1228, the London Episcopal Register (Gilbert, fol. 169–170) tells us that part of the profits from the Inns was due " to the altars of the Church of Ware and Chapel of

Thundridge ", so that they must have been already well established and flourishing.

In 1254, the Prior of Durham, with Robert de Insula, Bishop-Elect of Durham, came south to London. Their travelling expenses are preserved intact and have been printed by the Surtees Society. (Hist. Dunelm, Scriptores Tres., vol. ix, app. lxix, pp. 86, 88.) On their thirteenth day of travel, they reached Ware, the items of expenditure being : " Ware, the thirteenth day. Expenses in advance, 3s. 8d. (presumably for somebody sent ahead to make arrangements). In bread, 11s. 6d. In ale and wine, 35s. 10d. In provisions, 32s. 2d. In fodder, hay and litter, 23s. 4d." The expenses of the return journey are almost identical. " Ware, the second day, expenses in advance 3s. 8d. In bread, 12s. 1d. In ale and wine, 26s. 5d. In provisions, 24s. In fodder, hay and litter, 23s. 10d."

It is clear from the records that the most important of the Inns were : the Crown (87 High Street), the White Hart (75, 77 and 79 High Street), and, later, the George (Barclay's Bank, Ltd.) and, right up to the end of the coaching era, the Bull, upon whose site the present Post Office has, most appropriately, been built.

In Holinshed's *Chronicle*, 1557, we read : " The waie to Walsingham was through Waltham, Ware and Royston. Those townes that we call thorowfares have great and sumptuous innes builded in them, for the receiving of such travellers and strangers as passe to and fro."

John Taylor (the Water Poet) writing : " . . . a Relation of the wine Taverns either by their signes, or names of the persons that allow, or keepe them . . . " for Henry Gosson, 1636, tells us : " Ware is a great thorow-fare, and hath many faire Innes with very large bedding, and one high and mighty bed, called ' The Great Bed of Ware ' : a man may seeke all England over, and not find a married couple that can fill it. Ware hath 3 Taverns : Wil. Cross or Wil. Raste at the Crown, Shelton Amery, Christopher Robinson, Widow Hall at the George ; also she keeps a wine-seller at the Christopher."

Before passing on to the fuller descriptions of the great inns we will note the numerous smaller ones that have found themselves a place in the records, but whose sites are mostly unknown ; and the few references to inns where no name of the house is preserved.

The Angel.—Christopher Dixon and William Wiskerd, a

messuage called le Angell in Ware. (Recovery Roll. Mich., 7 Chas. I.) This Inn stands in Star Street.

The Bear.—Mentioned as early as 1494 (P.C.C. Will, Vox 11). In 1579, Gilbert Hill of Widbury was receiving quit-rents from the Bear, the Bull, and the Checker. (Rentals & Surveys (Gen. Ser.), portf. 8, no. 45, *V.C.H.*)

The Bell.—1606. (Pat. 3 Jas. I, p. 7, 22nd July.) To Robt. Earl of Sussex, Edward Sallus & others. Messuage called le Bell and rent, parcel of possession of Gelly Merricke, attainted.

The Bell and Dolphin.—Baptism, 1655, March 17. " William Boscocke ye son of William & Alice, a tapster at the Bell & Dolphin."

The Black Bell (Bull ?).—Paul Hogg, 1628, a musitioner. (Burial Register.)

The Bull's Head.—1572, Jan. 15. Robert, a servant, a stranger buryed from the bullhead.

1634, Dec. 27.   Gilbert Nicholss of the Bull-head.
1650, April 18.   John Whiskard of the Bull-head.
1696, Aug. 19.   John Gillham of the Bull-head.
                  (Burials.)

There is still an Inn bearing this name, No. 33, Baldock Street. John Flanders, of Enfield, was owner in 1723. (Will, Herts Muniment Room.) The fine " Parliament " Clock is still working.

According to the Chantry Certificates, this inn was held by Rich. Bromley and paid £4 13*s*. 4*d*. yearly. Reprises in rent to the manor, 3*s*. 4*d*. (Ed. VI.)

The Bluebell.—1690, Jan. 17. John Thornhill at the Blewbell. (Burial.)

The Black Swan (23 Baldock Street) has a mention among the Burials, 1654, March 22, Olliver Crosse, hoastler at ye Blackswan, and became part of the Elmer Charity. The house was owned by John Elmer who, by his will in 1622, bequeathed the annual value jointly to the churchwardens of Ware and Stevenage. The property was sold and the proceeds divided in 1906. This house has its original Tudor gateway, with beautifully carved spandrels.

The Black Bull.—In a House of Lords Cal. Petition we read that, in 1641, William Searle, late prisoner in the Fleet, complains that Abraham Hayne, clerk, having lent petitioner £100, secured upon an inn called the Black Bull at Ware,

H

seized the inn upon an extent, and let it at a far undervalue to Joseph Disbroe, who contrives to retain possession, and is allowing the inn to go to rack and ruin ; prays for relief. (Hist. MSS. Com. Report IV, p. 113.)

The Clarendon.—Now rebuilt and renamed the " Wine Lodge ", was very popular with the old East India College. (Haileybury.)

The Christopher (65 High Street) is probably one of the oldest remaining houses in Ware. (Exch. Dep. East. 14 Chas. II, no. 30.) This reference reads : " Arthur Sparke etc, & Thomas Bryan. Messuage lately an inn called the Christopher in Ware in the possession of deft. by purchase of the interest of the statute staple thereof of Sir Thos. Campbell." Lease of the Inn by Jas Pinkney to John Andrews.

" It has a large gateway opening into a courtyard. The wing running south in the E. side of the courtyard seems to have formed part of two 15th cent. timber and plaster houses which had a narrow alley between them running through what is now a coal cellar in the middle of the wing. The upper stories of these houses project and were apparently connected by a bridge from which a gallery ran on the west side of the south house. There are many 15th cent. details remaining in the building." (*V.C.H.*)

1655, Julie 15. Richard Chambers, Hoastler at the Christopher. (Burial Register.)

The Cock.—John Gillam, a bargeman, and probably owner of this inn, figures in a case in the Court of Exchequer, 1640. (Hertford Cor. Archives.) He issued his own token for $\frac{1}{4}d.$

Obverse—John Gillam at ye = A Cock.

Reverse—In Ware 1668 I. S. G. (Boyne's Tokens.)

1657, Dec. 8 William Busterd at the Cocke.

(Burial Register.)

The Coach and Horses.—Later known as the Waggon and Horses, Baldock Street. The Baptismal Register gives George Kilbee and Ann his wife, had a son George, Nov. 23, 1664 ; Ann, Dec. 1665 ; William, Oct. 1667 ; Susan, Sept. 1668 and Phillip, March, 1670. James Smith, writing at Melbourne, tells us that the head ostler and head chambermaid of the famous " Bull " married " and subsided into comparative seclusion as the landlord and landlady of the Waggon and Horses, a small inn, much frequented by country farmers, higher up the street ".

The Red Cow.—Till recently still stood in Crib Street. This good example of seventeenth century small inn, with over-hanging upper story and original chimney stacks, is described in the Herts Hist. Monuments Com., 230.

The Crane.—The Trustees of the Watton Road turnpike held a meeting here, 24th September, 1798. A much earlier reference to this Inn occurs in the Close Rolls, 3 Henry VII, probably dealing with a mortgage, "John Greene to John Elim gent. a tenement called the Crane." 28 Nov.

1634, Nov. 6.   Edward Meade of the Crane.
1644, Aug. 19.   Joan Thacker, a "made" Drown'd at the Crane.
1685, Jan. 31.   Thomas Walker of the Crane.
                 (Burial Register.)

The Golden Cross.—Burial Register, 1665, Sept. 14, "John Rowlie, a child of Dorothy Charnes buried in a garden at the Golden Crosse." This was evidently a plague burial, to save the child's body from being put into the common pit.

The Cardinal's Hat.—This inn must have been of some importance, but the knowledge of it is only preserved to us through the reports of the Chantry Certificates made in the reign of Edward VI. It was part of the Elen Brombles, or Bramble, Chantry, and stood next the Saracen's Head. "The Ferme of a tenemente or Inne called the Cardinall Hate with a Barne a Yarde and a Garden." The "Rente Resolute to the mannor or lordship of Ware" was 1d. The Inn may have been named after the great Wolsey who must have passed through Ware on his journeys north. Royston has an inn of this name also.

The Green Dragon is another seventeenth century house in Crib Street described among the Hist. Mon. Com. (230).

The Dolphin.—East Street, 1646, Jan. 7.   Robert Uffet, Inkeeper at the Dolphin.

1657, Sept. 9.   William, a servant at the Dolphin.
                  (Burial Register.)

In 1683, John Chauncey, Gent., paid 2/- p.a. to the lord of the Manor. (Ware Court Rolls. Add. MSS. B.M., 27/997.)

The Eagle.—This old Inn stood where the railway crossing is now. During a flood in 1824 (March), the water stood 6 ft. high in the tap-room.

1663, Aug. Henry Thorowgood at the Eagle.
           (Burial Register.)

The Flower de Luce. (The Fanshawe arms.)

1688, Feb. 24.   A stranger at ye Flower de Luce.
(Burial Register.)

This Inn stands opposite the French Horn, in the High Street.

20 Oct., 1736. Licence to Elizabeth Robinson Lytton to let the Flower de Luce Inn, Ware, the Malting belonging to it, and land in Wainges Field. (Lytton MSS., 23, 443. County Record Office.)

The Griffin.—(Opposite the old forge?)   1636, Sept 9. John Hornsworth, Tapster at the Griffin.

1636, Oct. 10.   John Howes, Inholder at the Griffin.

1640, Oct. 9.   Christopher Wilkinson, a servant at the Griffin.

1641, Aug. 26.   Elizabeth Spearpoynt, a servant at the Griffin.

1641, Nov. 1.   Will. Wilkinson, Chamerl. at the Griffin.
(Burial Register.)

The White Horse.—In the Abstract of Wills (Herts Gen. and Ant., ii. p. 85). " John Spencer, wheelwright, d. May 19, 1577, had a house called the White Horse." The will proved at Stortford, Nov. 18, 1577. Witnesses, Nicholas Thurgood, Thos. Claxon, Wm. Pike and Edward Nicolson. Friend, Thos. Cramphorne, overseer. A modern Inn of this name is in Crib Street.

1712, March 11. A strang woman from ye White Horse.
(Burial Register.)

The Eagle and Child.—1690, Feb. 23.   William Lowing of Eagle & Child. (Burial Register.)

This Inn is now a Bakery owned by Messrs. Jaggs and Edwards, and stands in West Street.

The Katherine Wheel was one of the larger fifteenth century inns and it is supposed that it stood near the Christopher in the High Street.

This Inn is mentioned in several Ancient Deeds (nos. 5193, 5198, 5202, 5200, 978, 1133, 1134, P.R.O.) as the property of the Pery and Hagar or Haggard families. William Pery, or Pyrrey, has a brass in the south transept of Ware Church, 1470. His will (P.C.C. 24, Milles) bequeaths the Inn to his son Thomas. The property is referred to in various forms of spelling, first in Chan. Proc. 153/60, as the " Caternw(e)le ", more often as " a Tenement or Hostel with a garden abutting on the water called le Ley, called le Kateryn Whele ". The dates of these deeds range from 1492 to 1548. A witness to the will of John Pery, 1492, was Sir Robert Lawe, curate of Ware. Thomas Byrche, who was granted the Franciscan Friary property in 1538, was also a part owner of the Katherine Wheel in 1529.

The Cross Keys.—In the Market Place, became a Chemist's shop in 1790 and has remained so. The old pewter pots are still on the premises. This Inn was the subject of a Chancery Bill in 1640 when Edward Packer (or Parker) sued his father, Humphrey Packer, for not carrying out an Agreement to hand over certain copyhold lands on the occasion of his marriage in 1633, the " Cross Keyes " being amongst the property. A Deed in Hertford Co. Record Office, dated 15th June, 1745, tells of the Cross Keys being moved to Land Row from Water Row, and that it was first known as the Ram. The Westminster Bank now stands on its site, which was between the Bull and the Coach and Horses, the latter is now also a chemist's shop, 61 High Street.

(P.R.O. Chancery Bills and Answers, Charles I.)

The Lion.—There is a token (not in Boyne),

Obverse—JOHN CRISPP AT THE = Lion ramp.

Reverse—IN WARE 1666 = I. M C

The White Lyon.—In 1683 Thom. Seager paid rent to the lord of the Manor.

The Half-White Lyon.—1663, March 18. John Dixon at the half-white Lyon. (Burial Register.)

The Magpie.—1657, Sept. 11. Francis Blewitt at ye Magpie.

1657, Oct. 30   Widdow Bluett at the Magpie.

1672, Sept. 13.   John Worland at the Magpie.

(Burial Register.)

In 1683, Wm. Crosse paid 4d. p.a. rent to the lord of the Manor for the Magpye. (Magpie corner and lane, Watton Road and Baldock Street.)

The Royal Oake (63 High Street).—1664, March 6. Steven Sekarman (Skerman ?) of the Royal Oake. (Burial Register.)

This is still among the finest of old Ware houses, with beautiful panelling in the sitting-rooms, and magnificent fire-places. The chief room on the first floor has a barrelled ceiling and above the overmantel are the initials H. I. S., and date, 1624. Another first-floor room has a recessed hiding-place, up the chimney, high enough to contain a man standing.

The Raven.—In the undated will of Elizabeth Hutchyn of Ware (Herts Gen and Ant., i, 71) is mentioned Goodwife Harvey at the Raven, whilst John Harvie of the Raven is executor. John Harvey, son, is mentioned in J. Harvey senior's will, 1562. (Herts Gen. and Ant., i, 356.) Also mentioned in a Chantry bequest.

The Rose and Crown.—A tenement in Baldock Street owned by George Rutt in 1683, paid 6*d.* yearly to the lord of the Manor. (Add. MSS. 27/997, B.M.) It stood on ground owned by the Rectory Manor called " Le Rose ", in 1676. (Rectory Manor Court Rolls, Trin. Coll., Cambridge.)

The Stag.—From the Diary of the secretary to Lewis Frederick, Prince of Wurtemburg : " Ware, a town where we lodged at the Stag. I slept in a bed of swan's down, 8 ft. wide." This refers to the visit of Prince Lewis of Anhalt, 1596, who visited one, Edelmann Johann Wrat, one German mile from Ware. This was probably John Wroth, who was sent to the Count Palatine and other German Princes, on the Queen's special service. (Cal. S.P.D., 1599, 4th July.) As there is no other mention of the Stag Inn perhaps the secretary mistook it for the well-known White Hart, which had many distinguished visitors.

The Star.—In *Proceedings in Chancery*, Q. Elizabeth (H.L., no. 50). " John Baker and several others, on the behalf of Eliz. Hill, daughter of Gilbert Hill, gent. decd. Defendant Ed. Meade and Philippe his wife. Claim under a will a messsuage called the Star, in Ware, and a parcel of meadow called the Star Holme, in Amwell, late the estate of said Gilbert Hill." There is still a Star Inn at the Bridge Foot, which gives its name to Star Lane.

The Wheatsheaf.—1762, Sept. 2. A soldier from the Wheatsheaf. (Burial Register.)

Apparently the Lion and the Wheatsheaf stood side by side in the market-place for the names were amalgamated into one sign and one house until the licence was withdrawn about 1930. Next door was the John Barleycorn, nearly next door the French Horn ; immediately opposite and all in a row stood the (old) Saracen's Head, another Rose and Crown, the Falcon, and the Roebuck, which joined the famous Bull. Nobody need have gone thirsty in the Market Place !

Before considering the larger inns, of which there are more lengthy accounts, a few references to the inns in general may be noted. In 1564 (23rd February), the will of John Holte, "Inholder," is recorded (Herts Gen. and Ant., ii, 85), also that of John Morgan of Ware, innholder, d. 14th July, 1576, and left "all to my wife for I broughte nothinge to her and therefore will geve nothinge from her ".

Two other wills of Innkeepers tell us something of their circumstances. In February, 1623, John Whiskett desired that his body should be buried in the church or churchyard. He left to his son William "one silver beaker, the best I have and one bedstead with the feather beds and furniture being the best in the chamber over the hall where I now lie and the table board and frame there likewise standing. The use of which bedstead and bedding and table my wife shall have during her life. I give unto Frances Palmer, the wife of Richard Palmer, my daughter one pair of flaxen sheets and ten shillings of lawful English money ". (PC.C. 36, Byrde.) And, in 1610, Richard Thomas, "Inneholder, within five days next before his death," was persuaded by some of his friends to make his will "and did say that his mynd and will was that his wife should have £300 more than she brought him or spake words to that effect. He married his wife (Anne) he being but a serving man having little and all he had came by her and her good means." (P.C.C. 44, Wingfield.)

In December, 1606, John Chambelain at Ware Park writes to Dudley Carleton that he "has no news but of husbandry. The king is at an inn at Ware with his hawks ". (Cal. S.P.D., 1605-6.) Another reference to King James I visiting Ware is found in a letter from Francis Morice, The Court, London, to Sir Bassingbourn Gawdy, dated 1604, 21st August. "Yesterday the King went to Somerset House about six o'clock . . . and from thence immediately took horse and rode post the same night to Ware, and so to his further delights." (Hist. MSS.·Comm. Gawdy MSS., p. 95.)

There are detailed accounts among the MSS. of the Duke of Rutland, Belvoir Castle, vol. iv, 1905, of old travelling expenses in connection with Ware. One account mentions the Crown Inn and it is probable that the other interesting bill was also paid at that Inn, but no hostelry is given ; the account runs (p. 290) : " The Account of Elizabeth Countess of Rutland, 1538. Dec. 8, 1539. Dec. 9.

" 1539 July. Item at Ware soper, in byffe, ij*d*. ; in calffes fyte, j*d*. ; in motton boled, j quarter, viij*d*. ; ij capons, iij*s*. ;

j dossen chekens, ij*s*. ; v rabyttes, viij*d*. ; in butter, vj*d*. ;
a pynte of wyneger, j*d*. ; a kylderkyne of bere, iiij*s*. ; a dossen
brede, xij*d*. ; iijlb. candelles, iiij*d*. ob. ; in drynke for the coke
and carters when they came to the inne vj*d*. ; in single bere
to my Lady, v*d*. ; in whyte wyne j pynte, j*d*. ; a potell of
claret wyne, iiij*d*. ; a pynte of sake, ij*d*. ; the carters beddes,
ij*d*. ; in fuell, xx*d*. ; . . . xx*s*. ob.

"Item in horsemet, as aperyth by a byll, xvij*s*. vj*d*. ; in
byffe boyled for brecfaste, vij peces, xx*d*. ; in bere, v*d*. ;
a pint of wyne, j*d*. ; iij dossen creves (crayfish), vj*d*. ; . . .
xx*s*. ij*d*."

(P. 326.) When the Earl of Rutland attended Parliament in
1542, he passed through Ware and paid 12/8*d*. for his " dener ".

(P. 367.) In 1550, there is mention, but without details,
of riding charges of the Earl to London : " Charges for 33
of my Lord's horses and 24 gentlemens horses at Ware,
Dec. 12." This item gives some idea of the amount of stabling
available when such a number of horses arrived in the town
for one party alone. No wonder the houses were built with
their upper storeys overhanging, it must have been worth
while to look out of the windows in those days.

There is a further interesting record of the Rutland
expenses in connection with Ware, on his return from the
seaside to London (p. 450) : " Account of John Brewer, 1602,
August 1 . . . 1603 August 1.

"Item payd to Mr. Pettingall which he layd out for post
horses from Huntingdon to Ware, £iij ix*d*.

"Item payd at Ware for the Baron of Walton's supper and
Mr. Screven's with that company that came to meet my
L.(ord) one Satterday night, xxx*s*.

"Item payd for his diner ther the next day and for them
that went befor xl*s*.

"Item payd for my L(ord's) supper one Sunday night at
Ware at the Crowne and for Sir William Constable's who came
after supper and for breakfast in the mourninge £vij ;

"Item payd for burnt wyne for my L(ord) which was left
unpayd at the Kinge's coming bye iiij*s*. [This would seem to
refer to the arrival of James I from Scotland, at the death of
Queen Elizabeth. He came by this route from the north and
stayed with Lord Cecil at Theobalds before entering London.]

"Item payd for Mr. Screven's supper that night at the
Hart and such as wear with him, xxx*s*.

" Item to the cookes and the maides at the Crowne, vj*s.* viij*d.*

" Item to the chamberlaynes ther, vj*s.*

" Item to the musitians, x*s.*

" Item for roods, vj*s.*

" Item to the poore, v*s.*

" Item given in the house at the Hart, iij*s.*

" (P. 451.) Item payd for post horses from Ware to Hampton Courte, £xiiij iij*s.*

" (P. 457.) Account of Thomas Scriven ; 1605 August . . . 1606, August.

" 1606. Hire of a horse to Ware for Anne (Manners), vj*s.* per Anne de Leto."

From these accounts it appears that the Crown and the White Hart were the Inns chiefly patronized by his lordship. It is much to be regretted that Samuel Pepys, who passed through Ware to Cambridge, and back, on various occasions mentions no particular inn, though he spent the night in the town more than once. On 15th October, 1662, he was returning from Cambridge to London when he " came to Ware about three o'clock in the afternoon, the ways being everywhere but bad. Here I fell into acquaintance and eat and drank with the divine, but know not who he is, and after an hour's bait to myself and horses he, though resolved to have lodged there, yet for company would out again, and so we remounted at four o'clock." On 14th September, 1663, with his wife and others, he was again passing through " a little bayte at Ware (I paying all the reckonings the whole journey)."

In 1756 (27th September), Ware Innholders and other public houses were granted £350 for the troops quartered upon them. (Herts Co. Records.)

Four inns, the Punch House, the White Swan, the French Horn, and the Saracen's Head, all good old houses, remain to this day. The three first-named were flourishing establishments in early Victorian days and are described, particularly regarding their social side, by Mr. James Smith, in the *Melbourne Argus*, about 1840. Of the *French Horn*, on the corner of Dead Lane and East Street he writes : " Every two or three years a company of strolling players visited the place, and set up their paraphernalia in the long room at the French Horn—a tolerably spacious apartment, with a row of stables underneath, and pervaded only by a fragrance which was neither that of new mown hay nor of any blossoms. I have seen Richard III performed by a company of three ladies and six gentlemen, with a Richmond who squinted abominably and a Lady Anne who was invalided—to put it delicately—three days after."

It was from this Inn that, following a challenge, a mock duel took place in 1836 (reported in the *Herts Guardian*, 5th January, 1836), between a gentleman named Jones and a jovial Exciseman. The affair was staged in a saw-pit, in Musley Dell. The Exciseman fired into the air and Jones dropped from fright, whilst a quantity of red currant jelly, which had been placed under the Exciseman's waistcoat, ran out in a most realistic way, terrifying the wretched man still further.

A delightful colour print in J. Hassell's *Picturesque Rides and Walks*, 1817, of Ware Market Place, or Plain, shows this inn with all its ancient gables, now partly hidden behind a yellow brick front and partly rebuilt.

The New Union Society was started at the French Horn in 1794, perhaps a rival to the Union society of the Saracen's Head. (Herts Co. Records.)

The Punch House, facing Rankin Square, was also well-known to James Smith, he describes it as follows—" One famous place of resort for the elderly gentlemen of that generation was the Punch House, and the landlord of it, Ellis by name, was himself a gentleman. To all outward appearances it was a substantial private residence ; but it had a small bar, a miracle of neatness and elegance, at which none but the regular habitués of the establishment ever dreamed of asking to be served, and there was a spacious coffee room in the rear, panelled with polished mahogany and divided into boxes, where white-headed patriarchs used to meet in the afternoon and evening and discuss politics and local topics."

The White Swan, nearly next door to the Punch House, was, James Smith tells us, " the favourite resort of the more convivial members of the middle class, kept by an elderly female familiarly known as Milly Dennis. The house was famous for its ale and for its ' long room ', in which malt liquors were never served except in silver tankards with glass bottoms. The oracle of that apartment was a gentleman named Yarrow, who occupied quite a mansion which he let out in suites of apartments to people in easy circumstances. He waited upon a limited number of respectable clients for the purpose of plying his calling each morning ; and as he was in independent circumstances he made it a kind of favour that he did so, and was received upon a footing of something like social equality by his constituents. The first of the day, or the greater part of it, was spent at the White Swan. Thither came the stationer, the principal grocer, Machon, the parish clerk, and the neighbouring draper for their ' beaver ' at eleven o'clock, and again in the evening for pipes and gossip, and the affairs of the whole town, and of everybody in the town, were discussed and rediscussed in that long room. We were all Radicals in those days, partly because we had not the franchise, and partly because the neighbouring town of Hertford, which had, was thoroughly Conservative. We were very jealous of our neighbours two miles off, as we considered that their largely-attended corn-market, held every Saturday, ought to be transferred to Ware. Did we not buy nearly the whole of the barley brought there for sale, and hadn't we built a Townhall with abundant accommodation for the farmers in the open area below, and had not they perversely refused to pitch their samples there, to the great detriment of our shopkeepers, who used to reckon up the amount of money diverted from their tills to those of their Hertford rivals and grind their teeth accordingly. Had we not every justification for our Radicalism ? "

The Saracen's Head.—The present house bearing the name is marked for demolition. The old inn is mentioned in a will about 1522, and an indenture of 1612 recites that an unknown donor gave a messuage or inn called the Saracen's Head, together with a piece of land called the Netherhoe to the poor. Also, in a Court Roll of 1542, it is mentioned as " Le Sarsen Hedde ". The present Saracen's Head was the last Ware home of the Great Bed.

In coaching days, the Rocket (from Hertford) called here every afternoon, except Sunday, at 3.30, and on Sunday at 4.30. To Hertford the Rocket called every day at twelve, and the Wellington from Newcastle-on-Tyne every afternoon (except Monday) at 3.30. (Pigot, 1839.)

In the Burial Registers we find :

1649, Nov. 28.   Antony Yong of the Sarasen's head.
1654, March 8.   William   Springe   Inkeeper   at   ye Sarazenshead.

1690, March 3.   Henry Hart of ye Sarazanshead.

1693, March 28.   An hoastler at ye Sarazenshead.

1804, March 25.   Vokes, John Thomas, a stranger, died at
                   the Saracen's Head.

In olden days there was a carrier, James Tillcock, who left
from the Saracen's Head every Monday, Wednesday, and
Friday for Hertford, Hatfield, and St. Albans.

A Union Society was started at the Saracen's Head in
1794, and at the same time a Friendly Society at the *Vine*,
the only mention of this house. (Herts Co. Records.)

The King's Head, 1681, the inhabitants of Ware complained
that Thom. Collup, being seized of an inn called the King's
Head, for which £100 or thereabouts may be procured, and
having besides sundry sums of money in the hands of Leonard
Battell and Edward Malyn, and although he had an infirm
daughter who had been charged to the parish for seven years
past, and his wife being aged and past labour, yet he himself
begs his bread from door to door, and despite his wife's impor-
tunities who is willing to give up her right in the premises, he
will neither consent to the sale of the inn, nor let or live himself
therein, or take steps to get the money out of the hands of the
person aforementioned, " but suffers the inn to drop down for
want of repair, and the timber and other materialls thereof
is stolen away by poore people, and the monies lies dead."

The petitioners desire that he may be imprisoned " until
he will yeild to take some care about the premises ".

1683.   The petition of the inhabitants of Ware : Shows
" that whereas one, Thos. Collup, of the said town is seized of
a certain messuage, or inn there, called the King's Head,
worth about one hundred pounds, and also hath in the hands
of one, Leonard Battell, of Gt. Amwell, in the said county,
yeoman, the sum of £200 or more or thereabouts, as security
against the claim of dower of Cicely, his now wife, in a certain
estate sometime sold by the said Thos. Collup, and the sum
of forty pounds more in the hands of one, Edward Malyn,
the elder, of the said parish of Ware, upon the like account.
Now although his said wife is ready to join in a fine or other
assurance for the giving up of her right in the aforesaid estate
and also to cutt of the intail upon the aforesaid messuage or
inn (shee being jointured in the same). And although a
daughter of his had been maintained at the charge of the said
parish for about twelve years last past, and his said wife being

ancient and past labour is now also become a charge to the same. Yet the said Thos. Collup being a wilful and obstinate person chuses rather to begg his owne bread from door to door, and to suffer his said wife and daughter to become a charge as aforesaid, and the above-said inn to fall down for want of repairing, and the timber thereof to be stol'n away than to join in the disposall of the said inn or getting in the aforesaid moneys to repair it withall, or to putt himself in some way to maintain his family as he ought to doe." The petitioners desire that Thos. Collup may be brought before the justices to " show cause wherefor hee should suffer such an heavy burthen to ly upon the said petitioners ".

Signatures on the back of the document. (Herts Co. Records, i, 36-7.)

 This petition was first brought up in 1672, April and July.

 1657, May 18. John Squire of ye King's Head.
 1661, May 9. Samuell at ye Kingshead.
       (Burial Registers.)
 1655-6, Feb. 2. Thomas Towne sonn of Edward & Elizabeth. a bardgman at the King's Head beyond the bridge.
       (Baptism Register.)

The Leopard's Head.—From the Herts Quarter Sessions Records, 1626.

 " 1626, 31st March. Examination of Thomas Phippes, who says that he and Nickolas Hilton took from a hedge beyond Burndwood, in co. Essex, two pairs of sheets, three shirts and one smock, which they brought to Ware and there sold them at the sign of the ' Leabord's Head ' to the woman of the house, who carried the finest of them to a certain brewer and told them that if they could get any more fine linen she would buy it of them. They afterwards brought her more goods and the deponent further says that this woman bought of a hat dresser, who was afterwards hanged out of Newgate, three great platters stolen from Widford, which she buried in the kitchen behind the door, and a flitch of bacon which she buried in a cloth under the buttery stairs, and the same man lay in her house for two weeks. Examinant says that Margaret Wilton, wife of Nicholas Wilton (Hilton), urged him to break into a house in Essex, nr. Royden, but he told her to do it herself ; and that she sold at Ward's Mylles at the White Horse, a cloak he had of her husband. Further he says, that there is at the Lepord's Head a privy place for hiding stolen goods and suspicious persons (suspects) and she (the landlady) says that at the press for soldiers she hid five men from the constables and that she can convey any man from chamber to chamber into the backside. She has an engraved cup which she had of a traveller. There is not such a house for the purpose within a hundred miles."

What a reputation ! And how one wishes that the " Leabord's Head ", wherever it may have stood, was still in existence that we might explore those secret places for ourselves.

The White Hart was undoubtedly one of the oldest and most important of the inns of Ware. It stood on ground now occupied by Nos. 75, 77, and 79 High Street, and was the property of the Guild of Jesus, bequests being made in wills preserved from 1490–1525, when the guild was dissolved. (Aug. Off. Misc. Bks., xiv, fol. 127.) In 1511, the White Hart was owned (or leased) by Rob. Rysley of Shelford Magna, Cam. (P.C.C. 5, Fetiplace.) In 1596, it was leased to John Abbot, yeoman, at his death it was occupied by Nicholas Bleake whereupon Abbot's daughter, Dorothy Bircheley, brought a lawsuit against him. (Court of Reg., 1, 103.)

Later the property was in the hands of feoffees and the income devoted to common town expenses, such as providing soldiers, paying taxes and tallages, maintaining a beacon by the Lea and a bridge over it.

This sign was the badge of the Hollands and probably dates from the time when, at the end of the fourteenth century, Joan, widow of Thomas Holland, Earl of Kent, and later wife of the Black Prince, held the manor or Ware. (The badge is repeated down both aisles of the church.)

The Inn has already had mention in the Duke of Rutland's accounts, 1603 ; a writer, Cray, in 1539, tells of travelling from the north : " Sun. Dec. 14. Rode out to Royston with 2 others while it was dark and could not converse for stumbling of our horses till we came to Ware within half an hour after seven. Refused to go to mine host in Ware and went with them to the sign of the Hart, where we broke our fast and the Bishop's servant (Durham) got a new horse." (L. & P., Henry VIII, 750.) In 1610, Prince Ludwig of Wurtemburg stayed at the White Hart (he called it " The Stag ") and saw, and slept in, the Great Bed.

It is not known when this ancient hostelry passed out of existence, part of the original buildings still stands.

1639. Feb. 3.   Robert Yardley of the White Hart.
(Burial Register.)

In 1684, John Searle, alias Savill, had to make answer at the Sessions Court, Hertford, to a charge brought against him by Nicholas Field, fisherman, and Thomas Philpott, bricklayer, both of Ware, "for severall abuses and ill language which he did in their hearing speake" against Sir T. Byde, Kt., and Skinner Byde Esq. at the house of Joseph Benson, at the White Hart, Ware, on the 31st March, about eight or nine o'clock in the evening.

In 1689, meetings for Religious worship were held at Joseph Parkers at the White Hart. (Herts Co. Records.)

The Crown, once considered the best known and most ancient inn in Hertfordshire, now 87 High Street, and generally supposed to have been the original home of the Great Bed of Ware.

References to this house in the Duke of Rutland's accounts (1603) and by John Taylor (1636) have already been given.

William Cross was landlord in 1646 (the initials W. C. on the Great Bed may have been his) and constable of Ware. It fell to his lot to conduct several unruly women from the Sessions Court at Hertford, back to Ware, duly assisted by "a certain number of fit persons", and to see that they were "well cucked tomorrow being markett day". (Herts Co. Records.)

From the Burial Registers :

1635, July 22.   John Crosse of the Crowne.
1639, March 6.   William Rastes, vintener at the Crowne.
1652, June 29.   Robert North, slain at the Crowne gate.
1653, March 31.   William Wales, a servant at the Crowne.
1654, Feb. 6.   A stilborne child of Edmond and Rebecca Rast's, Inkeeper at the Crowne.
1682, May 21.   William Roebucke at the Crowne.
   „   July 31.   John Thornhill at the Crowne.

This survey of some of the old Ware Inns comes to an end with the George, and the Bull which kept its place as chief posting-house to the very end of the coaching days and still carries on the tradition as Ware Post Office.

The George Inn.—This important establishment stood on the site now occupied by Barclay's Bank, Ltd., High Street, also Nos. 27 and 31 High Street.

The first mention of the name occurs in the Church Burial Register :

" 1570, Dec. 16.   Richards, ostler at ye George.

" In 1619 a rent charge of £5 0. 0. per annum out of this house is to be paid to the poor of Ware on the feast of St. Thomas the Apostle ; according to the will of George Mead, Doctor in Physick," dated in June of that year. (Char. Com. Rept., c. 1833, p. 323.)

In the Hist. MSS. Comm., Gawdy MSS., p. 114, is noted : " Nicholas Meade, the George Inn, Ware, to Framlingham Gawdy, West Harling, sends Gawdy's bay mare, her keep at 6d. a day comes to 13s. The farrier charges 5s. and advises her to be let run till March." 1622 (or 1611), 5th December.

It is not known exactly when the house ceased to be an inn. The historian Cussans says, " the inn has been pulled down for some years, and a large brick house, at present vested in the trustees of the late John Sworder, is erected on its site." About 1833, it was the property of Robert Sworder of Standon Lodge, and occupied by John Sworder.

It is one of the three Ware Inns mentioned by John Taylor, the Water Poet, in 1636 : " Widow Hall at the George ; also she keeps a wine-seller at the Christopher."

It is also noted by Defoe in 1724, and in Belsham's *Chronology*, 1765. The importance of the house is indicated by the fact of the local Justices meeting there. (Quarter Sessions Records.)

Isaak Walton is happily associated with the Inn, in *The Compleat Angler* he makes Piscator refer to the " great Trout that is near an ell long, which was of such a length and depth, that he had his picture drawn, and now is to be seen at mine host Rickabie's, at the George in Ware ". The very year that this immortal classic of angling was published " mine host " died. Judging from his Will, John Rickabe, " Inhoolder ", was a man of considerable piety, and he sets forth his religious convictions at some length, " nothing doubting but that for his infinite mercies set forth in the precious blood of his dearlie beloved Sonne Jesus Christ, our only saviour and redeemer, he will receive my soul into his glory and place it in the company of the heavenly Angells and blessed Saints . . . and according to the articles of my Faith when we shall all appear before the Judgement seate of Christ I shall resume . . . by the mightie

power of God . . . not a corruptible, mortal, weake and vile
body as it is now, but an incorruptible, immortal, strong and
perfect body, in all points like unto the glorious body of my
lord and saviour Jesus Christ " ; after which confession of
Faith he bequeaths his worldly goods, including the George
Inn and adjoining tavern, to his wife, Margaret Rickabie
and his son John. (P.C.C. 6, Brent.)

Ned Ward, a London Innkeeper, 1667–1731, wrote a
great deal of old inns, and his account of the George is both
quaint and interesting. It occurs in the second volume of
The Writings of the Author of the London Spy, 3rd ed., 1706,
pp. 252–5, and is headed " A Step to Stir-Bitch Fair ". The
travellers set out from London by coach and arrived at " Ware,
where we put in at the sign of the *English Champion*, who
Redeem'd the Maid from Jaws of the Dragon, to give Nature
the Refreshment of a Dinner, and to ease our tired Limbs from
that numbness, incident to those Cripling postures, the Number
of our Companions forc'd us to sit in : In this Inn stands the
great Bed of *Ware*, talk'd of as much among the Citizens,
who seldom travel beyond the bounds of the Home Circuit ;
as the Gigantic greatness of the *Herodian Colossus*, or the
Magnitude of the *Trojan Horse*, are among the Sober Enquirers
into lost Antiquities. The extravagant largeness of this Bed
is very much wonder'd at by all that see it, being wide enough
to lodge a Troop of Soldiers with the assistance of a Trundle-
Bed. In the same Room hangs a great pair of Horns, upon
which (insisting upon an old Custom) they Swear all New
Comers ; the form of the Oath being something Comical,
and withal very Ancient, I have presented it to the Reader,
hoping if it be not valuable for its Wit, it may be for its
Antiquity.

> " Take care thou'st thy self no wrong,
> Drink no small beer if thou hast strong ;
> And farther do thyself this Right,
> Eat no Brown Bread if thou hast white ;
> And if the Mistress thou canst Bed
> Be sure thou dost not Kiss the Maid.
> Show not thy Wife thy utmost Strength,
> Nor let her know the Purses length ;
> Never be bound for any Friend,
> But rather far thy Money lend ;
> For thou wilt find 'tis better he

I

Should break or be undone than thee ;
Trust no Man that is Proud and Poor,
Unless thou wilt forgive the Score ;
For he will never pay or own
The Kindness thou to him hast shown ;
Be just and Grateful to thy Friend
'Twill make thee happy in the end ;
But if thyself and thine Thou'dst save,
Take care thou dealst not with a Knave ;
Trust not thy Wife, tho' ne'er so good,
With no Man but thyself Abroad.
For if thou do'st, e'er she returns,
Thy Forehead may be deck'd with Horns :
What I have said do thou retain,
So kiss the Horns and say, Amen.

" After this very Useful and Cautionary Oath had been Administred to several of our Company, and amongst the rest my self ; our Twelve pence a piece was exacted for the Benefit of the rest of our Fellow travellers, who had been accustomed to the road ; which, in Fine, we were forc'd to submit to, or undergo the Rediclue of the whole House, for the Ill-natured Breach of an Old Custom. This Ceremony being ended, and the usual Dues Collected, and brought in such sundry sort of Liquor as might please every Bodies Pallat, spurred on by our Appetites, we began to enquire what sort of Provisions they either had in the House, or intended for our Dinners. To which the Master answered, *The only thing the Town was Fam'd for, was Eels* ? In the ordering of which they had so compleat a knowledge, they would undertake to dress 'em as many several ways as ever a *French* Cook did a Feast of *Frogs*, or a *Dutch* Skipper a Dish of *Pickled Herrings*. And it happening so Fortunately, that every one of our Company being great Lovers of this Fish, we readily united in one Opinion, and ordered that our Dinner might be all *Eels*, desiring the Cook might serve us up with as great Variety of this Slippery Food as her utmost Skill in the useful Art of Cookery would give her leave, wi'out further directing her to any Particularities, but left her wholly to her own Freedom and Discretion in the Business, which indeed, she manag'd so well to her Master's Interest, and to the Companies Satisfaction, that I believe never was a parcel of *Mud-worms* better serv'd up to the Table of an Epicure, and render'd more pleasing to the Pallat, with variety of Sauces than their Judicious Cookery had made our Slimy Eatables ; besides the ordinary ways of, Boiling, Frying, Baking, Stewing, Roasting and Toasting, we had 'em Coddl'd, Parboil'd, Sows'd, Dows'd, and the Devil and all.

" When we had plentifully Feasted on our Fish, like so many Cormorants, and wound up our Dinner as Decency requires, with a short Thanksgiving, we call'd for a Bill to inform us what we had to pay ; accordingly one was brought, wherein more Particulars were inserted, than ever was found in a Taylor's Debt-Book, or a Boatswain's Catalogue of Materials, for the new Rigging of a Vessel ; which, sum'd up, came as exactly to half a Crown a Head, and Twelvepence for the Cook, as if the Master himself had been well skill'd in Arithmetical Proportion, and knew well, upon Expedition ; how to prevent Fractions in a Reckoning ; tho' we told 'em we thought ourselves a little unreasonably dealt with, yet they so very much insisted on the Extraordinary Trouble we had put 'em to, that they Talkatively prevented any manner of Abatements ; only the Master very Politickly presented us with a Dram a piece of Right French Brandy, to wash away the Grumbling in our Gizzards, that we might not report to his Prejudice the hardness of our usage."

The " George " in the Burial Registers.

1570, Dec. 16.	Richards, ostler at ye George.
1608, Nov. 28.	A stranger from the George.
1640, Sept. 11.	Bernard Wright, servant at the George.
1653, April 25.	Mr. John Riccabie of ye George.
1654, Dec. 19.	Susan Flint a widdowe blowne up with powder at the George taverne.
1664, June 26.	Mr. Rob. Thomson drowned at the George, an Attorney.
1691, June 2.	Mr. Wooton of London was killed at the George by 5 Dutch troopers and another gentleman wounded. 3 of them sent to goale.
1691, Sept. 2.	Mr. Thomas Fotherby dyed at the George being hurt by a horse at Hayly.
1709, Jan. 16.	A stranger at the Gorge.

It was at the George, in 1691, that Matilda Lervex rashly declared that she did not care if King William were hanged, and was in company there with Roman Catholics. (Herts Co. Records.)

At the " White House ", 27 High Street, which was part of the George Inn, there was an interesting Royal Coat of Arms, carved in wood, part of the decoration of the over-mantel in the front sitting-room. This was found up the chimney some years back. Perhaps this was the inn where King James I used to stay, which would entitle the house to show the Royal Arms. They may have been hidden during the Commonwealth and forgotten. They are now in Hertford Museum, as is the fine " Parliament " Clock.

The Bull Inn.—This renowned establishment stood on the site of the present Post Office and was, in all probability, the headquarters of the postal arrangements for Ware and District since the inauguration of Ware as a post town in 1536, until the demolition of the old house in 1865, when for a few years the Post Office moved, first a little way down the street and then a little way up the street, until its return to the old site. Practically a continuous record of public service for just over four centuries.

In 1547, the inn is mentioned as the property of Michael Meade and Lady Eliz. Morris, widow. (Feet of Fines, Herts Trin., 1 Ed. VI.) And in 1683, the Bull was one of the inns paying rent to the lord of the manor : " Robinson, Gent. for the Bull, the Bridge and Signe on the Summer Howse 1/6." (Add. MSS., 27/997, B.M.) See also p. 4, under " The Bear ".

In 1741, Tuesday, 28th July, a meeting of the Trustees and Commissioners of Sewers for preserving and improving the Navigation of the River Lee was arranged to be held at the Bull Inn. (See chapter on " The River ".)

In 1760, 31st December, in the MS. Minute Books of the then Postmaster General : " Ordered that Mr. John Rayner of Ware be removed from the employment of Deputy Post-master there, and that Mr. John Thurston of the Bull Inn be appointed to succeed him, to commence on the 5th January next." (P.O. Record Office.)

It was in September, 1788, that the unpopular Excise Surveyor, Mr. Grand, was at the Bull and caused great indignation by appealing to the Military for support. (Hist. MSS. Comm. MSS. Earl of Verulam, p. 136.)

We are fortunate in having a description of the old house from the contemporary pen of Mr. James Smith (*Melbourne*

Argus), also an account of the halt made by Queen Victoria and the Prince Consort on their way through to Cambridge, Wednesday 25th October, 1843, written for the *Haileybury Observer*.

Mr. J. Smith writes : " The Bull Inn had tiers of galleries flanking the paved entrance and a little glazed sentry box on the right hand side of the gateway, commanding the long vista of the yard, where some scores of horses were stabled for coaching and posting purposes. The landlady was an institution—a strong minded elderly spinster with a cast in her eye and the most masculine business qualifications—a capital judge of horseflesh and gifted with an instinctive perception of the precise amount of courtesy to be exhibited to guests of all grades, from a prince of royal blood down to a bagman. Nobody spoke of her otherwise than as Fanny Brown. . . . At that time no railways disturbed the even tenor of our lives. Upwards of twenty York and Cambridge coaches—some of them famous for their speed—changed horses at the Bull, and sundry of the coachmen were important personages, notably those of the Rocket and Highflyer. . . . There was a good deal of posting in those days and we school-boys felt a considerable degree of pride in the horses which were furnished on such occasions from the Bull, and in the diminutive proportions and natty get-up of the postboys, who were generally withered old men with legs like pipe-stems and arms to match."

Well, those picturesque days are past and another little glazed sentry-box stands in the gateway now—labelled Public Telephone.

Pigot, writing of coaches in 1839, notes :

The Defiance from Peterborough and Stamford calls at the Bull every afternoon at a quarter before four.

To Peterborough and Stamford the Defiance calls at the Bull every Tuesday, Thursday and Saturday morning at eleven.

From the *Haileybury Observer*, 1st November, 1843, signed " Pawnee " :

" On Wed. 25 October, 1843, the youthful Queen Victoria, accompanied by her Consort, passed through Ware on her way to Cambridge. Immense excitement prevailed when the royal equipage arrived ; the band broke out with a splendid impromptu concerto of ' God Save the Queen ' and ' Rory

O' More ' simultaneously. The cheering and tumult were now immense. Alone amidst the general confusion, dignified and unmoved, stood the venerable landlady of the Bull Inn, bearing in her hand a humble tribute of superb grapes to be presented to her Majesty. The carriage dashed up, the horses were taken off, the Queen let down the window, evidently in expectation of some formal address (the authorities of the East India College at Haileybury had arranged to present one) when, to her agreeable surprise, a basket of grapes appeared, most timidly, but respectfully, insinuated by a neatly gloved hand.

" The horses were again put to ; the carriage approached the platform where the College folk were waiting—and then passed on. By some it was suggested that the Queen looked offended and disgusted by the strong smell of smoke which emanated from the front parlour of the Bull." The incident was commemorated in verse by " Pawnee ", who tells us he wandered to Ware and questioned a lad as to the crowds. He was told of the approaching arrival of the Queen and that :

> " There's Mrs. F. Brown
> And the rest of the town
> A-going to meet her here ;

> " I patted his head,
> And quickly I sped
> To a very large Inn called the Bull.
> I lit a cigar
> And went to the bar,
> Where at beer I took a slight pull."

Refreshed with :

> " Beer, good bread and cheese,
> A cigar and one's ease,"

the poet sees the unfortunate contretemps ; and blames the fates who :

> " Make the Queen prefer Fanny Brown's feast.

> " There's one cheer more
> And all is o'er
> The Queen has passed the Bull."

The Bull has a mention in Cooke's *Topographical Description of Herts.*

In the Burial Registers :

1641, April 1.   Will. Harrison, Tapster at the Bull.
1680, June 5.   Elizabeth Elsam drowned at the Bull.
1685, Nov. 26.   James Stimpson from ye Bull Inn.

Note.—Some of these notes on the Inns of Ware were collected by the late E. E. Squires, of Hertford, and are now in the possession of Reginald L. Hine, F.S.A., F.R.Hist.S., who kindly loaned them for reproduction here.

THE HIGH STREET
Past and Present

Fine, open gateways in an ancient town,
Whose weathered, sturdy timbers watch serene
The passing pageant of the years. There down
The street the coaches rumble in, gay scene
They raise. Horns blow, dogs bark, and ostlers run
As, clattering on the stones, the twinkling wheels
Turn in ; spent horses rest from work well done,
They're changed and off, then through the yard Peace steals.

Cool, shadowed gateways, slumbering through their days,
Hung low with Jasmine and the clustering Rose,
Thrice welcome oasis from sunlit blaze
And glare on tarmac road where ceaseless flows
The restless stream. Soft moss lies for our feet,
And rare hoof strikes upon the muffled stones ;
Although pale ghosts are all we seem to meet,
Is there, at midnight, still one faint horn blown ?

———————

" The Ware Constable's account of quartering three Companys of Lord Robt. Manner's Reg. men of foot at Ware. 1756 "

(Original in Hertford County Record Office.)
Ld. Robt. Manner's Regiment came in Dec. 13. 1755.
(One Co. draughted away in April 1756,
which reduced the House to the follg. numbers)

Flower de Luce	10	6
White Hart	4	2
King's Head	6	4
Black Swan	6	4
Old Crown	20	16
Bull Head	10	7
Saracen's Head	20	16
Bull Inn	20	16
Angel	8	6

Cow and Barge	8	.	.	.	.	6
Star	8	.	.	.	.	4
Hand and Flowers	6	.	.	.	.	4
Bay Horse	8	.	.	.	.	6
Dolphin	10	.	.	.	.	8
Cricket Players	10	.	.	.	.	8
Fox and Hound	6	.	.	.	.	2
Lyon and Sheaf	10	.	.	.	.	8
Grey Hound	8	.	.	.	.	6
White Swan	11	.	.	.	.	8
Bell and Sun	8	.	.	.	.	6
Fox and Goose	10	.	.	.	.	8
Old Coffee House	4	.	.	.	..	2
Vine	6	.	.	.	.	4
8 Bells	10	.	.	.	.	8
Red Cow	8	.	.	.	.	6
Magpie	0	.	.	.	.	0

And 45 men sent in to Amwell End by Order of Thos.
Plumer Byde Esqr. of the 4 Companys.

Crane	14 men
Cock	8
Adml. Vernon	6
Leather Bottle	2
3 Horse Shoes	2
Green Man (H. Heath)	2
Spread Eagle	4
Fox	3
Red House	2
Pipe and Pot	2

Besides a great Number of
Recruits Dayly passing thro'
the Town

(signed) John Game. Constable

TOWNSFOLK
The Witness of the Sessions Rolls

" Not the great nor well bespoke,
But the mere uncounted folk
Of whose life and death is none
Report or lamentation."

From " A Charm ", in *Rewards and Fairies*,
by Rudyard Kipling.

Old Charters, documents, miscellaneous items of information preserved through the ages, all contribute their share of historical data from which to construct a chronicle of Ware, but it is from the time (late sixteenth century) when the County Sessions Records began to be kept with order and precision that light is thrown on the daily life of the townsfolk, bringing to life many illuminating little incidents.

With the advent of these records, we see the population of Ware moving no longer as groups in a picturesque pageant (as, for instance, in an order given at Westminster, 7th May, 1485, " Warrant to the Baillife of Ware to prohibite men from neglecting Shoting (archery ?) a lawfull Game, and applieing them to the use of Carding, Dising, Boling, Playing at the Tenys, Coyting, Pikking and othre unleful and inhibited Disports ; and from diminishing the Game within the said Lordship, with Engynes contrary to the Lawes "), but coming alive as personalities that we may know and greet as friends. The Maltsters, Bargemen, Innkeepers, Apprentices, Yeomen, Pensioners, Tradesmen, Watchmen, and the rest, tell us their names and something of their circumstances, letting us into some of the secrets of their sins and troubles. (Is there not a note in the records for 1652 that " the inhabitants of Ware have not set up a cage in the said town for the securing of offenders " ?)

Among the pages of the Rolls, there is no crime of magnitude to rouse an unwelcome notoriety, but a rich choice of backslidings common to humanity in general which help to bring the past vividly before our sympathetic gaze, and we may regard them, surely, after this lapse of time with a degree of indulgent amusement, and even gratitude, for otherwise these distinctive personalities would have been lost to us for ever.

Details of local government that dealt with these offenders

are also set before us in these pages ; in 1646, it is noted (more particularly in connection with the upkeep of the highways) : " The parish of Ware is distinguished by the titles of Ware Infra and Ware Extra, and two several courts are kept by the Lord of the Manor.   From time immemorial Ware Infra has had the following officers, viz :—2 Churchwardens, 2 constables, 2 overseers for the poor, and surveyors for the highways as appears by the court rolls.   Ware Extra has had 1 Churchwarden, 1 constable, 1 overseer, and 1 surveyor."

The office of constable was held in addition to other callings, for in 1675, Henry Peach and Edward Fryer, maltsters, were also constables.   The title " Bailiff, of the liberty of Ware " was still extant in 1638, Richard Storey then holding the title.   He was succeeded, in 1639, by Christopher Robinson " appointed Marshall within the whole Division of Hertford and Braughin, to have such allowance as was paid to Rd. Storey, deceased, the last Marshall."

In 1648, differences arose between the late constables, William Love, Christopher Robinson, and Richard Asson, and certain inhabitants, including Captain Wilde, Mr. Edward Bromley, and Christopher Bagshaw, concerning arrears to the constables' rates.   The following year, 1649, Thomas Johnson and William Cousins were sworn constables.

In 1652, 20th April, the inhabitants of Ware met " at the Stone in the Parish Church ", and chose the following officers : Isaack Halden, Arthur Parnell, and William Cartwright for Churchwardens ;   William Collett, Richard Uthwayt the elder, John Grigges, and Robert Spencer of Upland for overseers—Yeallop, innkeeper, Edward Heath and Thomas Skyngle for surveyors for the highways.

In 1673, Mead Gardiner, late constable, refused to pay Thomas Spencer, present constable, divers sums of money which remained in his hands.

In 1692, George Waterman, nominated by Sir T. Byde, Lord of the Manor, to be constable of Ware Upland, prays to be excused from serving because he is very old and incapable of executing the office and asks that Edward Mayling may be sworn in his stead.

In 1756, Thomas Reed was exempted from all parish offices for apprehending and bringing to conviction Joseph Ruggles, who burgled the house of Eliz. Harden.   Reed assigned his certificate to Joshua Squire, maltster, for 5s. Witnessed by Thos. Hankin and Michael Pepper.

After this brief mention of the officers let us return to the townsfolk.

Anybody reading the full Calendar of these records will probably be struck by the continual mention of two items in particular : (1) The keeping of unlicensed ale-houses (a typical malting-town sin ?), and (2) The troubles caused by that unruly member, the tongue. The population of Ware, certainly during the seventeenth and eighteenth centuries, seems to have been markedly outspoken, sometimes with a sturdy independence of opinion, sometimes merely mischievous or quarrelsome ; the ladies easily holding their own with the men.

The prosecutions arising from the first item are far too numerous to quote in full, but among them we find John Greene, bargeman, who has the distinction of being first on the list, in 1619. He is followed, in 1625, by Elizabeth Armstrong, widow, and Humphrey Parker, gentleman, " who sold to Wm. Smith and Richard Retchford, unlicensed ale-house keepers, to each of them 20 barrels of beer, the price of each barrel being 8s." In 1633, again Humphrey Parker, or Packer, brewer, sold and delivered to " Christopher Hande, waterman, then being an unlicensed ale-house keeper, 10 barrels of ale, at 8s. a barrel. John Howe, labourer, was drunk there ". In 1638, John Whiskett alias Whiscard, brewer, supplied Edward Gouldsmith, labourer, with 6 barrels of beer. In 1643, indictment of Joseph Desborawe, late of Ware, innkeeper, for selling several wines, " namely, sacke, claret, and white wine " without a licence. In the previous year were prosecuted, for the same offences, Richard Catlyn, Robert Leake, Thos. Boose, and Richard Muske, and in 1661, Henry Robson, husbandman, John Baker, Thos. Lestridge, Edward Stones, Thos. Greene, Mary Harte, Priscilla Squire, Richard Gynn, James Salter, and William Smith, fine 20/- to be levied by distress. As a final example, in 1699, Elizabeth Sheppard, widow, was prosecuted for selling beer without a licence, for keeping a disorderly house and for harbouring rogues.

There are various prosecutions for fraud. In 1639, Isaac Fuller, maltster, " for keep and using an illicit measure, to wit, a bushel contrary to the assize " ; and, in 1667, John Richardson, for using " light and unlawful weights ". Evidently there came a time when this question of false weights had to be investigated seriously for, in 1673, it was ordered that the constables of Ware " shall be authorized to search all such houses, maltins, corn-shops, and other places which are lately informed of in this Court (Hertford) for using unlawfull weights and measures, for all bushells, weights and other measures and the same weights and measures to view and inspect whether the same weights are seized and sealed according to law ".

For dishonesty of a different kind in January, 1636, Nego Price, alias Bird, was committed to the gaol (Hertford) for a month " till he pays £20 for his fine for cheating Peter Weare, servant to Mr. Oagle. The said Price is to be carried to Ware and put in the pillory on the 18th of this month, being Market Day, the charges whereof he is also to pay ". Also Edward Bickerton to remain in gaol for a month " till he pays his fine, £6 13. 4d. for cheating Peter Weare whereof he stands convicted. He is also to stand in the pillory on a market day at Ware and to pay 9/4 Court fees before he is discharged ".

A few isolated cases are worthy of notice—such as that of John Collup, cordwinder, who in 1643 " played cards by night and day ", in spite of Richard III's order against " carding ". (We may speculate whether this John was ancestor to " Goodman Collup " of Ware, who was paid £17 4s. for timber and for the use of " pullies and roapes " for the construction of the beacon erected on Hertford Heath, in 1693.) There is a petition from Alice, wife of Edward Elsam, bargeman, in 1646, setting forth that she has been married to him for seventeen weeks, " but he spends his nights and days tippling at alehouses and has been absent from her for the past fortnight. He says that he has three wives besides petitioner and will allow her nothing." Then there is the case of William Gutteridge, tallow-chandler who, in 1626, converted a tenement formerly used for habitation in a place there called " le midle rowe ", next to the great street, being the common highway and still uses it as a " worke-house to trye his grease ", whereby all the surrounding atmosphere is polluted with a dreadful smell. Another offender at that time was James Game, labourer, who put " heapes of dounge and strawe " on the highway leading from Ware Bridge towards Amwell on account of which " the said highway is much annoyed ". And there was Robert House who, in 1660, " did keep one Mastiffie dog, which dog hath bitten divers persons of the kingdom which have occasion to pass the house of the said Robert."

Under the date of 2nd August, 1676, we find the entertaining account of Joseph Haynes who " doth acknowledge that he went out of London with a designe to assist James Domingo, and by naturall magicke and other artifices to tell fortunes, but denyeth that hee tooke any money and pretends whatever he did was without any designe but as a frollicke ". James Domingo " owneth that hee was at Bishop's Stortford with Joseph Haynes and a woman in man's apparrell " who he pretends is his wife and that he was also at Ware on 1st August. Information was given against them by John Hockley, John Grindley, Peter Holdsworth, and Rivers Dickinson. The prisoners came (the woman being in man's apparel) into Ware pretending to tell fortunes both by publishing papers to that end and also by doing of it, taking of Hockley and Grindley 6d. apiece. They also pretended to give physic and cure almost all diseases by an elixir, as it may appear by their bill ; they saying that " money came in very slowly at Ware by 6d. and 3d. apiece, but at Bishop's Stofford they got £20 ". Haynes boasted he had " gotten five pounds and three maydenheads at Ware and a broken shinne ", Domingo said he got about six and twenty shillings that day.

It is gratifying to find the good people of Ware less credulous than those of Stortford.

The Excise duty on malt was, naturally, a very unpopular charge and it is not surprising to read that, in 1648, on the information of George Thompson, one of the collectors within the hundreds of Hertford and Braughin, " William Wilkinson had threatened to beat him out of the county and burn his house as the Excise House in London had been burned ; and the same William Wilkinson said that those who established the Excise were rogues and rascals " ; and further, deponent says, that Alice Creed, sister of Wilkinson " spoke to the same effect for no other purpose than to rail at deponent and the proceedings of the Excise ". It is cheering to read that the downtrodden maltster occasionally received some redress for the wrongs he suffered, and there were successful appeals made at the Petty Sessions in 1705 by Whittlock Bulstrode, Esq.—" her Majestye's Sollicitour for the Revenue of Excise and Mault " against surcharges imposed by the Collectors on John Beale, Thomas Fish, Thomas Uthwatt, William Heath,

Hains Gregory, Thomas Grave, Francis Pryor, G. King, Thomas Page, George Hagger, William Tomson, and Elizabeth Brown, widow. Also, in the cases of malt being destroyed or damaged by accident, after duty had been paid, a proportion of the charge was refunded. In 1723, Ambrose Proctor, maltster, claims remission of excise duty because he put 150 qrs. of brown malt and 18 qrs. of pale malt on board a barge in Ware River and paid duty on this. Seven days later the barge sank in the River Thames, near London Bridge. The malt was greatly damaged and has cost him a considerable amount in " the charge of drying, lighting and portridge ". He claims £46 12s. and is allowed £7 7s. In 1748, Richard Dickenson, maltster, was remitted £16 7s. duty on 12 qrs. 5 bushels of malt totally destroyed and a " proportionable part of share " of duty on 152 qrs. greatly damaged when the barge upon which they were loaded sunk " at or near Bow Lock Standing on the R. Lee ". There is the certificate, in 1773, to Mr. Matthew Lothian, collector of excise, on behalf of Thomas Want and Thomas Harrison, maltsters, that they have lost two barge loads of malt upon which they had already paid duty, " by the inevitable accident of a Barge sinking." And, in 1779, Henry Page, bargemaster, was allowed half duty on 92 qrs. of malt damaged by his barge " strikeing against the Stump of a Tree at or near Enfield Lock in the R. Lee ".

During 1786, there was an extremely unpopular Excise Officer in the town, he was so disliked that he became the object of some demonstrations which scared him so badly as to make him lose his sense of proportion, and he applied to higher authority for military protection. This ridiculous action is the subject of correspondence recorded in the MSS. of the Earl of Verulam, Gorhambury. These notes are given on pp. 133, 136-9, as follows :

> 1786. Feb. 26. Mem. by Viscount Grimston of letter to Mr. Byde, informing him that " I had mentioned to Mr. Pitt the circumstances of the acquittal of the Ware people as a confirmation of the truth of our declaration that they had been extremely ill used ".

> 1788. Abstract of the state of facts presented to William Plumer Esq. and Lord Grimston on the oppression of the Excise Officers at Ware. " At Ware there are 33 maltings which make 1370 qrs. of malt per week. 70 men are employed in them. In Oct. 1787, Robt. Grand was appointed supervisor of Excise in the town

of Ware and neighbourhood, and soon after, in concert with
Sam. Veal, laid divers information against several maltsters
in order to recover penalties, which appears by their complaint
being so frivolous [sic] the crown not having been injured ;
nor has the maltsters gained any illegal profit.

All the informations which followed were quashed at the
county sessions. This conduct of the officers made them
obnoxious to the people, who have hallooed and hooted them
but never assaulted or obstructed them in the execution of
their duty. On 24th Sept. last the supervisor Grand, with the
exciseman Veal and another officer, went to examine the stock
of Worrall, a tallow chandler, and in so doing were hooted at.
They pretended to be alarmed and insisted on having a guard
home. On Sept. 26th a troop of horse entered Ware. On
Nov. 4th Grand, with a constable, whom he had appointed to
execute warrants, were at the Bull Inn, when he required a
party of the military to assist him, on which the constable
refused such assistance, declaring that there was no necessity
for it. Nevertheless the military did attend which induced the
inhabitants to apply to the commanding officer to know by
whose order such unconstitutional interference of the military
was directed, who answered at the requisition of supervisor
Grand. Thus the inhabitants have been alarmed in so much
that only 4 maltings have been employed. 2nd Dec. 1788.

1789. March 19. Thom. Steele to Viscount Grimston.
" The Treasury have given directions to the Board of Excise to
take the necessary measures for removing, without loss of time,
the supervisor who has lately been stationed at Ware, and
relying upon the assurances given that the inhabitants are
willing to suffer the revenue to be duly and peaceably collected.
Their lordships have ordered the troops to be immediately
withdrawn from the town of Ware."

Mr. Plumer took on himself the credit of having removed
the troops, whereas a Mr. Calvert received a letter from
Sir George Young, Secretary of War.

A further reference to Excise, showing the prosperity of
maltsters in the early nineteenth century, is given us by an old
cheque, drawn to the Commissioners of Excise in 1840, on the
Ware Bank of Adams, which reads :

" To the order of the Honble. Commissioners of Excise—
Thirty eight thousand pounds—being the Queen's money.
   Ware, 9th Sept. 1840   for Saml. Adams and Co.
                     (signed) Sam. Adams Junr."

This cheque is the property of Mr. G. Talbot, whose

premises, in the High Street, were formerly the site of Adams' Bank.

Only once does murder blacken the pages of the Sessions Records, and though the crime was committed in Ware it seems that the criminal was a stranger, for the entry reads : " 1678. Recognizance of Nathaniell Foard, chandler, and constable of Ware, and Humphrey Ives, bargemaster, for the former to appear and answer his neglect in not making hue and cry after one, John Kinnare, a soldier in Capt. Lawder's company, who committed murder on John Williamson, drummer in the same company at Ware." But in the *Gentleman's Magazine* for May, 1781, we are given notes on the George Inn—" now a private house inhabited by Mr. Lister. In the register is an entry :—'June 8, 1691, Mr. Wootten, of London, was killed at the George by five Dutch troopers, and another gentleman wounded : three of them sent to goale.' "

In the Summer Sessions of 1685, William Collett, Richard Searle, and John Lesteridge appear to answer a charge of being disaffected persons ; again, in 1689, on the information of William Gillham " on Tuesday, 27th August, last, being in company with one William Smart, of Hertford, webster, and talking about quartering of soldiers, the said W. Smart swore : ' D—— King William, a pox take him, for he and his souldiers oppressed the country more than ever King James did, and he wished that the devil had King William.' Being reproved by the said Gillham he swore he was not in the least sorry for what he had said and afterwards drank King James his health." Benjamin Patmore, " maultster," stated that he was with Wm. Smart on said date, at Ware, and heard him say the same, and that if King James were in the room " he would not hurt an hair of his head ". John Gillham stated that W. Smart asked if he were brother to William (Gillham) and on hearing that he was, said : " You shall drink King James his health," which John Gillham refused to do. In 1691, Matilda Lervex was presented, on the evidence of Ann Fryer, for saying several times " she did not care if King William were hanged ", and also being in company at the George Inn, with Roman Catholics, said " that they loved one another as well as they " (Protestants ?). Ralph Robins pursued her into Essex and charged a constable with her and she was carried before Capt. Wroch. And again, in 1695, William Hill and

Thos. Wren, yeomen, "indicted for refusing to provide a horse and carriage for the King's use at Ware, when called on to do so by Thomas Bray, a constable, under warrant directing constables to impress three carriages with able horses for a reasonable day's journey." Fined 30s.

Before the Toleration Act of 1689, illegal religious gatherings were rigorously suppressed, and prosecution for non-attendance at the Parish Church was sternly carried out. Many independent Ware folk fell foul of the law on these points and, apparently, the local authorities were not altogether unsympathetic.

Amongst the names of those fined for non-attendance at Church we find Thomas Basto, 1623, who had not attended divine service for one month; in 1641, Thomas Collup; in 1660, John Holland, yeoman, John Brestbone, yeoman, Robert Dawson, yeoman, James Grey, yeoman, Christopher Bagshaw, and Edward Grey, fined 4s. Further fines were inflicted, in 1662, Joseph Auger and Henry Peach, brewers, and in 1667, John Brestbone, husbandman, Henry Panke, maltster, Elizabeth Izard, and John Latter. One result of these prosecutions for illegal religious meetings was the order, 5th July, 1665, for the deportation to New England of several Quakers from Hertford Gaol, including John Brestbone, William Burr, Thomas Burr, and John Thorowgood. But it seems doubtful whether this fate was fulfilled, for Thomas May, master of the ship *Anne*, reports that the ship carrying the Quakers "arrived in the Downes, and wayting for a Winde the space of a Moneth, had so spent his Provisions that he returned to London to recrewt them, and in the interim his Passengers gott on shore in such manner as his Petition is suggested ". (Acts of Privy Council.)

In 1675, the constables of Ware levied fines on Thomas Burr, Gregorie Tingey, Mrs. Parratt, and Thomas Dockrell, convicted before Sir James Altham for being present at an unlawful and seditious conventicle held at the house of John Harwood, in Roydon. But, in the same year, Henry Peach and Edward Fryer, maltsters, "the present constables of Ware to appear personally at the next general quarter sessions for refusing to execute orders to levy distress on the goods of several persons at Ware, certain sums of money forfeited by them under the Conventicle Act." The same question arises in 1678, again we read " the Constables of Ware shall appear

at the next Sessions and show cause why they have not executed
a warrant to levy £20 of ' Phanatteck money ' upon several
persons ".   These illegal meetings seem to have taken place
outside the town for it is noted in 1682 : " They have noe
recusants nor popish priests nor Jesuits in the parish of Ware,"
but among the prosecutions for attendance at conventicles
that year are Mary Carter, widow, fined 5s. ; second offence,
10s. ; also, John Adams and wife, Job Tinge, and Thomas
Griper.   Thomas Burne (Burr?), maltster, was responsible for a
seditious conventicle held at Broxbourne, and at Patmore
Heath, for the worried constables complain that by order of
" the worshippful Esquire Allen " J.P., they had seized 26 qrs.
and 2 bushels of malt for a seditious conventicle of Th. Barr
(Burr ?) at Patmore Heath, in the parish of Albury, " which
malt they have still on their hands to their great damage for
shop rent, they having made an outcry for the sale of the
same, and nobody will give any money for it."   They also
present that by order of Sir Benjamin Mattox, J.P., they
seized a gelding of the same Th. Burr (clearly Thomas Burr
was an indefatigable sinner !), for a seditious conventicle and
meeting held in the street of Broxborne, " which in like manner
nobody would buy."

But by the Toleration Act of 1689, these religious difficulties
settled down and meetings for worship were held at Joseph
Parker's, at the White Hart Inn.   In 1697, there is an order
that the Meeting House belonging to John Worsley shall not
be rated to any of the parish rates unless the tenant or occupier
makes some profit out of it, and by 1729, the Quaker Meeting
House is built in Kibes Lane.   This building seems to have
fallen into disuse after the death of Mrs. Maria Hooper,
daughter of John Scott, the Quaker poet, who built Amwell
House with the Grotto in its grounds.

(*Note.*—In connection with the above references to malt
shop rent and the name of Worsley, it is most interesting to
note that the name " Worsley " still appears on the ancient
and most beautiful grain stores in Star Lane.)

Soldiers billeted in the town at various times brought
money to the Innkeepers, but their presence was clearly
responsible for much unruly behaviour and resented by many
of the inhabitants, particularly when Dutch troops arrived in
1689.   At this date, there is a petition of " divers of their
Majesties' officers and soldiers under their command of late

quartering at Hertford and Ware ". The petitioners under
obligation to appear at the Sessions to prosecute certain persons
of Ware for their offences committed against their Majesties'
guards of dragoons at Ware and their officers. Signed by
Capt. Podewills, late of Ware, and Capt. Fred. Hanbush,
lieut., Hertford. In 1756, the Innkeepers of Ware were
allotted £550 for the quartering of troops. (See full note after
" Inns ".)

Several old soldiers and sailors wander through the pages
of the records, applying for pensions. In 1622, Edmunde
Hopkins, an aged man, sometime a soldier in the service of
Queen Elizabeth, when he received many and sundry great
wounds and is now grown into want, prays for a pension. In
1627, we find that Robert Price, Thomas Hodge, William
Saward, and John Rolf are behind with their rates for maimed
soldiers, hospitals, and marshall's wages, and refuse to pay
the same. In 1630, Nicholas Bleake, a maimed soldier, gets
10s. for relief. A few years later, 1641, there is further
complaint, by Mr. Hoy, one of the chief constables for the
hundreds of Hertford and Braughin, that the Churchwardens
of Ware are in arrear with their money towards the hospitals
and maimed soldiers. Order that certain justices shall require
them to pay the said money, 41s. 3d., and also 2s. 6d., the
charges of this present order. In 1651, Elizabeth Casse, whose
husband was a soldier in Scotland and died in the parliament's
service, receives 10s. quarterly and 20s. for relief, but, 1653,
" for divers good reasons " the pension of Thomas Parker
shall cease. John Cooley, 1661, prays that a pension may be
allowed him, he having served his late Majesty during the
war, under the command of Sir John Watts, at Colchester,
during which time he received such injuries as prevent him
from earning a livelihood. In 1685, Joseph Finch, bargeman,
maimed in the late Dutch war, to have the pension of Nathaniel
Messinger, died. John Cross applied for a pension at the
same time but as it appears " that there are soe many
Pensioners already that it takes up almost all the yearly
stock of the Treasurers soe that there is no money in their
hands to answere other charges " it is resolved that his pension
be stayed until further notice. Joseph Finch has such a worthy
record behind him that his petition is supported and signed by
the Vicar of Ware and others. He states that he served " in
several shipps ; in the *Fame* a fyer ship, Capt. John

Gibbons ; in the *Amsterdam Bull* Capt. J. Gibbons ; in the *Royal James*, Prince Rupert and Sir T. Allen ; and in the *Old James* with Capt. Storey ". Being wounded in the wars he was set on shore and was attended at his own cost by Mr. Archer, of Hertford. He had a promise from Sir John Watts of the next county pension, " and this has now occurred by the drowning at Stansted on the previous night of Nathaniel Messenger." Another " barg man ", William Church, petitions : " It is not unknown but that your petitioner was in the late war against the Dutch, in the same shipp where Sir Thomas Leventhorp was in, called the *St. Andrew*, Capt. Pynes being commander of the said shipp, and did his Majesty true and faithful service, being wounded and much disabled therein. Your petitioner doth most humbly desire your wor-shipps to comiserate his condition, being very poore, ancient and crazy, and almost past his labour, to grant your poore petitioner to be admitted his Majesty's pension this sessions in the roome of Matthew Browne, his Majesty's pensioner, lately deceased."

The cases of Theft, including Petty Larceny and Poaching, supply some entertaining anecdotes and show how heavy were the punishments in the seventeenth and eighteenth centuries compared with our own day.

When we fall in with the poachers, we find those who robbed the waters as numerous as those who strayed on to private land for unlawful purposes. In 1623, James Grave, labourer, broke into the free fishery of John Clarke in the Lee river at Essenden, and with hooks and snares took away two trout worth sixpence. In 1660, John Gimber is prosecuted for keeping and using a net, not being 2½ ins. in " mashe " and having no water of his own. In 1672, James Middleton, Barge-man, William Blewett, and Thomas Thorowgood broke into the premises of Henry Jeas at Broxbourne and stole 7 eels, value 10d. Committed to gaol for felony and petty larceny till " Saturday next " and then to be well whipped in the public market at Hertford. Two years later, Abraham Sawell and John Hanchett, of Stansted, broke into the close of Thomas Ford and John Page at Amwell and Broxbourne and fished with nets and other engines and caught, and took away, 100 pike and 100 trout which were swimming in their waters, and, in 1719, we have the case of William Thorogood and William Battle, who broke into a fish trunk in the River Lee, belonging to William Edwards, R. Raynor, and Thomas Raynor, and took 20 eels, 20 gudgeon, 20 crayfish, 6 tench, 20 trout, and 4 carp, " to be whipped at the common whipping-post." An early land poacher was George Meade, the younger, yeoman, presented in 1618 for shooting " in a peece at conyes ". In 1639, John Hutchin, yeoman, carried a landgun charged with powder and shot and in a field called Scott's croft killed two pigeons. William Waller, Thomas Whittaker, and Edward Faircloath were convicted as common poachers in 1699. A little earlier, 1681, William Heard, tailor, and William Gardiner, yeoman, " with others " broke into the park of John Barnes, Esq., Gt. Hadham, and took a buck. One of the " others ", Edward Ashwell, husbandman, gives us a picturesque little account of this outing : " The deponent says that on the 2nd day of June, being Stortford faire day, William Heard, the son of John Heard, tailor ; William Gardner, labourer, and William Martyn, labourer came to the deponent and requested him to go along with them to Hadham. The deponent ask ' whether to any alehouse, they answered noe '. The deponent asked whether then ?—Heard replied ' to Esquire Bernerd, his parke, for to fetch a deere '. Then this deponent answered he could not goe nor did goe, so Wm. Heard desired this deponent to lend him a slipp to lead one of his dogges which dogg was the dogg of Thomas Bird of Ware, Esq. The said Wm. Gardiner did tell the deponent that he and Wm. Heard and Wm. Martyn did, the same night, take a deere which they carried to the house of Affabie Yardley at Widford Mill and that, the next day, a glover of Hertford, one—Edwards bought the skin of the said deere, which the said miller, of Widford, carried to the glover."

Among the petty thefts, in particular, are very severe and even brutal punishments. There is the confession of John Mogges in 1663, that " he went into the shop of Tobyas Greene, blacksmith, to warm himself by the fire, and, seeing his opportunity, he took away several parcels of old iron, but he knows not of what weight or value they were : committed to the House of Correction to be well whipped ". Another entry tells us that the iron weighed 20 lb., value 2s., and at the same time William Damper stole 6 lb. of iron, value 8d., from Edward Malen, and shared the same punishment. In 1676, Mathew Ayers, " going to meet his wife in Hare St. at the Dogshead and Pott, in his way thither in a lane called Holly

Bush Lane, on Shrubs Hill there, in the parish of Ware, was staid and secured by Thos. Cock, the elder, and Thos. Cock, the younger, and charged by them with stealing of one ew lamb." This he denies. For stealing 6 fowls, value 4*d*., 4 hens, value 4*d*., and a piece of beef, value 2*d*., the goods of James Hulls, in 1693, John Badcocke was sentenced to be whipped at a cart's tail on Tuesday next at Ware, "from the Crown Inn, through the town to the Great River there." In 1746, Sarah, wife of Thomas Sell, and Dorothy, wife of Thomas Mansell, were convicted for stealing wood from the park of William Freeman, Esq., "to be whipped at Ware between the hours of 12 and 1." For a theft of wheat, Charles Brown, labourer, in 1778, was ordered to work on the Thames for three years or go as a soldier. His choice of punishment is not given us. In 1776, Thomas Gillion was publicly whipped and imprisoned for three months for stealing a bushel of horse beans, value 3*s*., from Thomas Green. A few years later, 1785, William Francis, Labourer, stole a cock, value 1*s*., and 4 hens, value 4*s*. (a considerable rise in value since 1693) from May Griffin and was ordered twelve months' imprisonment and to be twice whipped. Another public whipping was ordered for Thomas Lee, who, in 1790, stole a copper tea-kettle from Mary Lambeth, also given a fortnight in prison, but the following year when Daniel Roberts stole 5 qrs. and 5 bushels of barley, value £6, from Aaron Green, he was transported for seven years. The same fate befell John Stalley, or Stallybrass, who also stole from Aaron Green 4 bushels of wheat flour, value £1 10*s*., and 4 bushels of pollard, value 10*s*., but William Samuel, who stole 1 bushel of wheat flour, was only given twelve months in the bridewell and a whipping. One of the severest examples occurs as late as 1814, when Thomas Haslam "deposes that having reason to think that some of his property had been stolen when he was at meeting of Sundays, he secreted himself in his shop when the rest of his family were at meeting. About a quarter to eleven Jane Head, mother of Ann Head, his servant, came to the door and was admitted by Sarah Collins, his other servant and went into the kitchen to Ann Head, who gave her mother various articles, including a bottle of oil, value 2*s*., 11 onions, value 3*d*., 3 lbs. of bread, value 6*d*., and ½ lb. of butter, value 6*d*." The daughter, Ann, was sentenced to a month in gaol, and the unfortunate Jane " to be transported seven years ".

Various entries concerning Apprentices, and those who carried on trades without having observed the necessary apprenticeship give us an insight into the strictly enforced regulations in the matter. We find Thomas Johnson presented for following the trade of a cordwinder and not serving seven years' apprenticeship, also James House for using the trade of baker, and Nicholas Barker, for exercising the art of a barber-surgeon, " not having been educated for that or for any other art, nor served apprenticeship," in 1666–7. In 1672, Thomas Newton was exercising the trade of a cloth dyer, and John Sheppard, glasier, traded as a painter, and in 1699, Thomas Millet, labourer, " exercised the art, mystery, or handicraft of a clockmaker, not having served as an apprentice thereto for a term of seven years." Certain difficulties between apprentice and master are shown in such entries as : " 1629, Richard Platt and his apprentice brought before certain justices that some order may be taken to end the differences between them " ; in 1630, " John Haynes, apprentice to John Collup, shoe-maker, discharged from his apprenticeship, as it appears that the said John Collup has much misused him." Collup to pay Mrs. Dorcas Newman, aunt of apprentice, £3, part of £4 paid by her for placing said apprentice. The Church-wardens of 1697, Richard Wharton, John FitzJohn, Henry Bawcock, and overseers, John Lammas, Thomas Town, Thomas Hulls, and Thomas Wrenn, bound William Cobham, a poor child, apprentice to Thomas Fish, maltster, " until he should be aged twenty-four years." Fish refused to execute a counterpart of the indenture and gave notice that he would appeal against it, also complained of over-rating, but " as he has not appeared the Court orders that Fish shall receive and provide for Cobham according to the indenture and that £10 shall be levied by distress upon his goods for contempt ". Similar orders were made in the cases of Samuel Hudson, a poor child, and James Manison, maltster, and of John Bradd, a poor child to John Allis, maltster. In 1704, there is an order adjourning the appeal of All Hallows the Greate, London, against a warrant removing Sarah Minors, aged thirteen, from Ware, where she was " endeavouring to settle herself " as apprentice to Daniel Skelton, " a poore barge man and not qualifyed by law to take such an apprentice." And, in 1708, Thomas Geagle, sack weaver or flax-dresser, was bound over for beating and bruising his apprentice John Holloway, " in

an unlawful manner and with unlawfull weapons " and for
" using reproachfull words and speeches and swearing several
prophane oaths " before the justices.

Misfortunes concerning the community in general are
reflected in orders occurring in these Sessions Rolls, in 1640
we read " that the inhabitants of Ware shall make a rate for
raising £30 to satisfy the arrears of money disbursed by William
Whiskerd, Robert Price and Stephen Land, as late constables,
in the time of the late visitation of that parish with the plague "
and again in 1667 : " Whereas Edward Godfrey, Robert
House, John Salisford and John Ansloe, late overseers, did,
in providing for divers infected persons during the last visitation
of the plague, disburse £26 1. 3d. more than was received by
them, it is ordered that the Treasurers and receivers of the
Towne-land moneys belonging to Ware, shall pay the said
sum to the overseers out of the rents and profits of the said
Towne Lands." Two years later this business was, apparently,
still hanging fire, for we find a note of " differences between
Mr. Alex Mead and inhabitants of the parish over money due
to him from the overseers in the time of the late great plague,
to be referred to certain justices ". A little later, 1747, George
Ballard is granted 5s. a week as inspector for Ware and
Thundridge to prevent the spreading of " the contagious
Distemper amongst Horned Cattle which now rages very
much ".

We are given, too, a fairly full account of the great storm
in 1738, as follows in a petition by certain J.P.'s to the Lord
Chancellor, when they pray for a grant of letters patent
empowering the sufferers to collect alms : " On 25 July last
there happened a most dreadful and terrible storm of hail
which fell about ten miles in length—for the most part in
a very rich corn country, the fields whereof were loaden with
exceeding good crops in the several parishes and townships of
Standon, Bengeo, Thundridge, Ware, Little Hadham, Harting-
fordbury, Bramfield, Furnix Pelham, Braughin and Albury—
the stones whereof were of a prodigious size and bigness the
like not known in memory, some of them being 6 ins. in
circumference and most of them an unusual size, attended with
a great storm of wind and thunder without intermission
which beat down and destroyed the growing wheat, rye, barley,
oats, pease, beans and generally speaking the whole product,
not sparing the clover, grass and pasture, besides the damage

done to buildings, the thatch being violently torn off and the windows broken and shattered and many cattle in the fields not escaping cuts and bruises." The loss was estimated at £5,122 12s. 3d.

Some thirty years later, we are given an account of other great storms in the diary of John Carrington, Bacon's Farm, Bramfield. He writes : " The great flood followed the dry summer of 1762. It commenced in October. We had had some rain before, but I remember it set in on Mon. 25th about 4 o'c in the afternoon and rained tremendous and on Tues. the 26th there was such a flood as could not be remembered for years past ; the river was swelled to that degree that all people who lived near it were great sufferers—(he gives details of damage at Hertford and continues) at Ware there was more damage done than at Hertford. It drove one house quite away with all the sheds, etc. and drowned an abundance of horses, cows, etc." Later he writes, " 1773. Account of the great flood which happened in harvest—we had had some rain for some days before but I remember it began to rain on Wed. about 3 o'c in the afternoon the 18th of August and rained all night and most part of Thurs. and at Ware and Hertford and all other places by the waterside such a flood had never been known, the water was a foot higher than it was at the flood of 1762. I saw it at Ware, the like I never saw."

Another Ware anecdote from Carrington's Diary is recounted in these amusing lines : " On one Battle, of Ware, who was swearing at the Spread Eagle on one Sunday afternoon, Amwell End, so Desprately he was desired not severall Times, but swore the more. He was instantly Struck helpless and Dumb, and was carried home in a chair and died about four Days after and spoke no more. In the year 1798. I knew him well, and as a Maricle or Judgment I wrote these lines :

" O Vaine man as thou art, when will you be wise ?
To curs and Damn yr. hart, and sware and blast yr. Eyes.
Remember ye are but Dust, and sertainly soon must Die,
And a count then give you must for all you sware and Lye.
O wt. Terable Dread must sease you with Supprise
That after such a Life you have led to Judgment you must Rise."

And now a few anecdotes concerning the brawlers and mischief-makers, who, in the absence of loud-speakers, must have contributed largely to the annoyance of their more peaceable neighbours. Riotous behaviour looms largely in the seventeenth and eighteenth centuries, " affrays " and " assaults " are numerous, but the only serious occurrence was the bargees' riot and strike in 1795, when the Hitchin Cavalry was brought over to quell the disturbance. The culprits involved were in the employ of Samuel Taylor, maltster and bargemaster. Among the lesser clashes with authority we read of the indictment of Thomas Logsdell who, in 1676, refused to assist in quelling an affray when called upon by Sir T. Byde, Kt., J.P. Earlier than this, in 1637, one Hancocke, " musitian," assaulted John Collup, shoe-maker. In 1658, John Ancell, tailor, and William Morris, maltster, assaulted Thomas Glynne and Henry Johnson, alias Brookes, and also stole one " stoned " horse and three geldings from Mary Allen. In 1706, Elizabeth Battle, also the wife of William Curtis, and Hannah Curtis, spinster, were indicted for assaulting Edward Thorowgood, servant of John Sale, gent., and for digging a pit in the highway. The following year, William Harding, Philip Mitton, John Humberstone, William Taylor, Philip Grindall, and —— Parratt, with people from Amwell, rioted at Ware and assaulted John Ramsey, constable of Bishopp Stortford, in the execution of his duty. James Hulls, bargemaster, was in trouble at the same time for assaulting John Bray and taking away a hare from him. A further case, in 1735, gives us the names of Jasper Pettytt, John Gillan, victualler, John Bray, farrier, Samuel Pountney, glover, Thomas Dollatt, corkman, who assaulted John and Mary Waterman at Thundridge. In 1749, Thomas Jennings, victualler, assaulted " Charmberalen " Thorrowgood, " ale-conner," in the execution of his office, and (1723) Thomas Toosaints, alias Mutton, bargeman, were also prosecuted for assaulting Joshua Page, whilst Thomas Clarke and William Chadwell were committed as " dangerous and incorrigible Rogues " to be kept to hard labour till next Session, and in the meantime to be publicly whipped on the market days at Hitchin, Hertford, and Ware.

There are a few instances of brawling in church, in 1620, Robert Swinsteed, smith, entered Great Amwell church whilst drunk and made a disturbance there during the service, and, two centuries later, 1825, Ann Hudson, wife of Abraham Hudson, bargeowner, was prosecuted for " unlawfully,

willingly, and on purpose maliciously, contemptuously coming
into the parish church of Ware and during the celebration of
divine service, disquiet and disturb one John Jones, gent. and
the congregation then assembled for the purpose of religious
worship, to the contempt of our holy religion, and to the evil
example of all others ". But long before this, we begin to read
of those unruly tongues, which seem to have caused much
trouble in old Ware, beginning in 1625 with John Grave,
gentleman (?), who, " was and still is a common barretor,
disturber of the peace and common fomentor of contumelious
discord as well amongst his neighbours at Ware as between
other of the King's people dwelling in the county." In 1646,
various ladies come into the records, Elizabeth Robinson,
Elizabeth Thacker, Katherine Philpott, Alice Ellsum, Mary
Bird, and Alice Creed, " being present in court did in a most
uncivil and irreverent manner in face of the said Court, scowle
and brawle one with another to the evil example of others and
to the great disturbance of the business of this present Session."
It is ordered that all the said women shall be taken into
custody by the constable of Ware " and there be well cucked
tomorrow being markett day ", that other women may be
warned not to offend in the like manner. The Constables of
Hertford, calling to their assistance a certain number of fit
persons, are to assist William Cross, constable of Ware, in
carrying the said women to Ware in case any of them should
break away before they have received the said punishment.
In spite of this example and warning, there is a complaint to
the Court by the inhabitants of Ware in 1683, " that there is
great need of a cucking-stool for the punishment of scolds and
unquiet people." It is therefore ordered that the constables
of Ware shall set one up in a convenient place. But the punishment was not always a ducking, for Mary Stratton, of Ware
Upland, who, in 1699, " swore by God several times," was,
for default of distress, set in the stocks three hours, and Thomas
Phip, victualler, also being convicted of swearing " By his
Maker ", paid 1s. to the poor of Ware Upland. In 1666, both
Nicholas Packer and William Bennett were presented as
" eves-droppers ", having stood under the windows of divers
persons to overhear their conversation with the intention of
spreading scandals amongst the neighbours. A few years
previously, 1660, both Ann Sickling, widow, and Anne Packer,
were indicted for standing as " eves-droppers " under the

eaves of Joseph Scruby and for repeating what they heard there with the intention " to sowe strife and dissencion " between the said J. Scruby and his neighbour. This brief survey of our late townsfolk, that has come now within measurable distance of our own day, may well end with a cheerful anecdote supplied by that gay roysterer, William Venables, who, in 1828, was indicted for disturbing and breaking the public peace by " whooping, holloaing and cursing in the public streets during the hours of keeping the watch at night, and for assaulting James Porter, watchman and peace officer, who did gently lay his hands on the said Venables to take him into custody ".

Finally, a short mention of the watchmen themselves (whose names are not always given to us), who no doubt did their best in trying circumstances to carry out the obligations of an unpopular post. That it was unpopular we know, not only from stories handed down to us of the disrespectful treatment they often received, but also from the evidence of the records. As early as 1620, William Little, musician, refuses to keep watch ; in 1636, Mary Scarnan, being a parishioner of Ware, kept no watch, by herself or deputy, between sunset and sunrise ; in 1679, presentments of Francis Dellow and John Martin, for refusing to keep watch, being warned by the constable. William Dale, watchman in 1811, tells us how he met George Day, between three and four in the morning, with a sack containing apples, turnips, and a fowl, and as he would give no account of them, deponent told him he must go with him to the cage.

In the early years of the East India College at Haileybury, the watchmen had particularly harassing times, each 5th November the young gentlemen came into Ware for a gay evening, all cellar gratings had to be protected with trusses of wet straw against the lighted squibs thrown down, and windows and doors barricaded ; many a time the unfortunate watchmen would be tied into their sentry-boxes, or the boxes overturned.

These watchmen, inadequate as they were for keeping the peace, leave us many a picturesque memory and we owe them something for that, particularly perhaps, Tubman, the last of his line, who gives us a picture that may rank high as any recorded. His description comes to us from the lips of those within whose memory he lived, so that we are enabled still to see him setting out on a bitter winter's night, in his well-known hat and coat with capes, with stick and lantern, having first (like a sensible man) taken something comforting to keep out the cold, and progressing, a little unevenly perhaps, from point to point, calling at intervals as was his duty : " Three o'clock on a fine, frosty morning, and two moons in the barge river ! "

A FEW CELEBRITIES

Though the celebrities of Ware are not numerous, the early ones, in particular, are of great interest, beginning in the thirteenth century with three natives of simple name— Robert, William, and Richard. William and Richard both became very distinguished men in the world beyond Ware, but Brother Robert's claim as a celebrity lies in the fact that, so far as is known, he is the only thirteenth century Ware man to have written an autobiography that has survived through the ages in a truly remarkable way.

Friar Robert.—" Preserved in the library of the Honourable Society of Gray's Inn, London, are the remnants of a Franciscan library of manuscripts that once belonged to the community at Chester. Amongst these is a Rosarium in MS. 7—' Twenty-five sermons on the Blessed Virgin, which are called the Rosary,' by Friar Robert of Ware. The style of the hand-writing (clear but considerably abbreviated) is late 13th or early 14th century, and at the bottom of the first folio is an almost obliterated notice in a later hand—' This book belongs to the Community of the Brothers Minor of Chester, the gift of Brother W. Gyn.' The ' Rosarium ' may have served as ' Collationes ' to be read to the friars ' in capitulo ' or in the refectory, where, as an old English preacher reminds his congregation, ' men of relygioun have a lessoun red at mete to fede the soule wyth gostly fode.'

" The actual sermons, on the Virgin, start off with the text ' Et nomen Virginis Mariæ ' (Luke i, 27), others follow on such topics as ' The sun was risen upon the earth ' (Gen. xix, 23), and ' He made the moon for seasons ' (Ps. civ, 19), opening themes which recall the rich symbolism with which praise of the Queen of Heaven was adorned at that time. In the Prologue, we are shown what occasioned more particularly the adoring eloquence of friar Robert, for here he sets his personal ' narration ', a vivid little sketch of his early life. The word ' Miraculum ' in the margin suggests at once a moral purpose, and its connection with the actual subject of the ' Rosarium ' is made clear when we find that the miracle itself which takes place ' in the Octave of the Assumption of the glorious Virgin Mary ' is ascribed to her influence. Friar Robert sends his ' Rosarium ' as ' a small gift ' to his beloved younger brother John, at the latter's eager request.

" Robert begins by telling us that he was the eldest son of fond parents who had planned for him a scholastic career from his earliest youth. Of his father's status or profession we learn nothing. But from minor references to his household, and from the vision subsequently told, in which we see him riding home ' on his horse, as was his wont, from a certain neigh- bouring town which is called Herteforde ', we can picture perhaps a prosperous merchant or franklin of the district, well known in the market-place. At Oxford, the domestic tragedy. opens, however, when Robert, the young under- graduate, fell under the spell of the Minors and joined their Order. The news of this sudden frustration of cherished hopes and plans came as a most grievous blow to the head of the family. Mother, brother, relatives, and friends, all were dispatched to do their utmost ' with entreaties and promises ' to make him quit. The disappointed man even went to the length of trying to get a formal release for his son from the Order, in the court of the Papal Legate in England, Ottobon— a little fact which gives us an approximate date for the episode between the years 1265 and 1268. It was of no avail. So now, as with the first Franciscan parent in Assissi, when prayers and schemes failed, grief gave way to anger and even a show of violence. In a few graphic lines, brother Robert revives an unhappy scene outside the old Ware homestead. After his father had refused to set eyes on him again, he ventured on one occasion to reappear at the gates, with a fellow friar, begging admittance. At once the servants were sent out to order him away, while the irate master within, drawing a sword, swore ' with a great oath ' to kill him if he dared to intrude. The separation between the two thus became complete. But, ' about the Octave of the Assumption of the glorious Virgin,' he who would not forgive was smitten down in his obstinacy by a mortal disease, and took to his bed, never to rise from it again. Yet in his worst plight the Mother of Pity was not unmindful of him. One night he dreamed that he was once again on his horse, riding the old familiar two miles home from Hertford to Ware. As he climbed a certain knoll that lay on his road, there met him three most fair ladies, ' exceeding white and glistering.' One of them, beckoning to him, bade him stay. ' Are you still in happy fellowship with your son, Robert ? ' she asked. ' Most assuredly not ! ' was the firm reply. But with an equal firmness the lady bade him not to proceed until first he had promised her faithfully that he would make amends. Awaking from sleep, the bewildered parent called a member of the household to him, and confided how that he had thus pledged himself solemnly to make peace and concord with his son, at the bidding of a most lovely woman whom he knew not. The ready explanation offered was that she could be none other than our Lady, come herself to put an end to the discord between them before he was finally called away. The sick man thereupon caused Robert to be fetched with haste from London, and the reconciliation followed. In the last hours of life he had lost power of speech and seemed unconscious. But Robert, entreating his father ' to turn to that so faithful Advocate ', managed to rouse him before the end came. With his dying breath he rallied, fervently completing the ' Ave Virgo ' at the point where his grief-stricken son had broken down in the prayer, and passed to his Maker with repeated cries of exultation on his lips. ' Therefore I ask you, dearest brother, that, when you turn again to these little gifts written for you, you recite at least one ' Ave Maria ' for my father and for me, most vile sinner that I am ! '

" So ends this little fragment of friar Robert's auto-biography ; nothing further appears to be left recorded of his works or of his subsequent career."

Note.—This translation of friar Robert's thirteenth century Latin story was made by Professor G. R. Owst, M.A., Ph.D., D.Litt., Lit.D., F.R.Hist.S., who generously permits it to be reproduced here from his article, " Some Franciscan Memorials," in the *Dublin Review,* April–June, 1925, and from a summary of that article in the Herts Mercury. Dr. Owst also refers to brother Robert's story in the *Transactions* of the St. Albans and Herts Architectural and Archæological Society for 1925.

William of Ware.—William was born in the thirteenth century, joined the Franciscan Order in his youth and finally achieved continental renown as a philosopher. It is probable that he studied at Oxford, but there is no direct evidence of this and the first reliable mention of his career comes from Paris, where he spent most of his life and was S.T.P. Here he was in close touch with that great scholar Duns Scotus, who went to Paris in 1304, and other schoolmen of that time.

A. G. Little, in *The Gray Friars in Oxford* (Oxford Hist. Soc., 1892. Part II), writes of him : " William of Ware,

born at Ware, entered the Order of Franciscans in his youth
according to Wm. Woodford (Twyne MS. xxii, 103.
Defensorium, cap. 62). Perhaps he is the ' Frater G. de Ver '
who was at the London Convent, *c.* 1250. It is not improbable
that he studied at Oxford, but there is no authority for the
statement. (Bale and Pits.) His name does not occur in the
list of Franciscan masters. He was S.T.P. of Paris, where he
spent most of his life. Said to have been a pupil of Alexander
of Hales (Dugdale, *Monast.*, vol. vi, part iii, p. 1529), and
master of Duns Scotus, who went to Paris in 1304. He was
called " doctor fundatus " by later writers. His *Commentaries
on the Sentences* were seen by Lelald in the Franciscan Library,
London (Collectanea iii, 51), and are now extant in the
following MSS.

Oxford. Merton Coll., 103, 104 (sec. xiv). Inc. " Utrum
finis per se et proprius theologie."

Toulouse, 242, § 1 (sec. xiv), anon. Inc. ut supra.

Troyes, 661 (sec. xiv), " Questiones super I et III lib.
Sentent." ascribed to Duns Scotus. Inc. ut supra.

Troyes, 661, § 2 (xiv), " Questiones Wareti super Tertium
librum Sententiarum." Inc. " Queritur utrum incarnacio sit
possibilis Quodnon." " Incarnacio est quedam."

Vienna. Bibl. Palat. 1424 and 1438 (xiv).

Florence. Laurentiana, ex Bibl. S. Crucis, Plut. xxxiii,
Dext. Cod. i (sec. xiii).

Padua. Bibl. S. Antonii, in Pluteis xxiv and xxii (Tomasin,
pp. 62a, 606).

A summary of this account of William and his works is
given in the *Dictionary of National Biography*.

Other information and certain items of William's philosophy
are given in De Wulf's *History of Mediæval Philosophy* translated by E. C. Messenger, Ph.D. (Longman's, 1926).
In Vol. I, p. 389—William of Ware (Varro) (Biographical and
bibliographical notes by E. Longpré, G. de Ware, in *France
Francisc.*, 1922, 1, and H. Klug, *Zur Biographie d. Minderbrüder
T. D. Scotus u. Wilhelm von Ware*). William probably taught at
Oxford, and whom Bartholomew of Pisa and a fourteenth
century MS. call " magister Scoti sine doctoris subtilis ",
was the author of " Quæstiones in IV Lib. Sentent."
(unpublished). (" Zu ben Beziehungen zw. Wilhelm von
Ware und Joh. Duns Scotus," *Franc. Stud.*, 1917, p. 221.)
In a fragment published by Daniels, William protests against

L

the special illumination theory as understood by several members of his Order and also by Henry of Ghent. (A. Daniels, *Wilhelm von Ware über das Menschliches Erkennen.*)

Vol. II, pp. 69, 188, 214.—According to Pelster (Hand-schriftliches zu Scotus mit neuen Angaben über sein Leben, in *Francisk. Stud.*, 1923), William was not master of Duns Scotus at Oxford. William holds that reason cannot con-clusively prove the Divine unity. He opposed the philosophy of St. Thomas Aquinas.

(*Note.*—Dr. Messenger also tells me that some of William's writings are being published in Germany now (1936) for the first time.—E. M. H.)

Richard.—It is not known whether Richard was actually a native of our town, but he is always mentioned as being " of Ware ". The name " Richard de Ware Senior " appears in connection with the Alien Benedictine Priory, 1231. Nothing is known of his early history, and we first hear of him at Westminster, in 1257. He became Abbot of that great Benedictine establishment in 1258, during the time of the rebuilding of the Abbey by Henry III, and evidently enjoyed the confidence both of that king and of Edward I, being made treasurer of England about 1283.

Most of the histories and books describing Westminster tell us something of Richard, the following notes give a broad outline of his career.

In *The Monks of Westminster*, Bishop E. H. Pearce, 1916, mention is made of a lease, 1257, containing Richard's name. Richard de Wara, or Ware, acted as Proctor to Abbot Crokesley in June, 1257. He was appointed a Papal Chaplain, 11th March, 1259, and permitted to borrow 1,000 marks for promoting the business of the Convent in Rome, 13th March, 1259. (Kal. Pap. Reg., 1, 364.)

In the beginning of December, 1258, Richard de Ware was chosen Abbot " by compromission or the choice by agreement committed to a few of the monks ". (*History of Westminster Abbey*, Richard Widmore, M.A., 1751.) He went to Rome for his consecration, where apparently expenses ran high, for he borrowed 1,000 marks from Florentine merchants, 20th March, 1259 (Mun. 12800), and a further 600 marks, November, 1259, to secure the election of Philip de Lewisham as Abbot. (Mun. 12802.) This led to a long suit with Carlinus Guiberti, of Florence, which was unfinished at Richard's

death.   From Widmore's history we learn, further, that
Richard went again to Rome, in 1267, when he brought those
stones and workmen for Edward the Confessor's shrine and
for the Mosaic pavement laid before the High Altar, which
was finished in 1268.   The design of the figures that were in it
was to represent the time the world was to last, according to
the Ptolemaic system.   When Richard died, in 1283, he was
buried to the north of the High Altar, beneath this pavement,
which was his gift to the great Abbey Church.   His simple
inscription is :

" Abbas Ricardus de Wara qui requiescit
     Hic, portat lapides, quos hic portairt ab urbe."

Richard was employed abroad on several occasions.   In
1271, he went to the King of France about the county of
Argent ; in 1276, to the Pope with powers from Edward I
to lay that King under an obligation to go himself to the
Holy Land, or to send his brother.   In 1278, he was sent to
John, Duke of Brabant, to treat of a marriage between Margaret,
the King's daughter, and the son and heir of the duke.   He
went again on the same business in 1279 ; the marriage took
place ten years later.

From Henry III, Richard obtained renewal of several
charters which the Londoners had obliged the convent to
give up, taking advantage of the King's imprisonment after
the battle of Lewes, 1264.   He obtained confirmation of
these charters from Edward I.

Westlake (*Westminster Abbey*, 1923) mentions that Richard,
in 1278, was appointed chief justice in eyre for Cumberland,
Westmoreland, and Northumberland.

Richard is also famous for his great " Customary ", the
daily routine of the monastery.   Unfortunately, this remarkable
document was much damaged in the fire at Ashburnham
House, 1731, where it was among the Cotton MSS. (Otho
C.xj.)   But enough remains (the copy of the original) to give
an illuminating picture of the monks' daily life.   Abbot Gasquet
writes that it shows " the utmost leniency in the inflictions of
punishments ", " prompt readiness to extend forgiveness to
the repentant ", and " courtesy observed in the relations
between inferior and superior ".   The whole " Customary "
has not been translated from the Latin, but in *Westminster
Abbey*, by A. L. N. Russell, 1934, enough is given to show

the extraordinary details into which Richard went, some of them being most amusing. We find that both hands were to be used when drinking " for this was the manner of our forefathers before the Normans came into the land " ; perhaps this Saxon custom was preserved as a tribute to Edward the Confessor. The monks had to shave each other, seniors first " because at the beginning razors are sharp and towels dry ". Bathing was restricted to four times a year (later to twice a year), for health and not for enjoyment, on entering the bath, one should sit down " humbly and in silence ". Linen nightcaps were permitted, but not scarlet or green or any other gaudy colour ! The discipline of silence at meals was strictly insisted on. Even visitors in the Refectory were not to be spoken to, but the hosts were " to make them as merry as they can in silence and cheer them by drinking with them ".

In spite of his strong character and the great thought he must have given for those under his rule, Richard was not popular on account of his austerity. (Chron. de Dunstaple, p. 494.)

(See Richard of Ware also in *Archæologia*, vol. i, p. 32, 1779.)

Thomas Fust, or Furst, martyr.—Foxe, in *Acts and Monuments*, records that Bishop Bonner, in 1554, left his retinue at Hadham and : " He rode that night to Ware where he was not looked for for three days after to the great wonder of all the country." It is not clear whether this visit to Ware was before or after the condemnation of Thomas Fust, who was burnt at the stake the following year. He was tried and condemned with George Tankerfield at St. Albans : " and as he had the same questions put to him so he gave or joined in the same answers ; when Bishop Bonner advised him to recant his opinions he answered, " No, my Lord, I will not, for there is no truth cometh out of your Mouth, but all Lyes ; you condemn me and will not hear the Truth. Where can you find any anointing or greasing in God's book ? I speak nothing but the Truth, and I am certain it is the Truth that I speak."

For his ill-advised and rude manner of speech, Fust was condemned to suffer the penalty of his day, and was burned at the stake in Ware market place, 26th August, 1555.

William Vallans, poet.—William Vallans has a brief notice

in the *Dictionary of National Biography*, where it is stated that he was born in Ware in the latter half of the sixteenth century. He carried on business as a salter, and was a friend of Camden and other antiquaries, but it was his poetry that has caused his name to be remembered. His poem, " The Tale of Two Swans," is one of the earliest examples of the employment of blank verse. His book is very rare. Another poem is preserved in the Harleian MSS. and complains of the injustice of suffering John Stowe to go unrewarded after compiling his *Survey of London.*

Vallans had some commendatory verses prefixed to *Wharton's Dreame*, 1578, and Hearne assigns to him the authorship of *The Honourable Prentice : or thys Tayler is a Man ; shewed in the Life and Death of Sir John Hawkewood*, by W. V., London, 1615. (Bodleian.)

Further notes, with the poem complete, are given in *Notes on the River Lee below Hertford*, by the late R. B. Croft, Esq., of Ware, and privately printed in Ware, 1907. The paper was first read to the Hertfordshire Natural History Society some twenty-five years previously.

Mr. Croft writes : " Vallans' poem was prefixed to Leland's *Itinerary*, vol. v., printed in London in 1590, and in 1711 considered very rare. In 1769, Hearne edited and reprinted Leland's *Itinerary* with the ' Tale of Two Swannes ', and gives some notes on Vallans, saying that ' he was a modest man, well versed in Records, an admirer of Mr. Leland (I think), travell'd into several Countries after he had published this Book '. Of the book he says, ' 'Twas printed at London (in three sheets in quarto) by Roger Ward for John Sheldrake, in the year MDXC, but 'tis so great a rarity that I had scarce so much as heard of it 'till late, when 'twas sent to me out of the well furnish'd Study of Thomas Rawlinson of the Middle-Temple, Esq., who gave me leave (if I thought proper) to reprint it.' "

William Vallans calls the notes at the end of the poem " A Commentary or exposition of certain proper names used in this tale " (those referring to Ware are given below), and follows the commentary with a letter to his beloved father, John Vallans, to whom he wishes " the Grace of God and prosperitie ", he then goes on to redeem a promise " to write a few words, concerning the matter whereof, at my being with you last, wee with certaine of our friendes talked ". The subject

being " that ships had been at Ware ", and one N. B. " had
kept astyr, affyrming, how it was unpossible that the river
which but of late was scarce able to bear a smal whyrrie shold
in times past beare big and mighty ships ".

Vallans then goes on to give an interesting account of the
Danish invasions, including the expedition up the Lea
valley derived from the *Anglo-Saxon* Chronicle, Henry of
" Huntinton ", Florence of Worcester, " and many moe,"
and adds that " O. Crosse did credibly enforme mee that at the
building of Stansted bridge " the remains of large ships had
been found. Vallans concludes the letter by hoping that by
the efforts of the " Lord Treasurer Maister Fanshawe " and
others who were " amending and scowring " the river they
might shortly see " though not shippes, yet good big boates
and vessels passe too and fro betwixt London and Ware to the
commoditie and profite of the whole countrey, which God
graunt ".

Probably Vallans' father is described when the Swans
reach Ware bridge, and a man " with silvery heares " makes
a little speech. (John Vallance, 18th April, 1603, Ware Burial
Register.)

" The guested town of Ware " refers to the numerous inns.
" Byrches House " was formerly the Franciscan Friary, and the
" rivulet " or " ril " from Chadwell was the natural course
of the overflow of that spring before the construction of the
New River ; all that remains of it now is the dock beside the
Victoria Malting. This allusion is the only note we have of the
spring's former course. We also learn that the newly-built
bridge was arched and of stone.

(*Note.*—The engraving reproduced by Mr. Croft from
Leland's *Itinerary* appears in that book as an introduction to
Leland's own poem of Swans, written in Latin, and bears no
relation to Vallans' story.)

Passing to a brief survey of " The Tale of Two Swans ", we
find a somewhat long, but interesting, introduction (not
referred to by Mr. Croft), in the course of which Vallans
writes :

" To the Reader.

" The reasons be manifold (good reader) that moved me to
publish thys present Tale. First, that I might (in what I was
able) illustrate, or make better known to the world, my countrie
or place of byrth : to which (as Cicero saith) each man doth

on the third part of his life, adventure his safetie, and hazard the dearest things hee dooth possesse. Neither yet was there ever any man so brutish, but rejoyceth to hear his countrie commended, and is delighted when he heareth the same wel spoken of and praised. . . . Thirdly, being fully resolved to leave my country, I held best before my departure Cigneum aliquid canere : not unlike the Swans, who before their death do sing. . . .

" The last and not the least motive was my friendes request, whose importunate demaund, without breach of amitie I could not gainsay : to whom, as also to thy favourable construction (curteous and friendly reader) I commit the same."

In the opening lines of the poem we learn that :

> " the Lady Venus viewed
> The fruitful fieldes of pleasant Hartfordshire
> And saw the river, and the meades thereof "

whereupon she sends for Mercury to fetch two " Cignets " :

> " And in the Laund, hard by the parke of Ware,
> Where Fanshawe builds for his succeeding race "

she waits for Mercury to bring the birds from " Cayster ".

When the birds are brought she throws them into " her river Lee " and flies to the throne of Jove, asking that her two " Swannes " may rule the rest as King and Queen. They reign for many years, until, growing old, they decide to visit all the waters of the Lea and its tributaries, inspecting their domain and the flocks of their descendants. They choose a troop as escort and set out on the royal progress. After negotiating the upper reaches of the Lea, the Mimram, and the Beane, they departed " towardes Edwardes Ware ". But ere they come unto the Meade or Laund :

> " Where Venus first did put them in estate,"

they pass up the river Rib, surveying the villages *en route,* then :

> " Returning backe againe, the companie
> Were marshalled and set in order brave.
> And this was done least that undecently
> They should passe by the guested towne of Ware.
> And so approching to the late built bridge,
> They see the barges lading malt apace ;
> And people wondering at so great a troope :

Among the which, a man whose silver heares
Seem'd to excel the whitenesse of the rest,
Bespake them thus :
' Long have I liv'd, and by this bridge was borne,
Yet never saw I such a companie :
So well beseene, so order'd and so faire.
Nay (as I thinke) the age that is by past,
Nor yet the same that after shall insue
Never beheld, nor lookt upon the like.'
   The people listened to this aged man,
As one they lov'd, and held in reverence.
And as they stoode, behold a sodaine chance :
From South-side of the bridge, hard by the same,
Two goodly Swannes with Cignets full fifteene
Present themselves . . .
       the Cock explains—
' A place there is, not farre from hence (O King)
A chalkie hill, beneath the same hole,
Cal'd Chadwell head, whence issues out a stream,
That runnes behind broad Meade that you see here :
A little rill, yet great inough for us,
And these our brede, yet (Gratious Prince) behold
A tale there is deliver'd unto us
From hand to hand, how that a haunted ducke,
Diving within this Chalk-well head or hole,
Was forced underneath the hollow ground
To swimme along by waies that be unknowne :
And afterward at Amwell spring (they say)
Was taken up all fetherlesse and bare.'
   The King and Lordes tooke pleasure at the tale,
And so made haste quite through the arched bridge
To Amwell, when they easilie did 'spie
The spring and rill that comes out of the hill,
And is suppos'd to rise at Chadwell head."

At the end of the poem, Vallans writes :

" A Commentary or Exposition of certain Proper Names used in this Tale :—

" *Fanshawe*.—One of the remembrancers of Her Majesties Court of Exchequer : an upright Justicer, and one that especially tendereth the profit of Ware, whereof he hath purchased the Lordship.

" *Ware*.—Builded in the year of our Lord 914 by K. Edward the sonne of K. Alfred. This towne since the building thereof hath greatly increased, and by procuring to themselves the free passage of their bridge greatly hindered the Shire-towne of Hartford. For in old time the bridge was chained and kept by the Bailiefe of Hartford, but in the time of King John, when the Barons warred one against another, and against the King himselfe, the townsmen, trusting to their Lord Wake, break the chaine, and have ever since enjoyed their passage, whereby it is greatly increased, and is likely still to doo, as well for that by meanes of the Lord Treasurer the .river is made passable for boates and barges, as also through the diligence of the Townesmen, who, with helpe of M. Fanshawe, have erected a new markette house, with entent to procure certaine Fayres to be helde there yeerely. The Bridge was reedified lately, and the arches made of stone at the charges, viz. 140 poundes geven by her Majestie. The rest by the Towne and Countrie."

(*Note.*—It was de Quincey, Earl of Winchester, who won the freedom of Ware Bridge in King John's reign, not Lord Wake.)

A few further notes are of interest in connection with this rare work.

In the title to the poem, Vallans mentions " the River Lee, commonly called Ware-River ", and his reference to the town as " Edwarde's Ware " is of particular interest when considered with Professor Skeat's remark in his *Place Names of Herts*, that the name " Ware ", by itself, is somewhat unfinished, as though a prefix had been lost.

But, by far the most interesting, the story of the " haunted " (hunted ?) duck, told by the swans from Chadwell Spring, carries us back to a legend whose origin is lost in the mists of pre-history. This story is found in at least two other places, as far apart as the Kettles of Hell spring, near Darlington (related by Daniel Defoe in his *Tour through Great Britain*, 1724, also by Manson in *Zigzag Ramblings of a Naturalist*, where he quotes from Leland's *Itinerary*), and in North Wales, where it is recorded .in a rare seventeenth century tract, " The Western Wonder or O Brazeel ", for N. C., 1674. The legend persists, too, at Tresco, Isles of Scilly. A common origin for these legends has been put forward by Dr. Rendel Harris in his *Sunset Essays*, No. 2, " Peg O'Nell," and No. 6, " Augmentation," where he suggests that the story may be derived from the Egyptian belief in the daily death of the Sun god, Osiris, who sank underground to rise next morning in the east. Dr. Rendel Harris founds his theory on the possible Egyptian origin of the place-names of Chadwell and Amwell ; Chad being derived from Tch-d, D-d, or T-t, one of the emblems of Osiris and said to represent his back-bone, and Am, An, or On, being another name for Osiris himself.

After these many ages the story is not likely to be proven, but the place-names, Amwell being east of Chadwell, in connection with a legend which was, as Vallans puts it, " delivered unto us from hand to hand," are certainly of striking interest and it remains for us to record our gratitude to Vallans who, in his turn, handed on so many items of interesting information in connection with the town he loved, and in such a delightful form.

(*Note.*—Although we are grateful to Mr. Croft for pointing out that the dock by the Victoria Malting was the original outlet of the Chadwell Spring, we should not overlook the fact that the Mill, a little east of Ware bridge (now the property of Messrs. J. W. French, Ltd.), stands beside the " Mill Brook ". As the Mill dates at least from the Domesday Survey, it is likely to be an older foundation than the Victoria Malting, and we may surely accept its site as having been chosen conveniently for the water supply.)

The course of the New River beside the London Road, past Amwell House, is still known to old inhabitants of Ware as " Mill Brook ", and it seems likely that the main flow of Chadwell Spring came as far east as this, and was then joined by the considerable spring from " Hog's Close ", or " Spring-field " (now a New River pumping station), before joining the Lea.

To this day, the low-lying ground between the back of the Mill and the railway station quickly reaches saturation point, and flood water appears when the river level rises ; this shows the course of the old " Mill Brook ", though Vallans would, naturally, choose the first " rill " for his " Swannes ", as they could not have negotiated the waterway past the Mill wheel.

Charles Chauncy, 1592–1672.—D.N.D., Brooks, *Lives of the Puritans.*

Charles Chauncy, great-uncle to Sir Henry Chauncy, the county historian, was born *c.* 1592. He became a fellow of Trinity College, Cambridge, obtaining his B.A. in 1613, and

M.A. in 1617. He incorporated on that his B.D. degree at Oxford in 1624. He was distinguished for oriental and classical scholarship, and made professor of Greek, or, more probably, Greek lecturer in his own college. In February, 1627, he became Vicar of Ware, until 1633 ; having already been before the High Commission Court in 1630, for disregarding Archbishop Laud's oppressive regulations, in 1635 he was again prosecuted in the High Commission for opposing the railing-in of the communion table at Ware, when he was suspended, cast into prison, condemned in costs and obliged to make the following degrading recantation : " Whereas I, Charles Chauncy, clerk, late vicar of Ware, in the county of Hertford, stand, by sentence of this honourable court, legally convicted for opposing the setting of a rail about the communion table in the chancel of the parish church of Ware, with a bench thereunto affixed, for the communicants to resort unto, and to receive the blessed sacrament there, kneeling upon their knees, saying it was an innovation, a snare to men's consciences and a breach of the second commandment, an addition to the Lord's worship, and that which hath driven me out of the town. I, the said Charles Chauncy, do here, before this honourable court, acknowledge my great offence in using the said invective words and am heartily sorry for them. I protest, and am ready to declare by virtue of mine oath, that I now hold and am persuaded in my conscience, that kneeling at the receiving of the holy communion is a lawful and commendable gesture ; and that a rail set up in the chancel of any church by the authority of the ordinary, with a bench thereunto affixed for the communicants to repair unto, to receive the holy communion kneeling, is a decent and convenient ornament for that purpose, and this court conceiveth that the rail set up lately in the parish church of Ware, with the bench affixed, is such a one. And I do further confess that I was much to blame for opposing the same, and do promise, from hence-forth, never, by word or deed, to oppose either that or any other the laudable rites and ceremonies prescribed and commended to be used in the church of England." Signed Charles Chauncey.

He read his submission " with bended knee ", and after being admonished by Laud was released on payment of costs. But Chauncy never forgave himself for this " scandalous submission " and went to America in 1637. Laud denominated him, " a most religious man who fled to New England for the sake of a good conscience."

These Altar rails are now restored to the Church, and form a Children's Corner.

Poor Charles also disagreed vehemently with the king's " Book of Sports ", and although he was not allowed to preach on a Sunday afternoon, when the drums beat in the High Street, encouraging the people to enjoy recreations, he spent the time in strict catechizing.

(*Note.*—" This prosecution was procured chiefly by the tyrannical power and influence of Laud ; and when Dr. Merrick, counsel to Mr. Chauncy, endeavoured to vindicate his client, because the setting up of the rail was done by a few parishioners, and without any warrant from those in authority, the archbishop, in a rage, threatened to suspend the doctor from his practice, for pleading thus in his favour."— Prynn's Cant. Doome, pp. 93, 95, 96. Rushworth's Collect., vol. ii, p. 316.)

During the Commonwealth, Chauncy was invited to return to Ware, and was about to embark for home when, in November, 1654, he was persuaded by the overseers of Harvard College, New Cambridge, to become president of that society and was inaugurated successor to Henry Dunster, the first president : he held the post till his death in 1672.

(*Note* 2.—" This submission is said to have been forced from Mr. Chauncy and designed only to deter others from opposing the archbishop's innovations. Though Mr. Chauncy was overcome in the hour of temptation, and enforced by the terrors and censures of his cruel oppressors to make the above recantation, he afterwards felt the bitterness of it, and deeply bewailed his sinful compliance. Though he obtained forgiveness of God, he never forgave himself and at the time of his death, nearly forty-four years after, he made the following humiliating declaration in his last will and testament :—' I do acknowledge myself to be a child of wrath and sold under sin, and one who hath been polluted with innumerable transgressions and mighty sins ; which as far as I know and can call to remembrance I keep still fresh before me, and desire, with mourning and self-abhorrence, still to do, as long as life shall last ; .and especially my so many sinful compliances with, and conformity unto vile human inventions and will-worship, and hell-bred superstitions, and other evil things patched to the service of

God, with which the English mass-book, I mean the Book of Common Prayer, is so fully fraught.' " Mather's *History of New England*, Bk. iii, p. 135.)

Simon Ive, 1600–1662 (D.N.B.), musician, was baptized in Ware, 20th July, 1600. He became lay vicar of St. Paul's till about 1653. At the restoration, he was installed as eighth minor prebendary. Whitelock chose him to co-operate with Henry Lawes and William Lawes in setting to music Shirley's masque " Triumph of Peace ". He had many more musical works to his name.

Thomas Fanshawe bought the manor of Ware, acquiring the park in 1575, where he built a new house, leaving the old town manor. He was Remembrancer of the Exchequer, and M.P. for Rye in 1571 ; in the five succeeding parliaments was member for Arundel, and in 1597, for Much Wenlock in Shropshire. He died at his house in Warwick Lane, London, 1601.

Henry Fanshawe, son of Thomas, succeeded him as Remembrancer of the Exchequer. He was M.P. for Westbury, Wilts, in 1588, and for Boroughbridge, Yorks, in 1597. He was a friend of Prince Henry, and became Knighted in 1603. His garden, at Ware Park, became famous for its fruit, flowers and herbs, and many of the trees were planted by him. The garden is described by Sir Henry Wotton. He also collected pictures, prints, drawings, medals, and stones, which he kept first at Warwick Lane, but by his will of 1600, bequeathed to Ware Park to be placed in the gallery or other fit place and not to be dispersed. He died at Ware and was buried in the church, March, 1615–16.

Thomas Fanshawe, son of Sir Henry, also held the office of Remembrancer of the Exchequer. He was made a Knight of the Bath at the coronation of Charles I in February, 1625, and was M.P. for the county of Hertford in 1661. During the Civil War he was an ardent royalist (smiths had been at work secretly at Ware Park before the actual outbreak of hostilities), and his property was sequestrated by Parliament. Charles II raised him to the peerage as Viscount Fanshawe of Dromore, in Ireland, but the Civil War had nearly ruined him and he sold the manor of Ware in 1668 to Sir Thomas Byde.

Jane Stretton, daughter of Thomas Stretton, a wheelwright, was baptized in Ware Church on 24th June, 1649. The curious misfortunes which befell her are related in a pamphlet

published in 1669 and reprinted, with an introductory note,
by the late W. B. Gerish at Bishop's Stortford in 1908, in his
valuable series on Hertfordshire Folk-Lore.

The title of the pamphlet is as follows :

THE HERTFORDSHIRE WONDER
OR
STRANGE NEWS FROM WARE

Being an exact and true Relation of one Jane Stretton the
Daughter of Thomas Stretton of Ware in the County of Herts
who hath been visited in a strange kind of manner by extraordinary and unusual fits, her abstaining from sustenance for
the space of 9 Months, being haunted by Imps or Devils in the
form of several Creatures here described, the Parties adjudged
of all by whom she was thus tormented and the occasion
thereof, with many other remarkable things taken from her own
mouth and confirmed by credible witnesses.

Job 1, v. 12.
" And the Lord said unto Satan, Behold all that he hath is
in thy power : only upon himself put not forth thy hand."
London : Printed for J. Clark at the Bible and Harp,
West Smith-Field, near the Hospital Gate, 1669.

All poor Jane's unhappy experiences arose from her father's
consultation with a certain " Cunning Man " over a lost, or
mislaid, Bible.   This " Cunning Man, Inchanter, Fortune
Teller, or what you will ", told Thomas Stretton that he
could tell if he would, whereat Thomas accused him of being
either a witch or a devil, which seems inconsistent, having
consulted him and, presumably, expected some helpful reply.
The man said nothing at the time but, " his heart inflamed with
the fire of revenge," he sent his wife later to Jane " desiring a
pot of Drink ".   This was given trustingly by Jane and, soon
after, her troubles began, with " violent raging fits ".

About a week later the woman came again and desired a
pin which Jane also provided, whereupon the fits " waxed
far more violent than before, her body swells like a bladder
puft up with wind ready to burst".   The last time the woman
saw this maid " she swounded away and lay for the time as if
deprived of life ".   For six months' space she ate nothing, "; but
such a wonder as this could not be confined, it was strait
spread abroad, and as we English are like the Athenians,
desirous to hear of News, and to be ascertained of what we

hear, so the report of this strange wonder drawes a great concourse of people to the house, to the disturbance not only of the maid, but also of Thomas Stretton himself, wherefore to purchase a quietness to himself, he removed her to the house of one John Wood a Neighbour of his." Friends and relations then began to suspect that the illness was of no ordinary nature, particularly when two flames proceeded from her mouth, " one of red colour and other blew," and eleven pins, in several crooked forms, also Flax and Hair were found upon her tongue. The girl (who had partly recovered her senses) complained of great pain in her back and a large knife was found in the bed. The room was also invaded by Frogs, Mice, Toads, and the like. " The report of these more strange accidents soon flew about not onely all over Ware but to the adjacent villages and more remote Towns, so that people came in multitudes to see her, some out of pitty . . . and some who were diffident of any such thing as Witchcraft, who being fully satisfied in the truth of what is here set down, went home fully convinced of their errors."

Finally, after about nine months, the wife of the " Cunning Man " was brought to Jane (presumably to undo the wrong with which she was credited) and although the ultimate cure is not recorded, the writer tells us that she was recovered sufficiently to take " surrups " and such like liquid ingredients. With which hopeful sign Jane Stretton disappears from her little turn of notoriety, the writer finishing his account with : " For the truth of this Relation I might (if there were occasion for it) insert the names of several Eminent persons both in Ware and London who freely offered to assert it, but the thing being so near hand and obvious to our eyes I count it needless . . . it being a vain thing to go to prove that which we suppose none will deny. . . . "

Sir Richard Fanshawe, distinguished diplomatist, became Ambassador to the court of Spain, and died there. He is buried with other members of the family in Ware Church.

(For fuller notes of this interesting family, see the *Dictionary of National Biography*. Memoirs of Lady Anne Fanshawe. Notes, etc., of the Fanshawe family. Shaw, *Knights of England*.)

Isaac Chauncy (D.N.B.). Isaac, son of Charles Chauncy was born and baptized in Ware in 1632, and went to America with his parents in 1637. He studied theology and medicine at Harvard and completed his education at Oxford. Before 1660, he became Rector of Woodborough, Wilts, but was ejected by the Act of Uniformity and moved to the Congregational Church at Andover. On 5th July, 1669, he was admitted as extra licentiate of the College of Physicians, and left Andover some time after the recalling of Charles' Indulgence, coming to London as a physician. In 1687, he accepted the pastorate of an independent meeting-house in Bury Street, St. Mary Axe, for fourteen years. But, though learned, he was an unpopular preacher and being somewhat bigoted he so tormented his hearers with incessant declamations of Church Government that they left him. He resigned in 1701, and later became divinity tutor to the newly founded Dissenting Academy in London, which office he held till his death in 1702. He was a voluminous writer on Theological subjects.

William Webster (D.N.B.), Vicar of Ware in 1740, was another prolific writer on theological subjects. Among his works were *The Fitness of the Witnesses of the Resurrection of Christ*, 1735, and *The Credibility of the Resurrection of Christ*, 1735. *A Complete History of Arianism from 306–1666. To which is added the History of Socinianism, translated from the French of the learned Fathers Maimbourg and Lainy*, London, also produced in 1735. At one time he fell into poverty and wrote *A plain Narrative of Facts or the Author's case fairly and candidly stated*, also *The Clergy's Right of Maintenance vindicated from Scripture and Reason*, 1726, London. Webster died in 1758.

Thomas Francklin, vicar in 1759 (D.N.B.), was a Greek professor at Cambridge. He was a popular preacher and was made a royal chaplain in 1767. He was a friend of Dr. Johnson and Sir Joshua Reynolds, and through their influence was made chaplain to the Royal Academy. He left Ware for Brasted in 1777.

John Trusler, 1735–1820 (D.N.B.), an eccentric genius, was curate at Ware in his early life. One of his schemes was that of sending circulars to every parish in England and Ireland proposing to print in script type 150 sermons at the price of 1s. each, in order to save the clergy both study and the trouble of copying. This plan met with considerable success.

William Godwin, author of *Political Justice*, was minister in Ware, 1778–9.

Alexander Cruden, compiler of the famous *Concordance*, was a tutor in Ware in his youth.

John Nickolls, antiquary, son of a Quaker miller, was born in Ware in 1710 or 1711. (D.N.B.)   He acquired the letters formerly possessed by John Milton, which he published as *Original letters and papers of state addressed to Oliver Cromwell 1649–58.*   His collection of 2,000 prints of heads at his house at Queenhithe, collected from the bookstalls about Moorfields, furnished the material for Joseph Ames's *Catalogue of English Heads.*

Nathaniel Hitch, sculptor. Born in Ware, 31st May, 1845. Fourth son of George Hitch, builder. At an early age he attracted the attention of the vicar, Mr. Blakesley, by constructing a perfect little card model of Ware Church. The vicar and others interested themselves in the lad, and arranged that he should become apprenticed in London, to learn stone and wood carving. After some years, Nathaniel was able to start business for himself, and executed many important works, chiefly for Cathedrals, Churches, and Colleges. He worked until he was 84 years of age, when he became blind. He died in 1938, in his ninety-third year.

Among his better-known works are figures and carvings in the cathedrals of Canterbury, Lincoln, Rochester, Norwich, Peterboro', Wells, Wakefield, and Truro ; in Calcutta, Sydney, Adelaide, and Newcastle (Australia) ; in Romsey Abbey, Southwell Minster, Lambeth Palace chapel, etc., as well as many lovely pieces of restoration at Westminster Hall, Hever Castle, and colleges at Cambridge and Oxford.

M

WARE AS A POST TOWN

Ware was among the first places in England to enjoy the status of a Post town, the first official orders being issued in 1536, and in this capacity is mentioned in various records and documents, as follows :

Lincoln Corporation MSS.—1536. October 9. Letter from Sir Brian Tuke, treasurer of the king's chamber, dated 6 October, ordering the mayors and officers of Waltham Cross, Ware, Royston, Huntingdon, Stilton, Stamford, Sleaford, and Lincoln instantly at their utmost peril to provide an able man well horsed to carry all letters as may be sent by the King or the Privy Council from post to post with all diligence by night or day. (Hist. MSS. Com. XIV, App. viii, 35.)

Acts of Privy Council.—1565. Order to the constables, officers and postes of Ware that no man be suffred to passe in poste to or from Scotland without license from the Queen's Majestie or the Lordes, and to signify wekely wither.

Cecil MSS., II, p. 214. (Hist. MSS. Com.)—1578, October 13. Letter from Richard Swynshed, postmaster, " Since Michaelmas he went to London to one Robert Parmentor, deputy to Mr. Randolphe, master of the Posts, thinking to have received his wages for three quarters of a year (which is very long for a poor man to forbear), but he was told that he could not have any money as the Treasurer of the Queen's Chamber had denied the payment thereof. As Burghley had always been good to him and all other ' posts ', seeks remedy through him. Would have come up himself (to Theobalds) but that the town of Ware of late hath been infected with the plague but ' farther off from my house than a man can shoot '. Letters and packets come so fast, at the least xxxiiijty [*sic*] times every month, and the charges so great, that, without payment, they shall not be able to continue the service."

Richard Swynshed, buried 29th July, 1597. Ware Church Register.

Calendar State Papers Domestic, 1581–90, p. 367.—November 13th, 1586. Thomas Randolphe (Master of the Posts) to Davison, in behalf of the Post and Constable of Ware, touching the taking of Mr. Quarles' horse to ride post.

Calendar State Papers Domestic, 1605.—November 5th, Thomas Swyned, post-master, informs Salisbury that Percy has not passed northward, but that he and his brother came from the north on Saturday last. Thomas Swinsted, buried 30th April, 1619. Ware Church Register.

Hist. MSS. Comm., 4th Report, p. 100.—August, 1641. Complaint of Mr. Rushworth, the clerk assistant of the House of Commons, against the Postmaster of Ware, for not supplying him with horses when carrying the letter for the speedy disbanding of the army from the House of Commons to York, in consequence of which he was forced to go some distance on foot carrying his saddle.

June 27th, 1660.—Joseph Strubie of Ware, co. Herts to Sec. Nicholas for the place of Post Master at Ware, Henry Beach the present postmaster being disaffected to Government and disarmed by order of the Militia Commissioners.

Calendar State Papers Domestic, 1665, p. 564.—September 16th, York. Sir Wm. Coventry to Lord Arlington. Thinks the general postmaster could trace by whom it is that packets have been opened as was formerly done about one to the Lord General, which came safe to Ware and left Royston broken.

Calendar State Papers Domestic, 1666.—February 24th. Jo. Mascall to Williamson (Secretary to Lord Arlington) : " The country still on their guard on the coasts. . . . It will be very material to waken the postmasters, for they have been 8 hrs. between London and Ware." (P. 266.)

Record Office of the G.P.O. MS., *Minute Books of the P.M.G.* " 1760, December 31st. Ordered that Mr. John Rayner of Ware be removed from the employment of Deputy Post-master there, and that Mr. John Thurston of the Bull Inn be appointed to succeed him, to commence on the 5th January next."

THE GREAT BED

This famous piece of Elizabethan furniture has been reported upon and illustrated and conjectured about so often that it would seem almost superfluous to attempt further description ; nevertheless it might be considered a serious omission to pass over this massive object in silence, linked, as it always has been, with the name of Ware.

There is no record whatever of its origin.

A marginal note in Sir Thomas Baskerfield's copy of Chauncey's *History of Herts* (add. MSS. 9062, B.M.) states that the bed came from Barnet. If, as is popularly supposed, the bed was made for the Earl of Warwick (the King-maker), this may be true. Again, there is a statement in James Thorne's *Rambles by Rivers*, 1844, to the effect that the existing bed is *not* the original " Bed of Ware ". If there were an earlier bed, constructed for the Earl of Warwick, it certainly could not be the late Elizabethan example now in the Victoria and Albert Museum.

All that is known for certain of this bedstead we gather from a few literary references, including Shakespeare and Ben Jonson, and accounts of the Inns. (See under " Inns ".) It is first mentioned at the Crown, then the Stag (White Hart ?) by a visiting German Prince, next at the George, and finally, until its removal to Rye House, at the Saracen's Head, where its height was cut down. It was barely saved from being shipped to America in 1931, since then, as already mentioned, it has become a national treasure under the Director of the Victoria and Albert Museum. It now measures 10 ft. 9 in. in length and breadth and 7 ft. 6½ in. in height.

It has been suggested that the Bed may have once belonged to Ware Manor, and that Sir Thomas Fanshawe, abandoning the old town house for his new residence in Ware Park when built, did not move so cumbersome a piece of furniture and it so passed to an Inn. The immediate predecessor at the Manor was Francis, Earl of Huntingdon, very deeply in debt, he may have had this extravagant piece of furniture constructed in the hope that Queen Elizabeth would stay with him. Or, it may have been in the ownership of Thomas Byrche, at the Friary (the great Hall would have contained it), who also owned the Bear Inn. This sign represents the badge of the Earl of Warwick (who had also held Ware Manor) and strengthens the idea of the original bed having been made for him, but throws no light on the origin of the present masterpiece.

The accompanying illustration is included by courtesy of the Director and Secretary of the Victoria and Albert Museum, and of the Editor of *Country Life*.

THE NAME OF WARE

In early documents, including " Domesday Book ", Ware is frequently spelled with a final " s ". Fuller, in *Worthies*, ii, 18, says : " Weare is the proper name of that Town (so called anciently from the Stoppages, which there obstruct the River . . .)."

In *The Place-Names of Hertfordshire* by J. E. B. Gover, Allen Mawer and F. M. Stenton (English P.-N. Soc., vol. xv), p. 206, the earlier explanation of Professor Skeat that " Ware " is the Old English " waras ", people or dwellers, is considered unlikely, as such a type of name with an earlier prefix lost to it would be without parallel. This book suggests that as Ware lies beside the river, the name probably goes back to O.E. " wer " from " waer ", a weir, and points out that " the inorganic ' s ' so frequently added to monosyllabic place-names by DB scribes probably does not point to an alternative plural form ".

Other spellings of the name include WARES, WARA, WAER, WARRE, WARAS. The final " s " is not found after 1200.

It should perhaps be noted that there are at least three other places in England called " Ware ", not beside waters, and that Vallans (see " Celebrities ") referred to the town as " Edward's Ware ".

Towards Ware Park lies Wengeo, an interesting contraction of the early " Waringhoe ", from the Old English " Waringa hoh ", " hill or spur of land of the people of Ware." In 1231, the spelling is " Waryno " ; in 1564, " Warengehoo." This small tract of land is of particular value and interest to the " people of Ware ", as it contains the clay-bed from which Ware bricks were manufactured for many centuries, quite likely, indeed, from the days of the Roman occupation.

Widbury, the camp on the white or chalk hill (see " Manor "), has been spelled variously as : WYTEBURWE, WHITEBERWE, WHITTEBERGH, and WITERBERWE in the fourteenth century ; WIDBOROW in 1598.

Old street names include : Baldoke Lane, Waterlane, Milstrete, Gerneslane, Cripestre—in 1231 (Trin. Coll. Cam., Box 44).

Later documents mention Cokylstret, Popislane (Musley Lane), Batistret, Grenestret, Dead Lane, Bowstret, Gardner

Lane, Magpy Lane, Star Lane is Sterlane, Kybuslane, le port way, the Highe forge, Water Row and Land Row (High Street), le Mydelrowe (East Street).

Hoe Lane comes down to Nedenhoo or Nethenhofeld, the marsh below the high ground.

" Pontem de Wara," Ware Bridge, occurs in the Pipe Rolls, 1191.

WARE IN GENERAL HISTORY

Mention of Ware in connection with the larger events of national history occurs from time to time, as the following references show.

1337. In preparation for the French War. Giles de Badlesmere, Wm. Band, John de Wanton, and Thomas Gubion instructed to lay before the men of Hertford, who have been summoned by the king to meet at Ware on Friday, after the Nativity of the Virgin Mary, the decisions of the coming council at Westminster and the king's intention for the safety of the realm. (Cal. Pat., p. 504, 1337, 11 Ed. III, Aug. 21.)

1402. Richard Mawardyn, king's servant, has shown that the late king by writ dated 28 June, 23 Ric. II, directed him (then sheriff of Wilts) to go in his own person with knights and esquires to the number of 60 well armed, and archers to the number of 100 of his county, to Ware, to go with the Duke of York, then Lieutenant of England, for defence of the realm, wishing that on his arrival at Ware the accustomed wages should be paid by the treasurer of England. And he went with no small number of men at arms and archers to the said Lieutenant at Ware and received from the treasurer £38 18s. and paid this sum to the men at arms and archers, but now he is called on to render his account for the sum at the Exchequer. The king grants that he be acquitted. (Cal. Pat., 1401–5, 3 Hen. IV, Apr. 1.)

Letters from the Mayor and Corporation of the City of London to authorities of provincial towns, 1350-70, at the Guildhall. (Originals in Norman French.)

1353. July 26. Adam Fraunceys, Mayor, and the Aldermen of the City of London to the Bailiffs, Constables, and Good Folk of the town of Ware.

Testifying to the good character of John atte Rofte, of Eueruyk [York] mercer, and desiring them for love's sake to restore the horse and other goods and chattels, to the value of 40s. sterling which had been taken from him, when travelling in their parts, on suspicion that he had unlawfully come by them.

The Lord have them in his keeping.

1353. August 12. Adam Fraunceys, Mayor, and the Aldermen of the City of London, to the Mayor, Bailiffs, and Good

Folk of Bristut [Bristol]. Peter Furlour, merchant of Bristut, had complained that Eleyne, the mother of Richard Neville, his apprentice, had maliciously accused him of having killed her son. The evidence of trustworthy witnesses, which they are asked to believe, showed that on Tuesday before the Feast of the Nativity of Our Lady [Sept. 8 and Ware Fair] in the twentyfifth year of the reign of the King [Ed. III] the said Richard had taken leave of his master to go to Ware on a visit to his friends, to return on the third day next ensuing ; that he had departed in good health on the said day one year, and had not returned.   The Lord have them in his keeping.

1369. July 26. The Mayor and Aldermen of the City of London to the Bailiffs and Good Folk of the town of Ware.

John de Lyncoln, corsour [horse-dealer] and citizen of London, had complained that one Marione de Clyf, who had agreed to serve him for the term of one year, has left his service without leave or reasonable cause, and was now residing in their town. Desire them to deliver her up to the said John, in such manner as they would wish a request of theirs to be respected in like case.

The Holy Spirit have them in his keeping.

From *Acts of Privy Council*, 1549, f. 504.

The exchequer had warrant for X£ to Sir Thomas Challoner for his costs and charges in ryding to Ware to take musters of Gamboa's band of Spanierdes.

1551. Benet of Ware, being examined before the Counsaill tooching the communication had betwene him and Griffithe and Portas, with certain other of Ware, confessed that a certein talke ther was emonges them howe my Ladie Marie wolde goo Westwarde to therle of Shrewsburye.

Warrants for the Great Seal, Chancery Series, 3, bdle. 16, file 979. 13 Jan., 1 Mary. (Lady Jane Grey proclaimed Queen in Ware.)

Warrant to Stephen, Bishop of Winchester, chancellor, to issue letters patent in form following—

Whereas Wm. Parr, Marquis of Northampton, late of Southwark was indicted with other false traitors in arms to depose us of our royal power and kingdom of England on 14 & 15 July, 1 Mary, at our town of Ware in our co. of Hertford in the intent aforesaid being assembled to the number of 500 persons in warlike manner at Ware and there falsely and traitorously in writing proclaimed the Duke of Northumberland to be lieutenant general and describing the Queen as the lady Mary the bastard daughter of King Henry VIII and proclaiming at Ware the Lady Jane one of the daughters of the Duke of Suffolk, wife of Guildford Dudley son of the said Duke of Northumberland undoubted and true Queen and other treason set out in the indictment taken at Ware before Sir John Butler, kt., on 10 Aug. 1 Mary, and afterwards at sessiins at Westminster.

S.P.D. Eliz.

1569. vol. lx. The Sheriff and Justices of Herts assembled at Ware and subscribed the articles for Uniformity of public worship. Inclosing " Declaration by the Justices of Herts of their obedience to the Act of Uniformity of Common Prayer, etc." Nov. 21.

Acts of Privy Council

1593. Letter to Sheriff of Co. of Hertford. " Wheras the present infection of the Plague is growne to be dangerouslie dispersed the fayres usuallie helde in the monethes of July, August and September next in sondry places nere unto any of her [the Queen's] saide houses and to that cittie of London shalbe forbidden to be helde." Ware, Sept. 7th

Hist. MSS. Comm., W. M. Molyneux Coll., 5 Nov.—Eliz.

Letter from R. Sothebie to Sir Wm. More, Kt., " The terme is kepte at Hartforde accordinge to the first appointment ; but howe longe the same shall continue it is doubtfulle, by reason their hathe deade of the plague in Ware, above the number of XXXti persons, which event hath caused lodginges to be so streight, as their offer made of V li a weake for a chamber, but can not be hade."

Cal. of Cecil Papers, VII, p. 303. Concerning Spanish Hostages from the Low Countries kept in Ware.

July 14, 1597. Thomas Crompton to Sir Robert Cecil.

" The speech Mr. Lindley and I had with the prisoners gave us no such hope as we could assure ourselves of good payment, for they offered us but 50,000 ducats for all, alleging they could go no further without a new conference with the rest. Whereupon we thought it not meet to speak any more with them, finding they did but trifle with us, and gave present order to their keepers to take them back to Ware and to keep them more straitly than before, and prescribed him the manner how to use them. Notwithstanding, we perceive by others and from some of their own company, that there is more hope than we can perceive from them, and that by good handling of the matter there will be a better payment than they make show to yield ; and yet I think there must be a good abatement. . . ."

P. 304. July 16, 1597. Eliano Calvo to Sir R. Cecil [written in imperfect French, with some Spanish] suggesting a meeting to confer and save further writing, and asking permission to confer among themselves. " Ware " spelled phonetically as " Varee ".

Cal. S.P.D., 1666. July 12, p. 258.

Sir Adrian Scrope to Williamson. " His troop, as good an one as ever raised, was mustered yesterday at Ware, but the commissary cannot close the rolls till all the commissions are given out and transcribed into the office. . . . "

1678, April 1, p. 85. W. Broxolme, Lincoln, to Williamson.

" I have my company full and am marching them towards Hull to receive their arms, and will have them next week at their assigned quarters at Ware."

Nov. 19. Warrants for impressing waggons and horses for conveying troops' baggage, for the Earl of Dunbarton's Regt.

One from Ware to Barkway

Two from Ware to Huntingdon.

It is recorded that during the Huguenot oppressions in France, a number of their refugee children were housed in Ware.

In 1618, Ware, with Hertford and St. Albans, were the only towns in the county to store munitions.

I turned the leaves of old Ware history back
Then took a malting shovel and a sack,
And as odd leaves fell, fluttering to the ground,
The shovel scooped them up, till there was found
A brimming, bulging sack. I pressed and shook,
And lo ! the sack and shovel made a book.

FINIS

INDEX

Alfred, King, 1, 16

Barge-owners, Elizabethan, 19
Beacon, 27
Blakesley, Rev. J. W., 15, 48, 72
Bourne, 36
Brasses, 52
Brawling, 138
Bridge, 3, 4, 20, 27
Bull Inn, 24, 116
Byde, Th., 11
Byde, Skinner, 13, 44
Byde, Th. Hope, 13
Byde, Th. Plumer, 13
Byrche, Th., 90, 101
Byrche, Rob., 90

Carrington's Diary, 137
Chantries, 60, 99
Charities, 65, 97
Chauncey, Ch., 70, 154
Chauncey, Isaac, 159
Church, Bequests, 64
Church, Plate, 56, 57
Clare, Lady Eliz., 85
Cromwell, Th., 88
Cruden, Alex., 160
Cudden, James, 13

Danish Encampment, 1
de Castro, Dan., 13
de Bohun, Joan, 5, 74, 75
de Quincey, Marg., 4, 74
de Quincey, Rob., 4, 74
de Quincey, Roger, 4, 74
de Quincey, Sayer, 3, 27, 38, 39
Domesday entry, 2
Durham, Prior of, 96

Edward the Elder, 1, 16
Edward, Black Prince, 5
Ermine St., 16, 26
Excise, 13, 125

Fair, 5
Fanshawe, Lady Anne, 91
Fanshawe, Sir Henry, 10, 157
Fanshawe, Sir Richard, 159
Fanshawe, Sir Th., 8, 20, 157
Fanshawe, Sir Th. (2), 11, 35, 157
Font, 6, 44
Ford, 3, 17
Francklin, T., 160
Fraunceys, Adam, Mayor of London, 168
Fust, Th., 70, 148

Godwin, W., 160
Grantmesnil, Hugh de, 2, 41, 74

Gubion, Th., 168
Guilds, 63

Halfhide, Wm., 73
Harold, King, 26
Hatchments, 55
Highwaymen, 35
Hitch, Caleb, 48
Horns, Ceremony of, 113
Hostages, Spanish, 170
Hudson, James, 48
Humphrey, D. of Gloucester, 37
Huntingdon, Francis, E. of, 8

Ive, Simon, 157

James I, 29, 103
Jane, Lady Grey, 169
Joan, of Kent, 5
Jones, Inigo, 10

Ker, Lord, 31

Lea, name, 25

Malting Trade, 13, 17, 31, 125
Manor House, 9
Margaret, Countess of Leicester, 17
Margaret, Countess of Richmond, 6
Margaret, Countess of Salisbury, 7
Market, 3, 4
Mary, Queen of Scots, 29
May Day, 14
Mills, 16

New River, 21, 37
Nickolls, John, 161
Nonconformity, 129

Pensioners, 131
Pepys, S., 33, 105
Plague, 20, 136, 170
Persecution, Relig., 70
Pulpit, 44

Rastrick, G., 13
Registers, 59
Richard II, 6, 168
Richard of Ware, 76, 146
Rickabie, John, 112
Riot, 13
Robert, friar, 142
Rutland, D. of, 29, 103

Scott, John, 4, 38
Storms, 47, 137
Street names, 166
Stretton, Jane, 157

Note.—As the majority of Inns are arranged alphabetically, they are not included in this Index.

OLD WARE MANOR, LATER CHRIST'S HOSPITAL

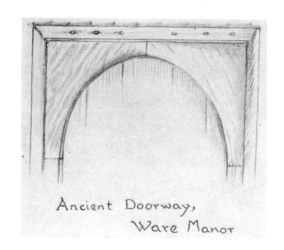

Ancient Doorway,
Ware Manor

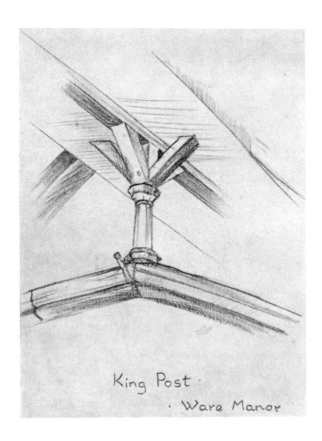

King Post.
Ware Manor

THE CHILDREN'S HOUSES, CHRIST'S HOSPITAL

OLD WARE MANOR, OVER THE ROOFS IN HIGH STREET

BRIDGE AND MALTINGS

" WARE RIVER "

SUMMER HOUSES BY THE LEA

THE OLD NORTH ROAD

BRIDGE FOOT

THE OLD FORGE

ST. MARY'S CHURCH, WARE

Print by J. Dibdin, 1849, from the drawings of Geo. Godwin, architect.

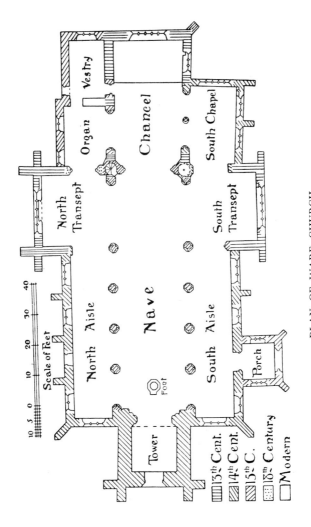

PLAN OF WARE CHURCH

By courtesy of the proprietors of the *Victoria County History of Herts.*

THE FONT

Sketch by G. Godwin. From *The Builder*, 1849.

THE SOUTH TRANSEPT WINDOW BEFORE RECONSTRUCTION
From a sketch by T. Baskerfield, 1803. (Add. MSS. 9062, B.M.)

THE CHURCH AND OLD LOCK-UP

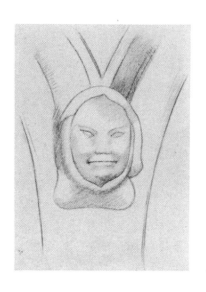

CORBELS IN N. ARCADE OF NAVE

CANONS MALTINGS. PART OF BENEDICTINE
PRIORY FARM

THE SEAL OF WARE FRIARY
(Add. Charter 36070 with the Obit.)

WARE FRIARY, *c.* 1820.

From a drawing by Thomas Fisher, F.S.A. 1771–1836. (Original in Haileybury College Library.)

WARE FRIARY GUEST HOUSE BEFORE ALTERATION
From *The Builder*, 21st July, 1849

FOURTEENTH CENTURY REFECTORY TABLE

BLACK SWAN YARD

TUDOR GATEWAY, BALDOCK STREET
THE BLACK SWAN

THE GEORGE INN. BEFORE 1760

A STABLEYARD. PART OF THE GEORGE INN

This Front perspective view of the High Street Wakefield taken during the Festival held on Wednesday the 3rd day of July 1832 in Celebration of the passing of the Reform Bill is respectfully inscribed to the Gentlemen and Inhabitants of the Town.

By their most obedient and humble Servant
John Stubbley

OLD HOUSES IN BALDOCK STREET
From a drawing by J. Buckler, 1831

CORN STORES, STAR LANE

CORN STORES, STAR LANE, c. 1620

CORN STORES, STAR LANE
Possibly built for Cavalry Barracks.

THE GREAT BED OF WARE